THE
GOLDILOCKS
MAP

A CLASSROOM TEACHER'S QUEST TO EVALUATE 'BRAIN-BASED' TEACHING ADVICE

ANDREW C. WATSON

First published 2021

by John Catt Educational Ltd

15 Riduna Park, Station Road,
Melton, Woodbridge IP12 1QT
UK
Tel: +44 (0) 1394 389850

4500 140th Ave North,
Suite 101, Clearwater,
FL 33762-3848
US
Tel: +1 561 448 1987

Email: enquiries@johncatt.com
Website: www.johncatt.com

ISBN: 978 1 913622 55 8

Set and designed by John Catt Educational Limited

PRAISE FOR
THE GOLDILOCKS MAP

If you are a fan of Daniel Willingham's clear thinking about education research, you will soon become a fan of Andrew Watson. Andrew walks you through a clear, step-by-step process you can use to figure out whether educational research might be useful to your teaching or school.

Rob McEntarffer, PhD
Assessment specialist, Lincoln, NE

A teacher who has studied learning science in depth, Andrew Watson is a perfect guide for teachers who want to know what works in the classroom and, just as importantly, what doesn't.

Nate Kornell, PhD
Professor of psychology, Williams College

The Goldilocks Map provides next-day-applicable guidance and pathways for educators to responsibly use "brain-based" research to enhance how we teach and how students learn.

Glenn Whitman
Co-author, *Neuroteach: Brain Science and the Future of Education*
Executive director, The Center for Transformative Teaching and Learning

The Goldilocks Map is an important addition to every educator's toolkit. Filled with real-life examples and amusing anecdotes, *The Goldilocks Map* answers one of the most pressing questions facing educators today: "What do we do with all that research?" Andrew Watson's Goldilocks equilibrium provides a common-sense approach to weighing the claims of edu-wizards and to assessing the efficacy of the "next best thing" in education.

For anyone who feels bombarded by the seemingly constant stream of contradictory educational research, *The Goldilocks Map* is a useful (and funny!) guide to how to effectively navigate the perplexing and exhilarating world of Mind, Brain, Education, the benefits and pitfalls of educational research, and the challenges presented by data-driven decision-making.

Eva L. Abbamonte
Dean of middle division faculty, Horace Mann School

The task of science translation can be so difficult that it's usually oversimplified. Andrew Watson pulls back the veil to help overwhelmed educators interpret claims made by self-proclaimed research experts. His unique dry humor and clever metaphors make this book a quick, enjoyable read. Educators will leave armed with a way of evaluating oft-heard advice; research translators will better understand the minds of their audience. *The Goldilocks Map* is a lesson in just-right critical skepticism.

Dr. Cindy Nebel
Lecturer, Peabody College
Learning Scientist (LearningScientists.org)
Faculty, Vanderbilt University

In a world brimming with misinformation and sensationalism, Andrew Watson's book is a welcomed salve. His cogent and balanced perspective offers a practical framework for educators to responsibly navigate scientific and pseudoscientific claims. A master teacher, Watson leverages his originality and penchant for metaphor to turn what could feel like a laborious task into an engrossing adventure.

Stephanie Fine Sasse, EdM
Founder and director, The Plenary

Andrew Watson's expert blend of knowledge, accessibility and humor make *The Goldilocks Map* an engaging and invaluable resource. This may be the first book of its kind: a practical handbook to evaluate brain-based educational claims, which will also leave you nodding, chuckling, and outright guffawing along the way.

Kristin Simmers
Elementary EAL teacher and team leader, NIST International School

Andrew Watson delivers a wonderfully accessible and entertainingly written guide for teachers to gauge "brain-based" teaching advice and apply educational research in the classroom. Whether you're a novice teacher or an experienced educator, you'll find this book more than useful. You'll find it essential.

Nick Soderstrom, PhD
Instructor of psychology, Montana State University

I have waited a long time to read a book on teaching and learning that I simply could not put down. This book is that book! Furthermore, the content on these pages encouraged my own self-reflection and self-evaluation of the decisions I make in the classroom on a daily basis. While there is no dearth of approaches to teaching and learning, there is a paucity of time to critically evaluate those approaches and their impact on student learning. Andrew Watson, through his engaging and entertaining writing style, walks readers through an internal dialogue that will support their decision-making at all stages of teaching and learning: planning, designing, implementing, and evaluating. And I thought Goldilocks was only a children's story. This book will inspire teachers to be more intentional, deliberate, and purposeful in their practice in such a way that brings back the passion and professionalism of what we do in the classroom.

John Almarode, PhD
Associate professor of education, James Madison University

In a noisy conversation around "brain-based" teaching practices, Andrew Watson's voice in *The Goldilocks Map* rises above the din to give readers concrete strategies to evaluate research. Andrew marries his experiences as a classroom teacher and administrator with his ability to analyze research studies, which allows him to move past a catchy article title to unearth a study's implications – or lack thereof – for classroom teachers. *The Goldilocks Map* is a useful go-to resource for teachers and school leaders to research regarding effective teaching practices.

Michael Wirtz
Head of school, Hackley School

It is vital for educators to ask: on what evidence is this based? Yet, do we know the validity of the answer or how to evaluate the research? How will I know if the studies being referenced apply to my students? Andrew Watson takes us on an enjoyable journey, tackling the ideas we wish we had been taught in our teacher education programs. Does the research apply? Is it a waste of time? Is it worth pursuing? Watson takes us, step by step, on the path that boosts learning for our students and leads us to become better-informed educators. *The Goldilocks Map* is not a fairy tale; it provides teachers and administrators with needed direction.

Patrice M. Bain, EdS
Educator and author, *Powerful Teaching: Unleash the Science of Learning*
and *A Parent's Guide to Powerful Teaching*

In the last few years, teachers have been inundated with research studies on the best practices that they should use to enhance their students' learning. Without a degree in cognitive neuroscience or psychology, it can be difficult to decipher the sometimes conflicting and often baffling advice. In *The Goldilocks Map*, Andrew Watson gives teachers the tools they need to ask the right questions and to become more sophisticated consumers of academic research. Engagingly written by a teacher for teachers, the book suggests that teachers use the Goldilocks principle: that is, they should be neither too skeptical nor too credulous, neither too critical nor too respectful, of every new study that promises to improve the learning outcomes of our students. Rather, Watson walks the reader through the questions to ask and the skills to use in discerning what might work and what probably won't. The book is an excellent resource for all teachers, whatever the age of their students.

Dr. Sheila Culbert
Head of school, The Loomis Chaffee School

By centering each chapter in plausible scenarios a teacher might encounter when wanting to incorporate brain-based principles, Andrew Watson's book will equip even the most novice teacher with the tools to wade through a sea of contradictory advice, supposed silver bullets, and know how to find the answers they are looking for.

Jasmine Lane
English teacher

The Goldilocks Map is a read for anyone who wants to understand how to use research to inform themselves, whether they are veteran educators, to-be educators, grad students, or even experienced researchers. The finesse with which Andrew Watson captures the distance between research and practice, and skillfully builds the bridge with numerous worked examples, is as insightful as it is useful. Pick up two copies, you'll want to gift one.

Dr. Kripa Sundar (NarayanKripa Sundararajan, PhD)
Founder and lead consultant, EdTech Recharge

Reading this book *will* help you become a better teacher. Andrew Watson distills essential cognitive and neuropsychological research and applies it to the classroom, while encouraging us to leverage our own experience and insights as we think about how this work applies not to every classroom, but to *our* classroom. He shows us that context is important and gives us the tools we need to understand how to apply the research he shares. Through the use of myriad examples and humorous anecdotes, Watson shows us how to use this information to help our students learn. He encourages us to think deeply about the students before us and appreciate the nuances that accompany research results. This book is an excellent resource regardless of how many years you have been teaching or how old your students are.

Susan Tammaro, PhD
Associate provost, Lebanon Valley College

As educators attempt to walk a line from neuroscience research to social and psychological adaptations to the realities of our classrooms, we need reliable guides. The path is hardly a straight one. Andrew Watson is a knowledgeable, engaging, and judicious companion. He understands the effort of professional translation that is required and is focused on what does (and does not!) move the needle in terms of research-informed teaching strategies. He certainly has the wit and insight to connect with educators and students in person and on the page.

Peter Welch
Head of school, American International School of Bucharest

To Richard Watson,
the kindest skeptic I've known.

And to H3,
Without Any Doubts.

"All models are wrong.
Some models are useful."

Attributed to George Box

CONTENTS

INTRODUCTION

Most teachers I know want to be better teachers. Happily, we live in a splendid time to improve our craft.

Back when I started teaching (in 1988), I relied on instincts and in-the-moment coaching. I drew on memories of the teachers I liked best. When my mentor teacher offered guidance, I tried to remember his suggestions. Generous colleagues shared their assignments and I borrowed the parts that sounded plausible. Mostly, I hoped that determination and humor would get the job done.

Today's teachers, however, can increasingly rely on **brain research** to inform and inspire their work. Specific fields within cognitive psychology and cognitive neuroscience give us precise and practical classroom suggestions:

- What's the best way to foster student attention? Michael Posner's **tripartite theory** points the way.
- Which study strategies foster long-term memory creation? Check out **retrieval practice** and **spacing**.
- What's going on when students mentally shut down? Research into **working memory** and **stress** offers surprising insights and inventive solutions.

Because learning happens in the brain, we teachers should benefit from psychology and neuroscience wisdom as we contemplate our classroom. Obviously. This optimistic realization, however, quickly runs into vexing difficulties:

- Brain research can baffle the most eager and determined reader.
- Those who offer "brain-based" teaching guidance often misunderstand or misapply the research they cite.
- Research-informed suggestions frequently conflict with each other. How can it be that brain research both requires and forbids the same teaching practice?

For these reasons, we teachers find ourselves both delighted and irked. We know that – on those groaning shelves of psychology and neuroscience texts – we might find enlightening resources to help us help our students. All those studies resemble a veritable Aladdin's cave, piled high with potential insights and wise guidance. And yet: what's the magic word to enter the cave? Once we're inside, how can we distinguish the real treasure from persuasive knockoffs? What riches should we share with colleagues and what debased coins should we leave behind? *The Goldilocks Map* will answer those questions.

First, I'll describe a balanced perspective that will help you approach and explore Aladdin's cave most wisely. Second, I'll give you a map that presents several specific steps to follow: questions to ask, traps to beware, treasure chests to open, mages to doubt.

I'll combine those two approaches with a loose extended metaphor. I see this process as a variant of **The Hero's Journey**, with several Joseph Campbell-inspired adventures along the way. You, as the teacher-hero, have been given a seemingly precious object: a "research-informed teaching strategy" bedecked in golden promises. Your quest will help you decide if that precious object is genuine or merely a gaudy fraud.

That is: you want to know if this teaching strategy is backed by authentic research, or if it results from misunderstanding or misapplication of research. When you reach your quest's conclusion, you will know whether this specific teaching strategy might truly benefit your students. This book won't provide "research-based" teaching ideas – that's not its primary goal. Instead, it will show you how to evaluate the advice that inevitably comes your way. When you hear the words "brain research shows…," you'll know exactly what to do.

Fair warning: I won't stick scrupulously to quest vocabulary. Heck, Aladdin has already made an unlikely appearance. Goldilocks will make her entrance in Chapter 1. Comic-book superheroes and television characters have cameos on upcoming pages. Our expansive metaphoric world will have room for them all.

Meet the Author

When you set out on this skeptical quest, you might well begin by being skeptical of *me*. Who am I to be offering this advice? How did I draw the map for this heroic journey? Bravo to you for asking those questions. I've got three answers: teaching experience, brain-science experience, and translation experience.

Teaching experience: I've spent my entire professional life in or near classrooms.

> Brief exception: after the Berlin Wall fell, I took a year off to manage a Beatles tribute band in Prague. No, really.

Specifically – when not in graduate school studying English and later studying brains – I worked as a high school English teacher for 16 years. I taught ninth through 12th grade at schools in Connecticut and Massachusetts: analyzing literature, calming parents; grading papers, soothing tempers; parsing sentences, advising teens. I especially enjoyed teaching 10th grade. Sophomores, I found, have the cognitive sophistication to think quite deeply, but don't yet feign jaded boredom about education and life. I loved their rambunctious energy and scattershot quest for emerging identities.

I also worked for four years as a dean of faculty. That job gave me daily chances to talk with teachers about their strategies and concerns and struggles and experiments. It also showed me the distinct challenges that different disciplines face. Teaching geometry, pottery, Arabic, pole-vaulting, and the Krebs cycle might sound the same to non-teachers. To those of us doing the teaching, however, they often require substantially different skills and insights.

If you ask me what I do for a living, the shortest answer is, "I'm a high school English teacher."

Brain-science experience: during my early teaching years, I paid little attention to pedagogical theory and even less to research. I was dimly aware of learning styles theory (now thoroughly debunked (Pashler et al., 2008)). I had seen the "learning pyramid," which claims that we remember 5% of what we hear, 10% of what we see, and so forth (claims never "bunked" enough to be debunked). I did work for two summers at a school that championed the Harkness method, but it never crossed my mind to ask, "Do you have any research supporting this approach?"

My conversion to brain world began in 2008. I attended a conference run by the organization Learning and the Brain and quickly came to several realizations:

- Psychology and neuroscience can fascinate even the most relaxed minds.
- They (especially psychology) provide teachers with fresh perspectives and practical strategies.
- In fact, cognitive psychology offers such useful guidance that it's shocking we don't require teachers to know more. (In all my years of teaching, no one suggested, much less required, that I should know anything about brain sciences.)

In 2011, I took a year off from classroom teaching to get a master's degree in Mind, Brain, Education – an interdisciplinary field that brings together psychology (mind), neuroscience (brain), and pedagogy (education) for interdisciplinary conversations. I studied with psychologists (Paul Harris, Nancy Hill), neuroscientists (Joanna Christodoulou, Gigi Luk), and experts in bringing it all together (Kurt Fischer, Todd Rose, Tina Grotzer).

To be clear, I'm not a practicing psychologist or neuroscientist. I've never run an experiment or held a brain. But in the years since my master's degree, I've continued my studies with a passion. For the past nine years, I've spent most of my days parsing brain research and discussing it with teachers and researchers.

In other words: if you ask me what I do for a living, the longer answer is, "I'm a high school English teacher, but a decade ago I got *really* interested in brains. I've been studying psychology and neuroscience ever since."

Translation experience: I've worked as a consultant since 2012, helping teachers and brain researchers understand each other's work. At times, I explain the complexities of classroom life to lab-based researchers – there are lots of good reasons why teachers can't simply do in the classroom exactly what their research suggests.

Mostly I visit schools and classrooms, explaining the practical uses of brain research to teachers, students, parents, administrators, and anyone else who'll listen. In this consulting work, I occasionally run into uber-skeptics who refuse all outside guidance. More often, I talk with uber-enthusiasts who can't wait to try out each new thing. As gently as possible, I try to explain why – even if their colleagues quote "brain research" to champion a new technique – they should ramp up their skepticism before they waste money and time. I frequently find myself saying:

- "The person who gave you that advice has cited research that contradicts it."
- "Research done with rats is essential to neuroscience and psychology. But until the theory is tested with human students, it should not shape classroom practice."
- "Brains don't 'light up.' They really don't."
- "The research you're quoting examined Finnish medical students learning how to complete insurance forms. You're teaching long division to fourth graders. Those med-school techniques just might not work with your nine-year-olds."
- "The strategy you describe has an uplifting name with the word 'brain' in it. Neither of those facts means that it has a good research basis."

Upcoming chapters will discuss each of these points in detail. But, as you can see, I've been exploring this book's questions and problems for almost a decade.

Other springs have fed the book's development. My deep interest in the topic flourished during several months' work with two thoughtful scholars: Stephanie

Fine Sasse and Maya Bialik. We developed and presented a framework – TILT – that charts the social, intellectual, and historical trajectories shaping modern research. This book does not draw directly on that work, but contains its influences in countless indirect ways.

For the past several years, I've practiced those TILTing skills as blogger for Learning and the Brain (www.learningandthebrain.com/blog), an organization that runs conferences on psychology, neuroscience, teaching, and learning. In preparation for those blog posts, I study scientific publications to discover practical classroom suggestions. With alarming frequency, I find that claims about brain research don't align with the research itself.

In a typical case, I might read a web headline saying, "Research shows exam-related stress damages teens!" If that's true, clearly high schools should stop requiring exams! When I click on the various links offered to support this claim, they show that:

- In certain circumstances, excessive stress can be bad for brains.
- Adolescent brain development creates both opportunities and vulnerabilities.
- In a recent speech, a prominent neuroscientist worried that England's national high-stakes exam might not be a good idea.

Those three statements might be true. But they don't remotely add up to "exams damage teens." After all, "damage" is quite a high bar. Of course, exams might harm teens. But if someone says "research shows X," *they should be able to quote research showing X.* If they can't, then they should acknowledge that they're assembling an argument, not quoting a settled conclusion.

This distinction might seem needlessly fussy, but I believe it deserves emphasis. In my life, I don't spend much time telling forest rangers how to range forests more effectively, because they almost certainly know their work better than I do. Likewise plumbers, dental hygienists, architects, restaurateurs, and chicken farmers. Most jobs require some kind of expertise. Lacking that expertise, I don't have the standing to tell someone else how to do their job better. Whenever I say, "You'll be better at your job if you do X," that's a **Big Ask**. Before I make that Ask, I should be as certain as possible that my advice will help.

The same truth applies to teaching. If you're a teacher, you know: effective teaching is hard. It requires experience, content knowledge, pedagogical wisdom, patience, people skills, and a magical something else. Whenever people say to us, "You'll be better at teaching if you do X," that's a Big Ask. And it's especially big if they're not experienced teachers themselves.

To boost their credibility, non-teachers who make these teaching suggestions often include the words "research shows." Those words seemingly convert a Big Ask into Entirely Sensible Advice. If they've got on-point research supporting this claim, then they're not being presumptuous – they're helpfully offering pertinent guidance. Given the magical powers of "research shows," we're right to ensure that *research really does show that.*

To return to the "Research shows exam-related stress damages teens!" example, an online paper – written by non-teachers – implies that schools should stop giving exams. That's a Big Ask gussied up with "research." When we discover that the sources only distantly imply that this Ask might be valid, that sleight of hand should thoroughly vex us. It should at least persuade us not to credit this advice (even if we ourselves don't much like exams).

As a consultant and as a blogger, I try to help teachers understand that brain research can profoundly improve our teaching. Just as important, I want teachers to see that misused or misunderstood brain research can impede effective teaching. We should take especial care when others make Big Asks decorated with "research."

In sum: if you ask me what I do for a living, the complete answer is, "Drawing on lots of teaching experience and years of studying brain research, I help people make wise use of psychology and neuroscience in classrooms. And I spend lots of time debunking exaggerated claims of research evidence."

Confession: my consulting work making Big Asks has provided an unexpected benefit for this book. I understand many of the mistakes described in upcoming chapters because I made so many of them myself. Having once relied too much on neuroscience research, I now recognize the dangers of doing so. Having paid too little attention to boundary conditions, I now obsess about them. In many ways, I'm writing the book I wish had existed when I started my conversion to brain world back in 2008.

A Unique Map

The map that I'll be sketching for you results from a decade of pursuing such quests on my own. No doubt other thinkers in this field would draw quite different maps. If you study statistics for a living, you would probably have included a lot more information about that field. (I'll talk a little bit about numbers and equations but won't dwell on those topics until Appendix I.) If you have a background in the theory of knowledge, you would probably prefer a more philosophical approach, with lots of explicit discussion of epistemology. (Daniel Willingham's excellent book *When*

Can You Trust the Experts? offers more of this helpful perspective.) Psychology researchers, I suspect, would prefer a more detailed review of methodology and object to some of my oversimplifications.

As I've drawn my quest map, I've kept myself within strict limits by asking two mundanely practical questions.

First, can non-experts take this quest step on their own? Can teachers, in fact, do what I'm encouraging them to do? In many cases, I've excluded questions and suggestions that – in my view – simply aren't practical. I'm told, for instance, that teachers who want to evaluate research simply must know the difference between ANOVA (analysis of variance) and MANOVA (multivariate analysis of variance). I understand why a statistician would make that argument, but I just don't think most of us have time to do that. Rather than create a complete but unwieldy system, I've focused on developing a process that, realistically speaking, anyone can use.

Second, does every adventure along this quest provide clear and useful information? Will each step help you sort genuine, research-informed teaching suggestions from the fakes? At the conclusion of each stage, I want you to feel confident about making an informed judgment call: to continue the quest or – having vanquished the misleading foe – to return home in triumph.

For that reason, I haven't explored broader philosophical topics or dwelt on the nature of scientific knowledge. *The Goldilocks Map* won't help you make an explicit argument about epistemology, but it will help you decide whether to trust the consultant who bantered so wittily at that recent conference. (He had such funny slides!)

Speaking of practical questions, this talk of questing through nine chapters invites a pressing one: exactly how much time will this adventure take? We teachers are a busy lot. We can't just drop everything and devote our weekends to heroic journeys. Happily, the journey requires less time than you might think. Several quest stages require brief minutes. Others will absorb as much time as you give them. However, you can decide how far along those branching paths you want to stray. You can draw your own reasonable limits. In short: the process will not take over your life. And, like everything else, the more you practice, the more quickly and effectively you'll accomplish these steps. You might start as a novice, but you'll develop greater expertise with each new adventure.

How Research Happens

Because this book focuses on brain research, it will be helpful to introduce the process that produces it. At the most basic level, researchers – often professors and their graduate students – set about a specific investigation. In common parlance, we speak of **experiments**. Researchers often use the word **study**, as in: "This study explores the effects of taking handwritten notes on lecture comprehension." These studies follow exceedingly rigorous steps to ensure, as much as possible, that the researchers can plausibly reach their conclusions. If I want to explore "the effects of taking handwritten notes on lecture comprehension," then I should take care in several ways:

- I need a precise method of measuring "lecture comprehension."
- I need to compare one group of students – who took handwritten notes – with another group of students – who used a plausible alternative. For example, I might compare the first group with a group that took notes on laptops, and another group that quietly spoke their "notes" into a recording app on their phones.
- I need enough students in both groups to ensure that my findings don't result from chance quirks. If my groups have only five people, then I might – simply by accident – end up with strong note-takers in one group and weaker note-takers in the other.
- I need to take detailed measurements and perform exacting calculations.

If I follow these (and myriad other) steps scrupulously, then I've earned the right to make a precise claim.

> Vocabulary note: researchers use the word **intervention** to describe the specific thing they ask students to do. In this case, taking handwritten notes is the intervention. In other studies, it could be mindfulness training, or naps, or exercise, or specific study techniques.

Researchers then write up all these steps into a document, colloquially also called a study. Before that study can be published, however, it must be vetted by other experts in the same field. Scholars who study stress might evaluate research by other stress scholars, but they probably wouldn't evaluate research into attentional blindness.

In theory, this **peer review** process provides quality control. A professional painter can tell you whether a colleague did a good job painting your house – certainly better than I could. A dentist can recognize a well-filled cavity better than most fighter pilots. A psychologist who spends her days researching sleep can spot a dodgy sleep study better than almost anyone else.

Unsurprisingly, this process results in lots of grumbling. Because peer reviews are typically anonymous, reviewers are occasionally quite mean. Professional jealousies, or fear of being scooped, might complicate the reviewers' motives. Twitter reverberates with complaints about peer review.

More substantively, we might ask pointed questions: does peer review guarantee excellence? Can we honestly say that all peer-reviewed research is good, and all research that isn't peer-reviewed is bad? Professor Robert Talbert answers:

> *"It's certainly true that a lot of peer-reviewed scholarship is bunk, and peer review is no guarantee of quality. Conversely a paper doesn't need to be peer reviewed to contain good scholarship. However, without peer review, what you're getting is basically a preprint [draft] that has not undergone systematic review by experts who have applied their expertise to detect and point out flaws – and those flaws most certainly exist simply because every study has flaws. Those flaws, having not been pointed out, are sitting there in the study, and they very likely affect the validity of the results."* (Talbert, 2020)

In other words: the peer review system has weaknesses and people sometimes abuse them. But, at present, we don't have a better way to ensure that researchers have met the standards that apply in their fields. For the same reason you wouldn't be treated by an unlicensed doctor (even though medical licensing has its flaws), and you want your certified public accountant to be genuinely certified, we shouldn't change our schools based on research that hasn't completed peer review. As Talbert says, "every study has flaws." We want experts to look for them before we do.

Because peer review can spot those flaws, this book mostly cites studies from peer-reviewed journals. I also quote a few books, an occasional blog or tweet, even an email or two. However, some of the examples I offer don't include citations. Let me explain why.

The Goldilocks Map uses specific examples to demonstrate steps along our heroic journey. When I present a *good* example – an expert drawing on strong research to offer wise advice – I credit that work in full. When I present a *bad* example – an "expert" misunderstanding or over-hyping research – I don't. *The Goldilocks Map* isn't intended to "name and shame" people who do this work badly. Instead, I use those examples to guide readers along a better path. Although I accurately represent the bad examples that I offer, I don't make their authors clear (with rare exceptions). Truthfully, their identities don't really matter. If the advice is wrong, it's wrong – no matter the credentials of the person offering it.

Skepticism 101

All this talk of peer review and studies and professional jealousy might sound daunting. I promise you: although the quest ahead looks scary right now, with common sense and determination you'll accomplish your mission with elan.

In fact, you've already got lots of useful skepticism skills right at hand. For one thing, you might at least notice the researchers' credentials. Do they have an academic degree? Is the advice they offer within that same field? (An anthropology professor might do important neuroscience research, but it doesn't happen often.)

Of course, researcher credentials give only a rough clue about the reliability of the teaching advice. Neil Lewis, an expert in science communication, warns specifically against relying on a researcher's eminence to weigh their advice (Lewis & Watson, 2020). As Lewis notes, scholars can gain eminence by publishing lots of studies quickly; however, longer studies probably give us deeper insight into learning. For an especially amusing analysis of this eminence problem, you might look into research on "pseudo-profound bullshit" (Gligorić & Vilotijević, 2020).

You've also got experience with many other day-to-day skepticism strategies. If I say to you, "I've got this awesome car that you can buy for just $10,000," for instance, you already know what to do:

- You would test-drive the car.
- You'd look on the internet to see if that make and model get good reviews.
- You would compare the car to others in its class.
- You'd find out if I had sold cars before and whether my customers had a good experience.
- You might look up the history of the specific car to see if it had been in an accident or used in a crime.

Likewise, when you read shocking claims on social media, you know how to look under the hood:

- You might (gingerly) click the link to see what other claims this news site makes.
- You might Google the claim to see if a better-known source is running the story.
- You might ask yourself what other sketchy claims have been posted by this friend.
- You might surf over to Snopes.com to see what their sleuths have deduced.

Some skepticism skills are so fundamental that they predate even the internet. As the most basic example, if an expert says, "Research shows that this brain-training program improves student performance," you will almost certainly ask, "How much does it cost? And how much do you make from the sale?" Yes, profit motives tempt even brain researchers to hype inadequate research. Lumosity, a much-loved website with "brain-training" games, was fined $2 million for making misleading claims about its products (Underwood, 2016).

In other words: the quest ahead will require specialized knowledge, and include several counterintuitive steps and strategies. But our common-sense skepticism will guide us along the way.

Despite the breezy tone of this introduction, I hope you agree with me that our quest has a special urgency. First, lots of false treasure circulates in our land. All too often, edu-wizards try to impress teachers with their Exciting New Idea; too often they claim that research supports their innovation. We're not battling a rare problem here. Schools launch "brain-based" initiatives all the time.

Second, this inaccurate information can have terrible consequences. If a classroom strategy does not work as promised, if the "brain-based" brand persuades us to change our teaching, *our students learn less*. That's bad for them. That's bad for our schools. That's bad for students' families. That's bad for our economy and culture and society. Every time we let flashy-but-false "brain-based" promises dilute our practice, we fail in our essential mission.

We simply must succeed on our journey. The next nine chapters unscroll the quest map before us.

Acknowledgments

I could not have written this book without: Eva Abbamonte, Pooja Agarwal, John Almarode, Patrice Bain, Maya Bialik, Tim Blesse, Christian Bokhove, Joanna Christodoulou, Mark Combes, Betsy Conger, Kate Conlon, Sheila Culbert, David Daniel, Kurt Fischer, Tina Grotzer, Paul Harris, Eric Kalenze, Nate Kornell, Dan LaGattuta, Jasmine Lane, Scott MacClintic, Kevin Mattingly, Rob McEntarffer, Isla McMillan, Steve Most, Jonathan Mulrooney, Cindy Nebel, Robert Payo, Brandon Peters, Andrea Poritzky, Alex Quigley, Kate Rudder, Stephanie Fine Sasse, Michael Scullin, David Silver, Kristin Simmers, Nick Soderstrom, Rob Stephenson, Kripa Sundar, Susan Tammaro, Amie Weinberg, Peter Welch, Glenn Whitman, Kelly Williams, Daniel Willingham, and Michael Wirtz.

I thank them for their guidance, insight, assistance, support, encouragement, and patience; and apologize to them – and my readers – for the mistakes that remain.

Andrew C. Watson, Somerville, MA
November 2020

PART I.
THE QUESTING
EQUILIBRIUM

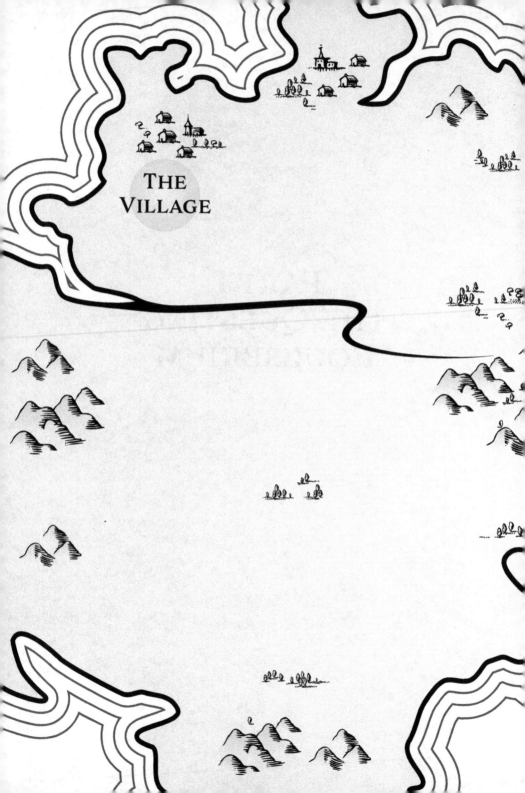

THE
VILLAGE

THE
GOLDILOCKS MAP

CHAPTER 1.
INTRODUCING GOLDILOCKS

Like quests of old, ours begins when a messenger unexpectedly appears. A rider clops up to our misty hamlet and unveils a magical object, gifted by a distant wizard. Secret words unlock the object's awesome powers. We must guard it zealously and wield it humanely. As abruptly as he rode in, the messenger vanishes – rarely (if ever) to be seen again.

That is: an outside expert enters our teaching world and gives us "research-based" guidance. A speaker might come to our building for a professional development day. Perhaps our grade team studies this year's must-read book. Our principal could return from an eye-opening conference with an exciting idea. Maybe a blog or a Twitter post inspires the leadership team.

Whatever the specifics, a seemingly knowledgeable specialist tells us to change the way we teach. He cites brain research to make that guidance sound persuasive. Sometimes implicitly, sometimes explicitly, the Big Ask includes this message: teachers need not question it because *research says so.*

Despite that message – "resistance is futile" – some villagers hold back. They admit that the mysterious object glows with a potent energy, but who was that stranger? Does he truly represent a famous wizard? Why should we believe either of them? How can they know what's best for our village? After an angry debate around a smoking peat fire, the village elders appoint us to undertake a quest: to learn more about the messenger, the wizard, the magical object, and its potentially awesome power.

That is: before we simply accept the "brain-based" approach offered by the professional development speaker – or the latest book, or the lively tweet – we should stop to ask some tough-minded questions. Can we trust the speaker, or the author, or the tweep? What does brain research actually say about this teaching method? What evidence suggests that this classroom strategy will help *our* students learn *our* curriculum in *our* community?

Like all first-time adventurers on a quest, we pause nervously on the threshold. How will we know the path? How can we best prepare ourselves? We feel perilously under-equipped for this weighty mission. I'm going to argue that, on our journey, we don't need supplies. Instead, we need the *right perspective*. In particular, we should strive for two kinds of mental equilibrium: the right balance of openness to new ideas, and the right balance of respect for expertise.

A Fine Balance: Openness to New Teaching Ideas

Perhaps you've seen a poster online: "The most dangerous phrase in education is, 'We've always done it this way'" (e.g., Harvard, 2019). Some of your colleagues, no doubt, rebuff well-intentioned suggestions with precisely that attitude. "I don't need others to tell me what to do," you hear them say. "If it was good enough for Gradgrind, it's good enough for me."

While this poster rightly mocks that "we've always" extreme, it does so by posing an extreme of its own. That's *the* most dangerous phrase in education? Really? (I would have thought "Today's faculty meeting will need a few extra minutes" portends considerably greater danger.)

Imagine that our department has a keystone project that truly brings together our students' understanding of a complex topic. Students love doing it. They rock that section on the final exam. Their subsequent teachers marvel at how well they remember the material. By all relevant measures, this project really works. And so, we do it year after year. In fact, it seems *we've always done it this way.* As long as we genuinely have good reasons to believe that this project helps students learn, a change might not lead to improvement.

And yet, we all have colleagues who latch on to every passing edu-fad, especially those fads with the word "brain" nearby: **brain gym** and **brain breaks** and **brain bag**. (I think I made up "brain bag.") Enthusiastically embracing all "innovative" guidance – particularly guidance with obscure terminology like "oxytocin" or "ventral tegmental area" – these colleagues are quite certain that classrooms require regular transformation.

If you don't work in a school, these two extremes may sound like parodies. If you do work in a school, you know exactly who I'm talking about. (Heck, you might have been one of those people. I might have been both.) Many of us – but not all – instinctively ally with one camp or the other. We might perk up when introduced to an exciting innovation, or we might roll exasperated eyes whenever we hear about some shiny new educational initiative.

These impulses, I suspect, come from basic drives built into the teaching profession. On the one hand, teaching allows each of us great independence. I can go into my classroom, close the door, and create a learning world as I see best. Little wonder I don't want outsiders telling me what to do. On the other hand, teachers regularly hear that we can shape the future. Today's children will be tomorrow's leaders, and that upbeat perspective can incline us to earnest optimism. Little wonder that I'm eager to try new things.

Before we begin our skeptics' quest, we should acknowledge this truth: *both extremes create palpable dangers*. Yes, my classroom allows me real independence and I don't want outsiders spoiling my relationships with my students. At the same time, other people do have good ideas: ideas that might help my students learn more – or, at least, more efficiently. Those ideas might contradict my training, or conventional wisdom, or my classroom hunches. And yet, if they truly improve schools and classrooms, I should move past my confident pride and accept outside guidance. Failure to do so harms my students.

And yes, my optimism about the future inclines me to experiment. At the same time, good teaching is hard. We shouldn't naively assume that every glossy new approach will benefit our students. Until we have asked difficult questions and considered unintended consequences, we should temper our enthusiasm with caution. Again: failure to do so harms students.

In other words: when a seeming expert says, "You should teach *this way* – research says so!" we should have simultaneous and conflicting reactions. We should feel excited about the possibility that research can improve our teaching. We should likewise feel wary about the potential exaggeration or misunderstanding of research.

As we gear up for our quest, we should deliberately pause and adopt this mental middle ground:

- Despite our instinctive doubts, we pledge to embrace the magical object if we see good reason to believe it works.
- Despite our excitement about its jewels and possibilities, we vow to toss it aside if we can't verify its magic.

I'm arguing that we should pursue our quest as Goldilocks. We don't want to be too skeptical; we don't want to be too trusting. We're looking for an openness equilibrium: a balance that's *just right*.

I have to admit that the image of Goldilocks on a quest looks jarring. With her pert curls and nosy innocence, she doesn't belong in a story with gory swords and touchy dragons. This incongruity, however, highlights an important point. Our culture's quest narratives emphasize good and evil, right and wrong, saintly and wicked. Such stories, in other words, typically focus on extremes. We don't have a national epic about questing valiantly toward a sensible middle ground.

For that reason, the quest decreed by the village elders creates a two-layered challenge. On the surface, it requires specific skills and technical knowledge. Deeper down, it requires a new mental model. We're not defying Sauron, or the Borg, or He Who Must Not Be Named. Instead, we seek out a moderate stance among hot-headed alternatives.

If you can picture yourself as Goldilocks on a Just Right Quest, you're already creating the perspective that will allow this journey to succeed.

A Fine Balance: Respect for Expertise

At the same time as we deliberately adopt a Goldilocks perspective on new ideas – not too skeptical, not too trusting – we should also contemplate a second, related middle ground: our response to expertise.

In a famous series of studies, two scholars tested students' *actual* skill at various tasks and their *perceived* skill at those same tasks (Kruger & Dunning, 1999). They had students take a grammar test, or a logic test, to measure their ability. At the same time, they also asked a straightforward question: "How many of those test questions do you think you answered correctly?" Justin Kruger and David Dunning wanted to compare the students' actual ability, as measured by their test scores, with their perceived ability, as measured by their predictions.

They found that, quite consistently, students who lacked a particular skill nonetheless predicted great success. On the logic test, for instance, the least successful students scored an average of 12%. Despite this painful weakness in their logic skills, they predicted a score of 62%. On the grammar test, they predicted an average score of 60%, when in fact – yikes! – they scored 17%.

Simply put: until we have an expert's knowledge, experience, and perspective, *we don't really know what we don't know.* We can't yet truly understand what we don't understand. John Cleese – one of Dunning's friends – sums it up in this way:

> "[Knowing] how good you are at something requires exactly the same skills as it does to be good at that thing in the first place. Which means, and this is terribly funny, that if you're absolutely no good at something at all, then you lack exactly the skills that you need to know that you're absolutely no good at it." (Monty Python, 2012)

The reverse holds true as well. Those who did the best on Kruger and Dunning's grammar test predicted that they had scored 77%; they had in fact scored 90%. The top group at logical reasoning predicted a score of 68%, yet achieved a score of 85%. The more we know, the likelier we are to spot – even exaggerate – our mistakes.

Figure 1 graphs this paradox. For those who know the least – the bottom quartile – the predicted score towers over the actual score. That is: the dotted line is much higher than the dashed line. For those who know the most – the top quartile – the reverse holds: the predicted score (dotted line) is modestly lower than the actual score (dashed line).

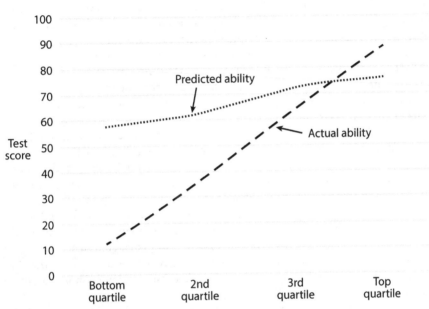

Effect of Actual Competence on Perceptions of Competence

Figure 1. (Source: Kruger & Dunning, 1999)

When we enter brain-research world, teachers often make both Dunning-Kruger mistakes. First, the allure of educational psychology and neuroscience tempts novices to enthusiastic overconfidence. For instance, when I attend my inaugural conference on the neuroscience of stress and memory, I might latch on to key ideas and terms: neuroplasticity, cortisol, hippocampus, amygdala, adrenal gland. Back in school, I zealously deploy those words to make my arguments more persuasive:

- "We can't possibly ask students to take that advanced course because *parietal lobe!*"
- "It's essential that every student have an adviser; we need to *raise their oxytocin levels!*"

These magic brainy words add seeming gravitas to the causes I champion. Trust me: experts would roll their eyes at my statements. Yet as a beginner, with only a weekend's worth of neuroscience under my mental belt, I don't understand how much I have misunderstood. I don't have enough knowledge to see the painful limits of my knowledge.

Our just-right Goldilocks perspective requires that we acknowledge the expertise that researchers bring. Psychologists have a profound understanding of the mind's baffling complexity. If a psychology researcher tells me that memorizing one thing (a poem) does not make me better at memorizing other things (properties of chemical elements), he probably knows better than I (Roediger, 2013).

So, too, neuroscientists explore an almost infinitely intricate map of calcium channels, glial cells, and Latinate terminology. If neuroscience researchers tell me that the inferior parietal lobe, the supramarginal gyrus, and the angular gyrus are associated with representations of semantic memory (van den Broek et al., 2016), I start by trusting their expertise.

Simply put, we should approach brain research respectfully, even modestly. When it comes to dendrites and long-term memory reconsolidation, scientists really do know more than we do. And yet, teachers often fall victim to the second Dunning-Kruger mistake as well. At the same time as we *overestimate* our knowledge of brains, we often *underestimate* our classroom expertise.

When a researcher makes a Big Ask, her fluency with neuro-terminology might scare me into needless timidity. If the person giving me teaching advice can say "corpus callosum" and "dosing effect" with casual confidence, that level of knowledge endows her with awesome authority. I take for granted that her suggestions will improve my teaching. I can't possibly know as much as these experts, so I should simply follow their instructions.

For instance, your average neuroscientist knows a lot more than I do about the ventral striatum. She might make emphatic teaching recommendations based on that brainy knowledge. But I know a lot more than she does about teaching *The Grapes of Wrath* to 10th graders. In my years of experience, I've learned to prepare students very carefully for the final chapter's fertile symbolism. If I don't, they'll be so grossed out by Rose of Sharon's breastfeeding that they'll completely miss her astonishing transformation – and Steinbeck's point.

Figure 2 highlights this paradoxical over- and under-estimation of our knowledge. At arrow A, we overvalue our knowledge of brain science – likely to be much lower than an expert's. At arrow B, we undervalue our teaching experience – likely to be quite meaningful.

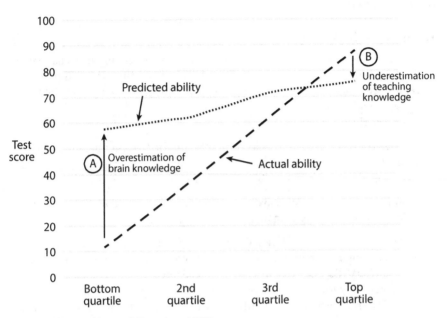

Effect of Actual Competence on Perceptions of Competence

Figure 2. (Source: Kruger & Dunning, 1999)

When we adopt our Goldilocks perspective, we remember to avoid both extremes. Brain researchers have one important expertise; teachers have another, equally important expertise.

In practice, the second Goldilocks equilibrium works like this...

A psychologist might say, "Research into the spacing effect shows that people learn more when they spread practice out over time. The same number of practice problems yields greater learning when spread out over days and weeks than when undertaken all at once. For that reason, teachers should rethink their syllabi and lesson plans."

We can start by respecting her expertise in long-term memory formation. We can assume she has good reasons to make this Big Ask. At the same time, we should respect our own expertise as well. For instance, as we'll discuss in Chapter 5, we should ask, "What are the boundary conditions for this research finding?" That question is entirely reasonable. The psychologist should answer it. In fact, a refusal to answer it would throw her teaching advice into doubt. Yes, her expertise encourages us to listen respectfully. And yes, our expertise encourages us to stand our ground. We should ask respectful questions – and confidently expect thorough answers.

Reverse Goldilocks

This Goldilocks perspective guides our thinking as we quest and helps us evaluate advice from messengers and wizards. For all the reasons that we avoid passionate extremes, we should beware others who embrace them. We value our Goldilocks compass so highly that we doubt others who ignore it.

Imagine the following exchange:

Teacher: Mr. Conference Speaker, thank you for that presentation. Now that you've shared your research with us, what plans do you have to gather feedback from teachers so you can learn from our experience as well?

Conference speaker: We have no such plans. We have done the research. We know what the right answer is. Teachers need to do it. So, *do it.*

This exchange – sadly, not fictional – presumes not a balanced equilibrium but uncompromising hierarchy. According to this conference speaker, teachers must obey researchers' directions, yet researchers need not even listen to teachers. In this view, teachers' day-to-day classroom experience has no place in shaping classroom practice. 'Tis not ours to reason why. 'Tis but ours to follow "research-based" instructions.

Our Goldilocks perspective tells us: ignore this speaker's extreme stance. We could imagine this dialog reversed:

Teacher: Mr. Conference Speaker, thank you for that presentation. I'm intrigued by your advice, but I've seen lots of psychology research that contradicts what you say. How would you go about integrating your years of teaching experience with research guidance?

Conference speaker: I wouldn't. I trust my gut and my experience and learn from my students. If researchers want to know what works in a classroom, they should come watch me.

I've never seen anyone say that at a conference, although I have seen such comments on Twitter. Here again, the speaker's extremity makes his argument unpersuasive. My classroom experience obviously informs my beliefs. But I've always got something to learn – especially from experts in cognitive science.

Most kinds of uncomplicated certainty should raise our doubts. If a book says that a teaching technique works for *all* students learning *all* topics in *all* circumstances, the very breadth of that claim makes it especially unlikely.

Goldilocks rarely believes "always"; she rarely believes "never." She prefers "most of the time, but with some important exceptions." And she straight-up loves "under these specific circumstances, but not those circumstances."

For this reason, scientists rarely use the verb "prove" – as in, "This research proves that kittens are cuter than puppies." They might say that this research "suggests" or "supports the hypothesis that" or "gives us further reason to believe that." The more often a conference speaker says "research proves," the deeper our doubts.

Here's the reverse-Goldilocks principle: the more absolute and inflexible the teaching guidance, the more confidently we believe that we shouldn't trust it. If someone makes a Big Classroom Ask and says, or implies, that teachers have to accede unquestioningly "because research says so," that absolutism alone makes the advice suspect. So too, if teachers refuse all outside guidance because "our experience by itself tells us everything we need," such tunnel-vision weakens their argument.

A more fruitful discussion starts like this: "Researchers found these interesting results under these specific circumstances. Let's use that research to launch a conversation: how do these findings intersect with your classroom experience? How might we bring our disciplines together into respectful and productive balance?"

At the end of such a conversation, teachers might adopt – or reject – a Big Ask in its entirety. We might blend, tweak, adapt, reschedule, or fiddle. In all likelihood, our students will learn more because we united the best of two perspectives. Goldilocks for the win.

And so, in Goldilocks garb, we prepare for our quest by purposefully adopting a balance of competing goals. We want to welcome new teaching ideas that might benefit our students, and to reject tempting possibilities that lack support. We listen to experts with deep respect for their knowledge and insight, *and* pointedly insist on answers to our reasonable questions.

At times, these contradictory goals require us to take a quirky, zig-zag path along our journey. In the chapters ahead, the path often doubles back to re-explore familiar ground and reopen once-settled questions. And yet, this mental compass ultimately gives us the truest guidance along the way.

Let the journey begin.

PART II.
RELIABLE SOURCES

BURIED TREASURE

DISGUISE SPELL

THE GOLDILOCKS MAP

CHAPTER 2.
FACING THE CHASM
OF SELF-DOUBT

A delicious piece of teaching advice has arrived at our school:

- In a fascinating blog post, a respected author advocates special handshakes at the classroom door; they foster deeper connections with our students.
- A professional development speaker champions the use of individual whiteboards to promote students' active recall.
- A colleague summarizes an inspirational book. By flipping the classroom, teachers can provide just-in-time instruction.

In every case, this transformational teaching advice is "brain-based." Whether focusing on the neurobiology of human connection, or retrieval practice, or working memory, these messengers offer classroom magic from brain-science wizards. Should our school follow their advice?

To satisfy uncertain village elders, we're on a quest to explore this magic. As seen in Chapter 1, we start by purposefully adopting a Goldilocks equilibrium. We pledge to be open to new ideas, but not credulous about them. We honor expertise, but expect honest answers to our frank questions.

Before we set out from the village, we need to decide on our immediate goal. We might be tempted to investigate the **magical object** itself. We could look into the research to see how much support – if any – the teaching strategy really has. We could see if other schools have tried it. We could assemble a task force to pilot the idea in one section or grade.

Alternatively, we might be tempted to start by investigating **the wizard**. These psychologists and neuroscientists whom the speaker quoted: are they leaders in the field? How seriously do other researchers take their work? How seriously should we?

For the time being, however, we must resist those temptations. We should instead start by investigating **the messenger**. We needn't worry so much about the teaching advice itself, or about the science behind it – not yet, anyway. Instead we should ask ourselves: *do we trust the person who gave us this suggestion?*

New teaching advice rarely comes to us directly from brain researchers. The conference speaker we heard or the blogger we read has studied someone else's research and translated it into specific suggestions. People who undertake those translations often combine rigor, insight, humor, and humility in reaching their conclusions. Alas, some don't. They might misunderstand the science, or over-extrapolate based on its conclusions, or overlook the very exceptions most relevant to our school. They might have a product to sell. Even with the best of intentions, they sometimes botch the job.

Because this research-to-practice translation requires expertise, nuance, and modesty, we have every right to ask pointed questions. These translators are making a Big Ask: "Stop doing what you once believed was right and start doing what I tell you is right – even though I'm not a teacher in your school." Before we say yes, we really must ensure that we can trust their judgment.

This request, however, immediately poses a problem. As Goldilocks, we scrupulously remind ourselves to be humble. Despite all our expertise in teaching, we have little in psychology and neuroscience. As novices, we can't easily distinguish between true brain experts and fake ones. If – as Dunning and Kruger remind us – novices don't know enough to know what they don't know, how can we possibly know enough to evaluate the messenger's knowledge?

Of course, we can't train up as brain experts overnight. However, we can solve this problem. We will ask that conference speaker **three precise questions**. Genuine experts typically offer recognizably right answers to those questions. If we hear those answers, we will choose to trust this advice. If we get wrong answers – also easily recognizable – we start to doubt this guidance. With these questions, even brain novices can easily distinguish between reliable and unreliable experts.

Each question sounds deceptively simple. And yet, each one includes enough Goldi-nuance to merit its own chapter. As we try to identify reliable sources, we might even have follow-up questions to ensure the messenger's answers are just right.

The messenger might be an author or a PD presenter; a tweep or a blogger; a colleague or a conference speaker. I'm going to call all these people "the source." As in, "When the source says *this*, we should do *that*."

A note on pronouns: to keep things clear, I'll use he/him/his pronouns for all *sources*, and she/her/hers for *researchers*. (Of course, although this shorthand is grammatically convenient, it doesn't express the full breadth of human gender expression.)

In the introduction to this book, we noted that credentials often influence our level of skepticism. If a conference speaker earned his PhD from a well-known university, if a blogger has published several books, if the mention of a Ted Talker's name causes our colleagues to whisper in awe – these accomplishments might incline us to trust him all the more.

Of course, such credentials often matter. Yale doesn't hand out psychology PhDs for no reason. At the same time, we should notice those accomplishments without being credulous about them. Not all degree holders, or books, or eminent people equally merit our trust.

To accomplish our first questing goal, we need to do better than credentials.

The Chasm Within

As we set out to test the source's credibility, we quickly arrive at the first quest obstacle: the **Chasm of Self-Doubt**. This obstacle, curiously, exists simultaneously outside the village and inside us. Simply put, we hesitate to ask the messenger bold questions because we doubt our own standing to do so.

What explains our strange hesitation? Why all this self-doubt? As we saw in Chapter 1, the source wields a seemingly awesome authority. When talking about those handshakes at the classroom door, he describes dopamine's journey from the anterior cingulate cortex to the prefrontal cortex (van Heukelum et al., 2019). When insisting on individual whiteboards, he cites a foundational study on retrieval practice and long-term memory consolidation (Roediger & Karpicke, 2006). All that scientific know-how makes our quest and our questions seem impudent. This Chasm of Self-Doubt blocks our path.

True enough, brain expertise certainly merits our respect. But the Goldilocks voice inside insists we press boldly forward. We should balance respect with determination. Sources don't get to tell us how to teach until we have asked – and they have answered – hard questions. We need to get over the Chasm. And it's surprisingly easy to do so.

To cross the Chasm, we start by (respectfully) asking our first question: "Your teaching suggestion sounds so interesting and helpful. *What's the best research you know of that supports it?*" This wonderfully simple question throws a bridge right over our self-doubt. What query could be more reasonable? If the source claims that brain research informs his teaching advice, then it couldn't be more appropriate for us to ask about that research.

An analogy might illustrate this suggestion. Whenever I buy a car, I ask a gearhead colleague for some guidance. He knows a great deal about the subject and always responds to my query with a lengthy – even wearying – list of cautions and suggestions. To answer my question, he doesn't summarize someone else's expertise. *He draws directly on his own deep knowledge.*

When a source tells me to change my teaching "because brain research says so," he too should draw directly on his own deep knowledge. He should not rely on someone else's summary. He should not say "I heard at a conference" or "I read a cool book" or "my favorite blog pointed to this cool tweet." He should, instead, know that research itself with scholarly richness. He should know why retrieval-induced forgetting complicates retrieval practice. He should know the relationship between the hippocampus and the medial temporal lobe. Like my car-loving friend, he should offer advice based on personal knowledge and expertise. Our first question – "What's the best evidence?" – helps us find out if he knows his stuff.

We can divide potential answers into three handy groups: the right answer, the wrong answer, and incomplete answers.

The Right Answer

Here's the right answer: "I'm so glad you asked! You should start by looking at *this* fascinating study, and if you want to dig deeper, try this other one as well. I hope you'll let me know what you think!"

Of course, the way we interact with the source shapes the way he can answer:

- If the teaching advice comes from a book, then we should easily find supporting research in footnotes and reference pages. All that small print at the bottom of the page or the back of the book – all that counts as "the right answer."
- If the advice comes from a PD presenter or a conference speaker, we can approach him at the end of the talk to ask our question. Speakers often include citations on their slides; occasionally, they have a final slide with a list of references.
- Those presenters who have bad memories might say, "Ugh, I wish I were better with names. Lob me an email (here's my card) and I'll send you the links." As long as the follow-up email happens, it's all good.
- Trustworthy blogs usually include links to the research they cite. If a blog post doesn't include such a link, then we can email the author to ask for the best research evidence.

- Social media platforms, like Twitter, don't feature links as frequently as blogs do. However, we can – and should – follow up with a direct message or tweet.

The words might be different in each medium, but the result and the attitude should be the same. Trustworthy sources *want us to want more information*. We should expect some degree of enthusiasm and a specific answer to our question. When the seeming expert offers this information, he behaves just like a reliable expert. He gives us an initial reason to follow his guidance. We can, with this reference in hand, continue our quest with renewed confidence. First mission accomplished.

We can pause here, on the far side of the Chasm of Self-Doubt, to notice how easily we overcame the first obstacle. If this were a movie, uplifting violin music would swell and the camera would pan up to a bucolic valley vista. It may be hard to believe that the quest's first step has already been completed. Yet because we had a Stubborn Goldilocks attitude as we approached it, and because we knew what question to ask, a problem that seemed insurmountable practically vanished. This entire process took longer than a minute only if the source wanted to give us lots of research to explore.

The Wrong Answer

At the same time, we should prepare for wrong answers to our question at the Chasm. The wrongest answer sounds like this: "I won't/can't share that information with you, because [insert excuse here]." Let me be succinct: sources *never* have a plausible reason to decline to answer. Such reasons do not exist.

This answer, although wrong, makes our quest extremely simple. We have, in fact, completed it already. Given a chance, the seeming expert has conspicuously failed to act like a genuine expert. We can turn right around and return to our village with a triumphant conclusion: "The messenger refuses to name his wizard. His refusal clearly means that the 'magical gift' has no value. We should give it to the neighboring villagers who stole our sheep last season."

In other words: this answer is both wrong and useful. We know exactly what to think of this "brain expert." We think he hasn't earned our trust.

You won't hear this wrongest answer very often, but you might hear it. I once asked a source for research supporting his claim that "brains don't multitask well because the corpus callosum is too small." He responded, "I can't give you that information because you don't have a PhD in neuroscience." Notice the strangeness of this excuse: "because you don't have a PhD in neuroscience." That non sequitur tries to put the responsibility on me, as if my own shortcomings somehow deserve the blame. And yet, obviously, the source could share the research with me whether I have a high school diploma or not. If he's going to make a claim about the relationship between brain regions and multitasking, he should be willing – and eager – to support that claim.

As an analogy, let's imagine this dialog between me and my doctor:

Doctor: Take this medicine; you'll feel better.

Me: I'm curious, how does it work?

Doctor: I'm not going to tell you. You're not a pharmaceutical company.

That irrelevancy doesn't work for my doctor, and it doesn't work for sources. They can't simultaneously ask us to follow "brain-based" teaching advice and refuse to specify the research. The refusal removes the base on which their "brain-based" advice rests. The structure collapses on its own illogic.

In case you're wondering, the source himself *did not have a PhD in neuroscience*. And I should add that his claim was bogus. Brains do multitask badly, but not because of the corpus callosum – one of the brain's largest structures. When a research group tried to find the neural basis for multitasking difficulties, they concluded that "the corpus callosum does not seem to be a plausible multitasking locus" (Nijboer et al., 2014, p. 65). The source couldn't give me any supporting research not because I don't have PhD, but because it doesn't exist.

Like right answers, this wrongest answer will sound different in different media:

- If a speaker refuses to cite research, obviously, we have ended our quest victoriously.
- If a blogger or tweep doesn't answer our polite request for more information, that tells us everything we need to know.
- If a book claims that its suggestions are "research-based" but doesn't cite research, that failure counts as a wrongest answer.

In every case, these answers mean we have successfully completed the quest. (Whenever a quest concludes in this way, we might decide to relaunch it independently in Chapter 8. By then, we'll have lots of vital skills that will allow us to blaze our own trail.)

Incomplete Answers

At the Chasm of Self-Doubt, we might get right answers ("Here's the information you asked for!") or wrong answers ("I can't tell you"). Or we might get incomplete answers. In that case, we draw on our Goldilocks stubbornness and ask our follow-up questions.

Incomplete Answer #1

"I'm so glad you asked! You should read this book."

At first this answer sounds promising. Unlike the wrongest answer, it provides a concrete resource and presumably lots of information. At later stages in our quest, books will prove immensely useful. By the time Chapter 8 rolls around, we'll be reviewing books with gusto.

However, this answer doesn't satisfy our immediate goal. Remember: we don't (yet) want to look at the *research*. Instead, we want to ensure we can trust the source. That is: we want to know with confidence that he has studied the research directly. We don't want the source merely to have read so-and-so's book – one author's explanation of someone else's research. We want the source to have engaged with the scientific studies knowledgeably, himself.

This requirement might sound unreasonably stern. However, we are currently in Stubborn Goldilocks mode. The source has made a Big Ask. He strode into our classroom and told us to change our teaching. He has standing to do so if and only if he knows a great deal about minds and brains. To prove he wields that knowledge, he should be fluent in its language: fluent enough to cite specific studies.

For that reason, if we get this incomplete answer, we should follow up with: "Thanks for that suggestion. I'm curious, *which study* in that book did you find most persuasive?"

If, in fact, the source speaks this language fluently, he will enthusiastically follow our lead. We should hear at least one specific citation. Ideally, we would hear several more than we plan to read. That answer would clearly give us reason to trust the source.

If the source starts hedging, however, we reluctantly arrive at this troubling conclusion: he's giving us advice *without having studied the research on which it's based*. We wouldn't let our doctors do that. So, too, with "brain experts." Anyone offering suggestions based on research should, obviously, know that research in detail.

This incomplete answer comes in other guises. A book by a well-known Ted Talker assures readers that its parenting suggestions rest on brain research. However, all its citations point to popular magazine articles. Of course, magazine writers might do an excellent job of explaining brain research. Alas, these citations don't provide the reassurance we need. At this point in the quest, as you recall, we want to know that our source can evaluate research. If all his citations point to magazines, we simply can't have confidence that he has explored the topic directly. Without that reassurance, we can't rely on his judgment.

There's an important exception to the "don't accept books as citations" rule: if researchers wrote the book, then we're good. Books written by brain scientists explore and explain the very details we want our sources to know. For example, if a source suggests we read *Make It Stick* by Brown, Roediger, and McDaniel (2014), we can accept that suggestion because Roediger and McDaniel have done vital research in long-term memory formation.

Incomplete Answer #2

"Don't worry. *All* the research shows that."

This answer troubles us for two reasons. First, common sense says that it doesn't inspire trust. It sounds like the source can't think of a specific citation, so is trying to ward us off with vague but comprehensive reassurance. For that reason, we should follow up with: "That's certainly reassuring! Which studies do you find most persuasive?"

Here the decision tree forks. If the source says, "A great question! I'd start with X and Y, but P and Q struck me as interestingly helpful," then he regains our trust. We were (appropriately) determined to get an answer and he was (ultimately) helpful in giving us one. We have the citations we asked for and a healthy dose of reassurance that the source knows his stuff.

If, however, the source says, "No, trust me, all researchers agree on this," our quest has reached its successful conclusion. We can return to the village in triumph, announcing that the magical object has no real value.

In part, the source's refusal to name names persuades us that he doesn't know the research well enough to make strong recommendations. This incomplete response, after all, is simply a politer version of "I won't tell you because you don't have a PhD." In both cases, the source declines to name the research basis of his teaching advice – advice we were listening to only because he claimed it had a research basis.

Second, more importantly, this incomplete answer reveals a profound misunderstanding of psychology research itself. In psychology, it is simply never true that "all the research" agrees on a finding. That *never* happens. For the source to insist on this point reveals that he doesn't understand how psychology research functions. This insight is so important that it will be a core principle of Chapters 5 and 6.

For the time being, as we make our way back to the village, we can content ourselves with the fact that our quest succeeded so quickly.

Incomplete Answer #3

The third incomplete answer causes us the most confusion, because it dazzles and hypnotizes. It sounds like this: "I'm so glad you're asking about research. So-and-so's study shows the essential connections between the prefrontal cortex and the basal ganglia. You'll find that GABA and glutamate are vital in this discussion."

When we first hear it, that answer sounds utterly compelling. So many brain terms in so few sentences! We feel that we've been invited into an exclusive club, where the elect deploy Latinate vocabulary in hushed tones. At the next faculty meeting, we'll be sure to slip the word "glutamate" into a rebuttal.

To understand why this captivating answer shouldn't satisfy us, we need all our Goldilocks nuance: a just-right balance of humility and determination. And some history will help, too.

For most of the 20th century, neuroscience and psychology eyed each other from a wary distance. To outsiders they sound roughly alike; so far in this book, we've been lumping them together under the banner "brain sciences." After all, both study "stuff going on in the head." During the 1900s, however, neuroscientists and psychologists concentrated on their bedrock differences. Neuroscientists primarily studied physical, biological objects: mostly the brain itself. They studied cells and neurotransmitters and electrical current. If they wanted to know, say, how memory functions, they would look at activity in neurons and synapses. A neuroscientific description of learning sounds something like this...

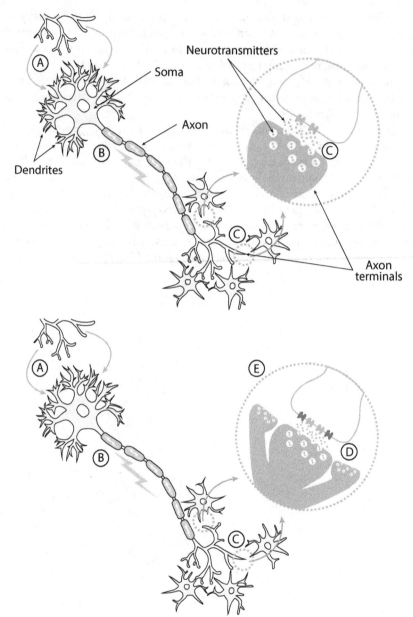

Figure 3. (Source: Kandel, 2006; Squire, 2004)

When we create new long-term memories (that is, when we learn something), thousands of neurons join together in a complex network (Kandel, 2006; Squire, 2004). (See Figure 3.)

A. A chemical signal enters the neuron through the dendrites.

B. When enough chemical energy builds up in the soma, it releases that energy as an electrical signal down the axon.

C. The axon terminal then sends another chemical signal (neurotransmitter) to the dendrites of the neighboring neuron.

D. If this process happens enough times in the right ways, the axon and the dendrites undergo physical changes. The axon, in effect, grows more branches. Each branch releases more neurotransmitters when stimulated by the electrical charge. And the dendrites respond more strongly to those neurotransmitters.

E. There's an oft-quoted neuro-saying that "neurons wire together if they fire together." That is: repeated signals down this neural chain create lasting physical changes at the magical place where axon and dendrite communicate: the synapse. The concept comes from the neuroscientist Donald Hebb. The neuro-saying, although often attributed to Hebb, comes from Lowel and Singer (1992).

In brief, in the 20th century, neuroscience was a highly specialized kind of biology. Neuroscientists dissected brains and stained slides and zapped cells. Requiring scalpels and gloves and microscopes, neuroscience was often cool and occasionally sticky or gross.

While neuroscientists studied their specialized biology, psychologists during the 1900s focused not on the brain but on the *mind*: on mental behaviors. I can, for instance, pick up a brain and weigh it. I can't pick up *attention* and weigh it – attention is a behavior, not a thing. I can study a neuron with a microscope. I can't study *introversion* with a microscope – introversion is a behavior, not a thing. In fact, 20th century psychologists largely rejected the idea that examining the brain might elucidate the mind. The brain was a "black box" – no amount of fancy biology could reveal useful truths about mental behavior.

Whereas a neuroscientist studies memory formation by slipping on gloves and prodding neurons, a psychologist studies memory formation by investigative cognitive activity. Here's a fun and useful example.

The psychologist Doug Rohrer's research team had students learn about a mathematical process called permutation (Rohrer & Taylor, 2006). Some students did all their practice problems at once; a month later, they scored 32% on a permutation quiz. Other students *spread their practice out over several days*. A month later, these students scored 64% on the same quiz, even though they did the same number of practice problems. In this study and in many others (Brown et al., 2014), spreading practice out over time was found to increase learning. Hence the phrase **spacing effect**.

A note on methodology: you might think that 64% sounds like a lamentable score. But notice the improvement – it's twice as good as 32%. When students use this spacing technique in courses with meaningfully developed and connected content – not a freestanding topic like permutation – they'll probably learn more. Students who once scored Bs might now get B+s, and so forth.

Notice here that Rohrer and Taylor looked at mental behavior. Students who *studied* one way *learned* more than students who studied a different way. Both "studying" and "learning" are cognitive processes, not damp biological objects. In this psychological study, there isn't a neurotransmitter in sight.

As we contemplate these related but distinct fields – neuroscience and psychology – we consider this Goldilocks question: which perspective offers us the most useful classroom advice? A sports analogy provides helpful perspective.

As a soccer coach for starting players, I might tell my team about an amazing leg muscle called the **gracilis**. Located in the thigh, it helps move the leg toward the body's midline. Because soccer requires lots of leg, my team members will use the gracilis constantly. Hence, I routinely coach my players by shouting, "Remember: use your gracilis!"

A coach for the other team – to my surprise – does not tell her players about the gracilis. When she coaches from the sideline, she shouts, "Remember: kick with the inside of your foot! Run to open space! Trap first, then pass!"

Care to guess whose players will improve at soccer?

To be clear: when players kick and run and trap, they do indeed use their gracilis. I didn't give my team incorrect information. However, while my anatomy lesson accurately describes the mechanism of movement, it doesn't tell my players *what to do*. As my players contemplate their gracilis, opposing team members will be running to open spaces, trapping the ball, and shooting. Because the other coach went *beyond anatomy to action*, her team has a much higher chance of success.

The same statement holds true on our quest. When we move from brain anatomy and physiology (the traditional focus of neuroscience) to mental action (the traditional focus of psychology), we have a much better chance of getting practical teaching advice.

Let's go back to those two explanations of memory formation.

If a PD speaker described the neural process behind learning – dendrites and synapses and neurotransmitters – most of us would find that fascinating. We would have eager questions about the details of each stage. How do the dendrites receive the neurotransmitters? How does the soma convert chemical signals to electrical signals? What's this thing called myelin?

Emulating my rival soccer coach, let's move beyond anatomy to action. Now that we know more about these brain mechanics, *how will we teach our classes differently tomorrow?* What will we teachers do with that information? After we ponder that arresting question for a few minutes, our answer goes something like this: "Well, we want to teach in ways that cause that amazing neural transformation to happen!"

Indeed we do. However, that brain information hasn't given us any new strategies to accomplish that goal. We know more about what *happens* in brains when students learn. But we have no additional information about the teaching strategies that *cause* them to learn. This information – like my cry "Remember the gracilis!" – *intrigues* teachers but doesn't *help* them.

If a second PD speaker described Rohrer and Taylor's research into the spacing effect, we might repeat our earlier question: "Now that we know all this, how will we teach differently tomorrow?" In this case, answers come thick and fast. We need to adjust our syllabi to ensure that students practice their work over longer periods of time.

In the past, perhaps, I scheduled my students' homework in 20-problem blocks. When I taught grammar, students practiced identifying nouns and pronouns on Monday. On Tuesday they identified verbs. Wednesday: adjectives and adverbs. The homework on my syllabus looked like this:

Traditional Syllabus

	Monday	Tuesday	Wednesday	Thursday
In class	Topic A	Topic B	Topic C	Topic D
Homework	20 A problems	20 B problems	20 C problems	20 D problems

Figure 4

But Rohrer and Taylor's research might encourage me to adapt my syllabus to spread out that same number of practice problems. On Monday, students would do five practice problems with nouns and pronouns. Tuesday: identify five more nouns/pronouns and five verbs. Wednesday: identify five parts of speech from several categories. The specifics will differ, depending on a great many variables:

the grade and subject I teach, the daily schedule my school follows, the other topics we're discussing. But, conceptually speaking, my homework syllabus now looks more like this:

Spacing Syllabus

	Monday	Tuesday	Wednesday	Thursday	
In class	Topic A	Topic B	Topic C	Topic D	
Homework	5 A problems	5 A problems	5 A problems	5 A problems	
		5 B problems	5 B problems	5 B problems	→
			5 C problems	5 C problems	→
				5 D problems	→

Figure 5

This second PD speaker, in other words, offers teachers *practical guidance*. We might not find it as sexy as all that talk of the inferior parietal lobule, but we certainly can use it right away. In brief: for soccer players, the gracilis might interest my players, but coaching advice about it doesn't immediately help them. For teachers, neuroscience (à la 20th century) might *fascinate* them, but psychology (à la 20th century) *helps* them.

As those parentheses suggest, that summary requires some contemporary nuance. In recent decades, the relationship between these brainy fields has become cozier. Neuropsychology and cognitive neuroscience use gross/cool/damp neuro-tools and neuro-terms to describe mental behavior – once the exclusive kingdom of psychology. In a Venn diagram, two wholly distinct circles now overlap to allow for some cooperation. (Of course, much work in these fields remains obviously distinct. Molecular neuroscience, for instance, largely maintains its biological focus. Over pizza a few years ago, a psychology grad student warned me sternly not to be drawn into too much brain talk.)

This evolving cooperation means that, to draw wise distinctions, we should focus less on the *label* and more on research *content*:

- Does the study focus on cognitive behavior? Then it might prove useful to teachers. (This work probably has the stem "psych" in it somewhere, but might have a dollop of "neuro" as well.)
- Does the study focus principally on brain anatomy or physiology? Then, with some exceptions, it probably won't help us change our teaching. (This work

almost certainly fits in a "neuro" category, but might occasionally have some "psych" influence as well.)

We can feel Goldilocks straining to get this balance just right.

The distinction between psychology and neuroscience merits so much attention because *sources frequently emphasize brain anatomy*. Alas, they often do so inappropriately. Drawing purely on neuro-research, they offer classroom advice. And yet, by our rough-n-ready terminology, they shouldn't make Big Teaching Asks unless they can cite psychology research: research into mental activity.

For instance, that first PD speaker might correctly explain the neurobiological process of memory formation. He might then say, "Therefore, you should spread students' practice out over time rather than bunching it all together." In this case, his *advice* is correct. But he didn't cite *research* supporting it. Until he gives us Rohrer and Taylor's study – focusing on studying and learning – he shouldn't make this Big Ask. The neuroanatomy was fascinating, but not directly helpful.

Here's another example – this one a true story. Teachers often hear debates about **cold-calling** students – that is, calling on a student who hasn't raised her hand. I once heard a conference speaker make this argument:

Students who have been cold-called feel great stress. Bruce McEwen's research (1998) has shown the terrible effects that stress has on the brain. It raises cortisol levels, and cortisol actually damages the hippocampus. We all know that the hippocampus allows students to form new memories. When we cold-call, we weaken the hippocampus and make learning harder. And so, teachers seriously violate their professional responsibilities when they cold-call. Research says we must never do so.

This argument sounds alarming indeed. If a teaching technique literally damages brain regions, we obviously shouldn't use it. Notice, however, that the speaker's claims here focus on brainy things: cortisol, hippocampus. His account certainly sounds neuro-plausible. Cold-calling *could* raise stress, which *could* elevate cortisol levels, which *could* damage the hippocampus, which almost certainly would hamper learning. But before we change our teaching, we want to know if that plausible process really happens under specific circumstances – circumstances that resemble our real classrooms.

A study examining that question would (substantially) rely on psychology. We would cold-call a group of students, measure their actual stress, and measure their actual learning. We would compare this group with a second group of students who studied in identical circumstances, but without the cold-calling. Such a study would provide useful classroom advice.

That study might include some neurobiological measurements; for instance, we might track students' cortisol levels as an indicator of stress. But we would surely ask them to rate their own stress (psychology). And we would surely see how much learning took place (psychology). That is: we would focus on their mental behaviors – stress and learning. Such research might confirm the fear that cold-calling inhibits learning. But it also might refute that hypothesis. We don't know until we check. In this case, "checking" means "psychology."

When sources name brain parts and functions and then tell us to change our classroom work, they skip the essential step. Before we accept that Ask, we need to hear about the psychology research that buttresses their specific teaching suggestion. After all, many classroom experts consider cold-calling an essential strategy to check for understanding (e.g., Lemov, 2015).

Confession: I understand many of the mistakes described in this book because I have made them – none more often than over-reliance on neuroscience. Early in my consulting career, for instance, I devoted lots of time to a study called "The hippocampus is coupled with the default network during memory retrieval but not during memory encoding" (Huijbers et al., 2011). Based on the title, you can understand my fascination with it. I'm now here to tell you: it's super-interesting – and has no direct teaching implications.

Because neuroscience has such social currency, you'll hear this sort of information quite frequently. Three claims often receive outsized attention:

1. "When students do X, you can see how much more of their brain lights up!"

As neuro-novices, we respond with enthusiastic nods. In that fMRI image, we *can* see how much more of their brain lights up! However, this claim disguises two conspicuous problems.

First, brains don't "light up." Images from fMRI scans use different colors to represent changes in blood flow. Honestly, nothing is lighting up. The psychologist David Daniel jokes, "If you don't believe me, go into a dark room, *think hard*, and open your mouth. See what I mean?" (D. Daniel, personal communication, November 2019.)

Second, this enthusiastic statement suggests that *more* brain activity results in *better* thinking. If an fMRI scan spots additional blood flow, surely our students must be thinking more! Alas, not so. In some cases, more brain activity results from *inefficient* cognitive processing. Dyslexic readers, for example, use considerably more neural real estate than neurotypical readers (Gabrieli, 2009). More brain activity isn't unambiguous good news. People who understand neuroscience know that.

You might also hear this enthusiastic cry:

2. "When students do X, it actually changes their brains!"

Here again, as beginners to brain research, we might find this fact astonishing. The speaker's awe implies that brains rarely change. We should be ever so impressed that X causes them to do so.

Alas, this premise doesn't hold up. Brains change all the time. **Neuroplasticity** is, in fact, a basic part of human brain function. A speaker might announce that studies of Tibetan Buddhist monks show that "over the course of meditating for tens of thousands of hours, the long-term practitioners had actually altered the structure and function of their brains" (Davidson & Lutz, 2008, p. 176).

No doubt that's true. To change our brains, we might spend tens of thousands of hours doing *anything*: playing the piano, learning sign language, singing opera, juggling chainsaws. I suspect – although I don't know of research on this topic – that my brain will change if I get into the habit of napping. (It's possible I'm already in the habit of napping.)

In brief: we shouldn't be impressed by giddy claims that "brains change." And we should be wary of sources who make a big deal of this entirely routine process.

3. "When you give your students a handshake at the door, you give them a hit of dopytocin!"

OK, I made up the word dopytocin: an unholy marriage of dopamine and oxytocin. Sources talk about both these neurotransmitters with breathless excitement, implying that getting a "hit" of either should be a first-order classroom goal. At times, sources describe oxytocin's function correctly. Indeed, handshakes at the door might raise oxytocin levels. But, as teachers, we don't care about oxytocin; we care about students' mental behavior. Are they *learning*? Are they *paying attention*? Are they *making friends*?

I know of one study showing that positive greetings at the door increase students' attention and reduce their disruptive behavior (Cook et al., 2018). As long as those classroom improvements happen, then the neurotransmitter blend honestly doesn't matter. Yes, oxytocin might be involved in the process, but focusing on the oxytocin doesn't make us any better at this teaching strategy. (Yes, my soccer players use the gracilis to trap the ball and run to open space, but focusing on the gracilis doesn't make them any better at executing.) Instead, teachers need to know the specific steps that the researchers developed:

- First, greet the student by name: "Good morning, Dan. Great hat!"
- Second, offer **precorrective guidance**: "We're starting with flashcards, so be sure to have them out right away."

Assuming that teachers have limited amounts of time and memory, sources should focus on useful teaching specifics, not neural mechanisms.

Equally troublingly, sources regularly get neurotransmitter information wrong. With alarming frequency, for instance, sources describe oxytocin as "the love hormone." Apparently, nursing mothers boast unusually high oxytocin levels. Because oxytocin = love, the logic goes, we want to increase its levels by shaking hands at the door.

Alas, oxytocin heightens negative emotions as well. Some researchers, for instance, describe it as a "crisis hormone"– one that increases when emotional investments in a relationship differ (Grebe et al., 2017). A "hit" of oxytocin might help connect students warmly to each other, or it might stress them out. When sources imply that oxytocin *always* benefits students, they make fundamental mistakes in describing its function.

In other words: we can understand why sources make mistakes about neurotransmitters. The topic can baffle the most scrupulous researcher. (If you want to explore the astonishing complexity inherent in neurotransmitter function, Robert Sapolsky's dense and excellent book *Behave* (2018) walks you through layers and layers of intricacy.) However, I struggle to understand why sources devote so much time to neurotransmitters. Information on the topic is always incomplete and often incorrect; in either case, *it doesn't help us teach any better.*

In brief: don't let mere talk of dopytocin persuade you to accept a Big Ask.

Fair warning: this argument about the limitations of neuroscience (à la 20th century) is highly unpopular. Several people whose work I respect, and whose guidance I follow, rely heavily on neuroscientific terminology. I wish they wouldn't. But, because they can cite psychology as well as neuroscience, I ultimately trust their advice.

Many researchers – both psychologists and neuroscientists – share my frustration and worry that sources extrapolate too zealously from brain regions to classroom advice. This debate rages hotly in the field of Mind, Brain, Education.

With this neuro/psych balance in mind, let's return to the Chasm of Self-Doubt. When the source answers our first question ("What's the best research to support that teaching strategy?") with a neuroscience study, his answer might enthrall us but it doesn't help us. The answer isn't wrong, but it isn't persuasive either. When we get that incomplete answer, we should follow up with: "That neuroscience research sounds fascinating. I'm more focused on research into classroom practice. Has this strategy been tried with students in classrooms?"

Imagine that a conference speaker makes this claim: "Teachers should encourage simple calisthenics during classroom mini-breaks; they promote learning." When you ask for research evidence, he says, "So-and-so's fMRI study shows that exercise oxygenates blood flowing through the prefrontal cortex – a brain region essential for self-regulation. You should check that out." This claim is plausible and rich in enticing terminology.

However, it doesn't answer the key question. After all, exercise might oxygenate blood in the prefrontal cortex, but does that extra oxygen truly *help students learn more*? The source claimed that it does, yet this research doesn't directly support that precise conclusion. For that reason, we follow up by seeking the psychology research: "That sounds fascinating. I'm curious, has this calisthenics suggestion been tested with students? It sounds so simple and practical; I'd love to try it. And I always like to see classroom research on a teaching technique before I start using it in practice."

If you, like me, hear a conference speaker claim that McEwen's research forbids cold-calling, you might send a follow-up email:

> *The potential neural effects of cold-calling sound terrible. I had no idea that stress could do lasting damage to the hippocampus.*
>
> *I'm interested, has this relationship been studied directly? Do you know of classroom research where teachers did (or did not) cold-call? Perhaps this research measured the students' stress levels? That kind of research would complete the picture and help our school create a research-informed cold-calling policy.*

Sources' responses to our questions about calisthenics and cold-calling will help us decide if we can trust them or not.

The first source might say: "Weren't you listening? Exercise oxygenates the dorsolateral prefrontal cortex. FMRI data show that conclusively. Of course calisthenics will improve focus!" The second might say: "Research shows that cold-calling shreds the hippocampus! If you're not willing to give up a 19th century teaching practice that damages students, I don't know what to say to you."

These answers have a troublingly familiar ring: "I can't give you psychology research because [insert excuse here]." In this case, the excuse is: "I've given you neuroscience; you don't need psychology." As we've seen, however, neuroanatomy rarely provides sufficient classroom guidance. It offers a fascinating potential explanation for the learning and teaching world in which we work. But it almost never tells us how to teach.

The source's refusal to acknowledge this truth makes our decision easy. We shouldn't trust him enough to accept his Big Ask. Because we persistently asked the right questions, we successfully accomplished our quest.

Of course, we might get a different answer if we ask the source to go beyond brain function. The first source might say: "Yes, of course, you're right! Neuroscience can give us some helpful predictions and pointers, but we really do need to test these ideas in the classroom. You should check out Barbara Fenesi's recent study on mid-lecture exercise breaks; it's the best I know" (Fenesi et al., 2018).

This answer promptly restores our trust. By acknowledging that neuroscientific predictions must be supported by psychological findings, the source shows how well he knows this field. His initial answer made us worry he was trying to distract us with merely decorative neuroscience. By combining neuroscience (brain research) with psychology (mind research), he has instead elevated his credibility.

"But," you ask, "what about **both**? Wouldn't teachers benefit from knowing psychology *and* neuroscience?"

We have two ways to think about that question. First, in Chapter 8, we will invite neuroscience to partner with us as we quest. For the time being, we typically *end* a quest by looking at brains, but rarely *begin* a quest that way. Second, to understand when we might wisely *begin* with neuroscience, turn to Appendix IV.

To sum up this chapter so far, Figure 6 sets out the decision tree you'll follow to cross the Chasm of Self-Doubt.

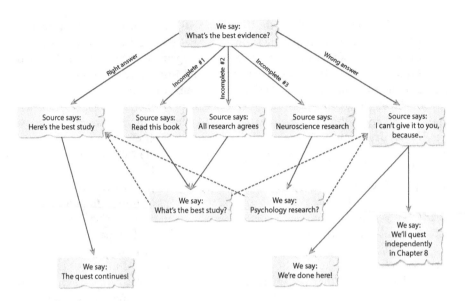

Figure 6

Two important points merit emphasis.

First, I've argued that if we can't trust the source, we shouldn't accept his teaching advice. If he says, "Believe me: science says I'm right," but won't share the science, then he's probably not right. When we therefore reject his advice, our quest ends quickly and successfully.

In some cases, however, that conclusion might feel like a failure. We might want to believe him. His advice might resonate deeply with our teaching experience and our school's philosophy. We might wish to adopt this new method in our school, and tell our students and their parents that brain research has inspired us to do so. The quest's abrupt ending brings no satisfaction.

In this case, we can follow an alternative path: we must, in effect, morph into our own source. We must set out to find supporting brain research ourselves. In Chapter 8, we'll consider the strategies to use when we start that improvisational quest. By that point in our investigation, such free-form questing can be great fun.

Notice, however, this crucial distinction. We might continue investigating the *research*, but we're done with the *source*. We might be tempted to follow unreliable guides who occasionally point us in the right direction. We must firmly resist that temptation.

Second, I've emphasized that the Chasm of Self-Doubt can be quickly overcome. We ask the source one simple question. If we get the right answer, we carry on almost without breaking stride. If we get the wrong answer, we celebrate the rapid conclusion of our mission. If we get an incomplete answer, we know how to deploy our Goldilocks stubbornness and ask our follow-up questions.

My breezy tone disguises a curious fact. Although this step is that easy, it often *feels* remarkably difficult. The Chasm of Self-Doubt really does inspire dread; it really does deter most teachers from even beginning their quest.

I learned this lesson many years ago. A colleague and I led a four-hour teacher workshop on effective skepticism. We discussed several strategies for seeing past exaggerated research claims, and described the techniques teachers need to expose them. We had rich discussions and offered several opportunities to practice. The teachers – who had all chosen to attend a workshop on effective skepticism – were not only curious, experienced, and thoughtful, but also well-prepared.

My colleague and I ended the workshop with a hands-on exercise: attendees had 30 minutes to skeptically investigate the claim that "students remember material better when they take marginal notes in their books." We were curious to see how long it would take them to get to step #1: ask for research that supports the claim. In those 30 minutes, *not one* of the 45 teachers asked. They put their effort into later steps, even though we had discussed that first step at great length. It was, in fact, on the projector screen behind us.

In our concluding discussion, we pointed out that they had all skipped this step. This room full of teachers looked at us, amazed and abashed. To a person, they said they hadn't fully realized that they'd missed it. They might have felt a brief mental hitch when they started the process. But it seemed somehow impertinent or impermissible to ask. They felt that they didn't have standing to question the authority figures in the room. They preferred working quietly at their tables. Brain research has such social currency these days that it seems simply beyond questioning.

For that reason, I encourage you to start practicing now. When you hear a factual claim, inquire about the source. Perhaps a friend says, "I read online that cats are smarter than dogs." You might respond, "I'm intrigued! Do you remember where you read that? I'd love to follow up and learn more." If a neighbor tells you that the mayor's salary has *doubled* in the past five years, you can be sympathetic and curious: "I must say, that sounds outrageous. I really want to know more about this. Where can I get specific information?"

In asking these questions, we don't need to be unpleasant or overtly skeptical. Instead, we're simply practicing a skill: braving the Chasm of Self-Doubt. Every time we inquire politely about a source, we build muscle memory to help us ask more easily the next time. When a conference speaker tells us to try his exciting new method, we'll have lots of experience in making inquiries. The self-doubt that once resembled a chasm will hardly slow us down.

And because we can leap over that Chasm of Self-Doubt, we can turn quickly to the second stage of our quest: digging for Buried Treasure.

CHAPTER 3.
DIGGING FOR BURIED
TREASURE

Our quest has started well. By emulating Goldilocks, we've got the right mental equilibrium in place. Having crossed the Chasm of Self-Doubt, we feel a rising sense of confidence in our source.

Before we tackle the next obstacle, let me encourage a brief but important mental exercise. Take a few minutes to recall the key concepts of the previous two chapters. While you're at it, consider definitions and specific examples as well. You might ask yourself:

- To have a Goldilocks equilibrium, I need to strive for two different kinds of balance. What are they, specifically?
- Why are they difficult to achieve?
- What's an example of being conspicuously out of balance? Of being wisely in balance?
- What is the self-doubt I might experience at the Chasm?
- What question do I ask to bridge the Chasm? What answers might I receive? How should I respond to each one?
- Are there exceptions or special cases to ponder?

In a moment, I'll answer those questions and explain why this exercise is valuable. But, for the time being, *don't read ahead*. Instead, push yourself to answer the questions as best you can. Remember: you're not allow to keep reading unless you've thought hard about the questions above. Once you have, your answers might sound like this...

A Goldilocks equilibrium begins by balancing openness to new ideas with a healthy skepticism about them. We don't want to resist every teaching suggestion we hear, but we don't want to adopt them all either. That balance can be difficult to achieve because our personalities probably incline us one way or another. And, truthfully, our culture valorizes extremes: those who insist on fierce independence, and those who instinctively and relentlessly innovate.

At the same time, we should balance a deep respect for expertise with a stubborn confidence in our own right to ask reasonable questions. As brain beginners on the Dunning-Kruger graph (Figure 2; see p. 33), we shouldn't think we know as much as researchers simply because we've read a psychology book or two. As classroom experts on that graph, we shouldn't think we know nothing simply because we don't understand the nuances and the fancy terminology. In this collaborative effort to improve teaching, we should listen to wise guidance *and* ask pointed questions.

In fact, it's this self-doubt that we face at the Chasm. Brain research somehow seems so far above our pay grade that we dare not act presumptuously. Yet we can raise our confidence with a reasonable question: "What research best supports this 'brain-based' teaching suggestion?" If we get a specific answer, we continue with heightened trust in the source. If we don't – despite polite and persistent questioning – then we should decline that Big Ask.

In less than one minute, our first magical question encouraged us to believe in ourselves, gave us reason to trust the source (or not), and provided useful information for later stages of our quest.

I promised to explain why I insisted on this try-to-remember exercise. We have lots of robust research showing that trying to remember something promotes long-term learning of it. That is: you'll remember this summary much better if you tried to answer those questions on your own. We now call this strategy **retrieval practice**, and it has ever so much research behind it. In fact, I encourage you to try this technique with your students. Don't have them merely *review* information or processes. Instead, have them *try to remember* first.

As you read that last sentence, I hope that a small alarm bell went off in the back of your head. After all, someone (me) just made a Big Ask (use retrieval practice) and claimed that we have "ever so much research" to support that advice. If the ideas in this book have started to take root, your internal thought process might have sounded like this:

That sounds like an interesting teaching idea. I'm open to trying it out. But I don't want to rush in and accept every new suggestion. This book's author claims to have expertise and I should listen to it. But I have expertise too, and I'm not going to change my approach to teaching just because he says so. I need to send him an email and ask for some sources. If he responds, I'll start to trust him. If not, well, this "retrieval practice" thing just might be a cleverly branded dud.

Let me save you a step. Research into retrieval practice (under different names) has been around for more than 100 years. In 2006, Roediger and Karpicke published a study called "Test-enhanced learning: Taking memory tests improves long-term retention," and it revived interest in the topic. If I had to pick my favorite study on the subject, I'd point you to "The value of applied research: Retrieval practice improves classroom learning and recommendations from a teacher, a principal, and a scientist" (Agarwal et al., 2012). This study looks at retrieval practice in actual classrooms, so it gives us confidence that the technique works in the real world. And, by the way, Agarwal and Bain have written a great book called *Powerful Teaching* (2019) that offers lots of examples and research. (Remember, I'm allowed to cite a book if it's written by the researchers themselves.)

Peer Review and Beyond

Let's resume our quest.

At our journey's outset, we identified a conundrum. In Goldilocks mode, we pledged to listen both respectfully and critically when a source makes a research-based Ask. Alas, being psychology and neuroscience novices, we struggled to deploy our skepticism effectively. How could we – who know relatively little about nodes of Ranvier and theory of mind – distinguish scholarly advice from bunk?

Happily, we've found a clever strategy. If we ask the right questions, we can evaluate our source's answer. True experts, we know, answer these questions in recognizable ways. If we don't get the right kind of answer, we know not to rely on the source – even if his fancy terminology sounds ever so impressive.

So, for instance, we reasonably asked for the source's best evidence. We know that reliable sources willingly supply us with pertinent psychology research. If we hear any kind of refusal – "You don't have a PhD!" "I've already given you neuroscience research!" "Look, squirrel!" – we know not to rely on that source's advice and not to honor his Big Ask.

That strategy has enough fine points to require its own chapter, but it really is that simple.

Having received that information, we now ask our next strategic question. We know that – except in unusual circumstances – reliable experts depend on published, peer-reviewed research. Now that the source has given us his best evidence, we check: has this study been published in a peer-reviewed journal? The source told us of Buried Treasure; now we unearth it to test its value.

As noted in the introduction, **peer review** cannot claim perfection. Its misuses and mistakes invite entirely reasonable criticism. Hasty peer-reviewers might overlook ugly errors. They might reject strong research because of petty jealousies. We should not – and will not – simply obey every conclusion supported by peer-reviewed research.

At the same time, peer review can – and often does – benefit scholars and practitioners. I recently saw this exchange (which I've edited for simplicity) on Twitter:

Thoughtful tweep (asking an honest question, not being a troll): I just don't understand why people who have tenure publish in journals. Why not escape the hassle and "publish" on your own website?

Highly esteemed cognitive psychologist #1 (responding): Two times in the last year, reviewers gave feedback that helped us rethink our evidence. Their comments made our analysis better.

Highly esteemed cognitive psychologist #2 (responding): Peer review also helps us know which studies make important contributions to the field. Papers that aren't peer-reviewed won't have the same influence as those that are.

For these reasons, reliable sources make recommendations based on peer-reviewed research. In those rare cases when they depend on unpublished research, they explicitly alert us to this exception. If we find the source's best evidence in a peer-reviewed journal, we have even greater reason to rely on his judgment. If we don't, however, we doubt him all the more.

Like the questions that helped us cross the Chasm of Self-Doubt, this one seems perilous and daunting. How can we enter the world of scientific research to find such arcane information? Surely dusty libraries permit access to credentialed insiders only. Even if we have permission to enter this world, where do we look? The treasure could be tucked anywhere in Aladdin's vast cave.

As was true at the Chasm, this seemingly daunting obstacle quickly diminishes in scale. In fact, *we know exactly where to dig*: an online search engine called **Google Scholar**. We can hop on to the nearest computer, surf over to Scholar.Google.com, and use our everyday search skills to find the cited study. In barely a minute, we'll have the information we need.

This sounds too good to be true, so let's excavate an example. Imagine that we read a blog post with concrete advice about flashcards. The blogger says that students benefit more from one large flashcard deck than from several small decks.

According to this source, research suggests that – to a reasonable degree – students should resist the temptation to divide and conquer; better to take on one tall stack than several short ones.

Being open to new teaching suggestions, we want to know more about this advice. Yet being cautious consumers, we want to investigate the reasoning behind this suggestion. Steeling our nerves and facing our self-doubt, we return to the blog post asking: "What's the best research in support of this suggestion?" Happily, the blogger anticipated that question and cites research by Nate Kornell called "Optimising learning using flashcards: Spacing is more effective than cramming" (2009). Relieved to discover that the Chasm wasn't even a ditch, we start digging for this Buried Treasure. We surf over to Google Scholar and type a few key words into the search box: perhaps "Kornell," "flashcards," and "2009."

The results look like this:

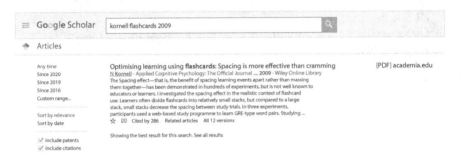

Figure 7

We'll return to Kornell's study in later chapters. You might make a mental note to recall its general outline.

As we get used to Google Scholar, we'll learn more about all the exciting options when we're digging for Buried Treasure. For now, let's keep things simple. At the center of the webpage, we see the study title. When we click on the hyperlink, we find ourselves in the Wiley Online Library, on a webpage for *Applied Cognitive Psychology*, the journal in which Kornell's study was published.

Ensuring that an official-looking journal does, in fact, peer-review its studies takes some improvisational sleuthing at this point. With *Applied Cognitive Psychology*, for instance, the "author guidelines" clearly state that "the journal operates a double-blind peer review policy" (*Author Guidelines*, n.d.). On other journals' webpages, you'll need to hunt about in likely looking spots. Unsurprisingly, the "About" tab often reveals this secret. (Note to journal publishers: please come up with a consistent system to make this part of the process easier.)

Returning to the Google Scholar search result, we spot another hyperlink on the right; it begins with [PDF]. We click on the link and, voila, we have the PDF we just started digging for. Yes, we found our Buried Treasure that quickly. The movie music swells again; birds are chirping in trees overhead. Like the first obstacle, this one can be cleared in less than a minute.

Question: What if I can't find peer-review information on the journal's website?
Answer: Surf over to Google proper, and search using the name of the journal. The information box on the right almost always tells you if this journal uses peer review.
Question: Why didn't you just tell me to do that in the first place? It sounds much simpler.
Answer: Trust me, Google Scholar repays all the love and attention you give it. You'll be delighted you know about its powers. For instance, it's far and away the easiest strategy to get hold of a PDF of the study – and you'll need that PDF very soon.

By the way, we can always find information about peer-reviewed research on Google Scholar. But, alas, that PDF link won't always be there; some research hasn't yet made it on to the internet. In this case, we have backup strategies.

The journal's webpage will identify one of the researchers as the **corresponding author**. It will, almost certainly, include her email address. We can simply email the corresponding author:

Dear Professor Agarwal,

I've read about your 2012 research into retrieval practice and am curious to learn more. Unfortunately, Google Scholar has let me down: I haven't been able to locate a copy of the study. Could you send me a PDF?

My students and I thank you.

Researchers can, entirely legally, send us those PDFs. And, in my experience, they're often thrilled that we ask.

Pro tip: you can also Google the researcher's academic website. They often post their studies there.

Like researchers, sources should also be willing to share the PDFs they cite. If you can't find Kornell's flashcard research on Google Scholar, you can instead email the blogger:

I'm intrigued by your recent post on the size of flashcard decks. I teach lots of vocabulary and my students love using flashcard programs. I wasn't able to locate the Kornell study you cited. Could you send me a copy?

This strategy takes a bit longer than Google Scholar, but it almost always works.

If you can't get hold of the study after trying these strategies, you might start feeling extra-suspicious. I know just that feeling...

Back in 2018, researchers in Australia developed a font with a deliciously clever name: Sans Forgetica. They claimed that this font itself helped students remember information (RMIT University, 2018). How splendid! Simply by adopting a specially designed font, it seems we can help our students learn. Because this claim drew on earlier research traditions – **desirable difficulties** and **disfluent fonts** – it certainly sounded plausible. However, I couldn't find any supporting information on Google Scholar.

Curious, I switched to my next strategy and emailed to ask for supporting information. To my surprise, I heard back not from the researchers but from the university's publicity department. In fact, I had no way of getting hold of the researchers themselves. In other words: the university was making a "research-based" claim, and it even made the font itself available for others to use, but it made neither the research nor the researchers available. Those facts alone raised suspicions.

Sure enough, two years later, those suspicions flowered into contradictory evidence. Researchers in New Zealand found that "although Sans Forgetica promotes a feeling of disfluency, it does not create a desirable difficulty or benefit memory" (Taylor et al., 2020, p. 850). I was not wholly surprised to see that result. When we can't look directly at the research itself, we shouldn't trust that its purported conclusions will withstand later scrutiny.

Unearthing Treasure: Teaching Vocabulary

We've covered a lot of ground in these opening chapters, so another example may help to pull the pieces together. Imagine that, scrolling through our Twitter feed, we come across this intriguing tweet:

For students learning vocabulary, direct instruction is less efficient than listening to stories. Vocab learned from listening to and reading stories lasts longer, too. Less "drill," more storytelling.

Because we've got Goldilocks in mind, we're open to the idea that stories might beat direct instruction as a way to teach vocabulary. Perhaps we should accept this Big Ask and follow the source's tweet advice. At the same time, we don't give up on our well-established methods without asking a few questions first. Screwing our courage to the sticking place, we ask, "What peer-reviewed research supports this recommendation?"

In this case, the tweet answers that question directly with a link to the underlying research. That discovery raises our trust in the source: he anticipated our question and seems to want us to know more. So far, at least, the source behaves like a reliable expert.

We click on the link and find a grim discovery. The link does not take us to the webpage of an academic journal. It does not provide a PDF of the published research. Instead, it takes us to a Word document that's been uploaded to the internet. Nothing about this document gives us reason to believe the study has been vetted and published by an academic journal. We followed the quest map for Buried Treasure, but all we've found are glass shards and rusty nails.

When we see this online Word document, lacking all hints of peer review, we have only two logical conclusions to draw.

- Either: the source understands the importance of peer review, yet willingly cited this unvetted Word document. His willingness to do so means that he forfeits our trust.
- Or: the source does not understand the importance of peer review. He does not, in other words, understand fundamental standards in psychology research. Here, again, he forfeits our trust.

Whichever conclusion we draw, we can bring our quest to a successful close. When we find the treasure chest empty, we know what to tell our fellow villagers. We should not change our teaching based on research that hasn't been evaluated by expert peers. And we should not rely on those who encourage us to do so.

As in Chapter 2, this success might feel like failure. When we first read the tweet about teaching vocabulary through stories, we might have felt a sudden rush of excitement. Perhaps this suggestion aligns perfectly with our school's pedagogical culture. We really want to believe the source and the "research" he has cited. What would happen if we kept going and tried to find research that *does* verify the source's claim?

One answer to that question is that doing so would overlook our primary goal at this point in the quest. We're not (yet) trying to verify scientific claims. We're (still) trying to decide if we trust the source. In this case, the source encouraged us to teach in a particular way, implied that research supported his suggestion, and then cited unvetted research. Sources who do that don't deserve teachers' trust.

Another answer to that question is: "OK, let's give it the old college try." I've spent a lot of time old-college-trying and I have gotten nowhere. In this case, the online Word document claims that the research is published in a particular journal. I've looked on Google Scholar; I've looked on Microsoft Academic; I've reached out to scholarly friends – none of us can find evidence that this journal even exists. You can find *anything* on Google except, apparently, this journal.

The research cited by the source is written by two scholars. I've emailed them both to ask about their research. More than a year later, I still haven't heard back. I even emailed the administrator of the website that hosts the Word document. No response.

I also reached out to an expert in vocabulary learning: Alex Quigley, author of *Closing the Vocabulary Gap* (2018). When I asked about the claim that students learn vocabulary better through stories than through direct instruction, he responded in an email:

> *"It is a flawed claim that isn't substantiated by evidence that I know. ... The evidence is solid: direct instruction of vocabulary helps develop vocabulary. ... The [tweeted] claim is wrongly oppositional: you need both [teaching strategies] in unison, neither is sufficient in isolation."* (A. Quigley, personal communication, April 2, 2020)

Even if we divert our attention from our primary goal (which is to vet the source) and give it the old college try, we still can't find good support for this claim.

Since Chapter 2, we've been wrestling with a conundrum: how do we – lacking expertise in brain research – evaluate "expert" advice flavored with psychology and neuroscience? We might, as I just did, give it the old college try. When a self-proclaimed expert offered "research-based" teaching advice – "teach vocabulary with stories, not direct instruction" – I threw questions at plausible targets. I emailed the scholars and the website host. I reached out to the author of a well-known book. In brief, I made a nuisance of myself until I gathered enough data points to satisfy my curiosity.

Now that we have our quest map, however, we realize that we don't need to go through all that bother. We can save time by following a simple rule. When our source cites research that hasn't been peer-reviewed – or, in this case, even published – that fact alone means that we've completed our quest. Genuine experts just don't do that. More precisely, in the rare cases when genuine experts do, they proclaim the absence of peer review quite loudly and explain their reasons for relying on the research nonetheless.

We ask the questions "What's your best evidence?" and "Has it been published in a peer-reviewed journal" precisely because the answers save us time. We can recognize the right answers. When we get the wrong answers, we can celebrate our quest's successful end.

Always With the Nuance

Although we've embraced Stubborn Goldilocks, we always seek out a nuanced middle ground. For that reason, I should emphasize that the format of the "research" in this example – a Word document – doesn't necessarily trouble us. Occasionally, once researchers' work has been vetted and accepted by a journal, they make this final draft public before it has been published. That document will say something like: "This study has been accepted at *Journal X*." We will know that the research has been peer-reviewed and we can trust our source when he cites it.

Spoiler alert: in Chapter 6, we'll look at research that, although not published in a peer-reviewed journal, merits our attention. We'll discuss this exception when we get there.

A second example requires even more nuance. In recent years, researchers have started to make drafts of their results public *before* they have been accepted by peer-reviewed journals. Websites like PsyArXiv.com (that's webspeak for Psychology Archive) host these **preprints**. In this case, our willingness to trust the source depends on the claims he makes about those preprints.

A source might say, "You should use this teaching practice; research says so." When you approach the Chasm of Self-Doubt and ask for a citation, he cites a preprint. This not-fully-vetted reference should make us nervous: "research says so," yes, but that research hasn't been peer-reviewed and accepted for publication. The source should know better. Our trust meter ticks down.

However, the source might say something like this: "I've seen as-of-yet unpublished research suggesting that this teaching practice might help students learn. If that research is peer-reviewed, we'll be on even firmer ground in recommending it." In this case, the source has acknowledged the difference between pre- and post-peer review. By highlighting different levels of research certainty (and uncertainty), he gains our confidence.

The Joys of Paradox

One final example highlights the efficiency of digging for Buried Treasure. In Chapter 1, we reviewed the Dunning-Kruger effect and the graphs that illustrate it (Figures 1 and 2; see p. 31 and p. 33). If you had already heard of Dunning-Kruger, you might have expected a different graph: one that looks like Figure 8. This graph, after all, accompanies most popular explanations of their work.

The Dunning-Kruger Effect

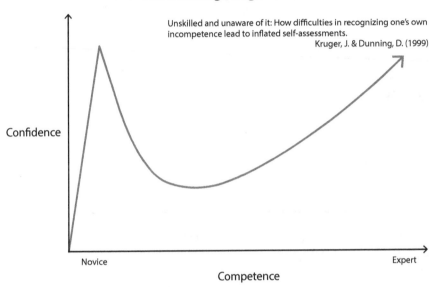

Unskilled and unaware of it: How difficulties in recognizing one's own incompetence lead to inflated self-assessments.
Kruger, J. & Dunning, D. (1999)

Figure 8

If a source makes a Big Ask based on this graph, we can unearth the study he cites: Kruger and Dunning, 1999. And because that graph features so prominently in the source's analysis, we can scan the study to confirm the graph's existence. This process couldn't be easier. We have downloaded the PDF from Google Scholar and can briskly scroll through its pages to locate the graph.

When we do so, we arrive at an arresting discovery: *it's not there.* Kruger and Dunning's 1999 study includes four graphs that resemble Figure 1, but nothing that looks like Figure 8. By digging for this Treasure, we have found that our source – as he ribs novices who overestimate their confidence – has made a rookie mistake: providing an inaccurate source for his graph of overconfidence. The irony could not be more shocking.

For some reason, Dunning and Kruger's insight into novice behavior has a paradoxical effect on people. Novices want to explain it to others; as they do so, they make lots of novice mistakes. Believe it or not, Figure 9 features in several online explanations.

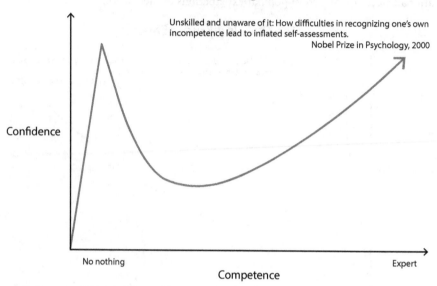

Figure 9

The source who created this graph wants to tease overconfident novices. In doing so, he misspells the word "know." And he suggests that the study was done by the Nobel Prize in Psychology. (It was done by Kruger and Dunning.) Furthermore, he suggests that the Nobel Prize in Psychology *exists*. (It doesn't. Honestly, there is no Nobel Prize in Psychology.) To be clear: Dunning and Kruger won the *Ig* Nobel Prize in Psychology in 2000. Of course, the Ig Nobel prize is a parody, its name a pun on the word "ignoble."

Dunning and Kruger's research might inspire us to change our approach to teaching in some way. However, we should absolutely not trust a source who makes such deliciously ironic mistakes.

Curtain Up

As we set down our shovel and dust off our hands, we can pause to contemplate the speedy progress we've made. If the first three chapters of this book were a play, it would go like this:

~ Lights come up on a humble village square ~

(The Hero packs up saddlebags)

Hero (to self): I should adopt a Goldilocks equilibrium. I'll be neither too cranky nor too credulous. I'll listen to brain experts and I'll stand up for my own expertise.

(Hero rides out of village)

Hero (at Chasm of Self-Doubt): What's your best evidence?

Messenger: Here's the best evidence!

Hero: Many thanks! (Hero crosses Chasm, picks up shovel.) I wonder if I'll find that Buried Treasure/evidence?

Google Scholar: Here's the Buried Treasure/evidence!

Hero: Many thanks!

~ Curtain ~

Mere minutes after we first contemplated the messenger's Big Ask, we've already found important reasons to trust him. Back in the village, as we were cinching up our saddlebags, we didn't know if we could make any progress at all. But with the right mindset and the right questions, we've already impressed the village elders.

Emboldened by these rapid successes, we prepare for the most perilous step yet. We start by opening our Book of Spells…

CHAPTER 4.
BREAKING THE
DISGUISE SPELL

Doing our best Goldilocks impression – not too trusting, not too skeptical – we traversed the Chasm of Self-Doubt, then excavated for Buried Treasure. In both cases, an obstacle that once looked formidable easily gave way before us. We asked a few questions and persisted if we heard incomplete answers. We clicked about on the internet and downloaded a peer-reviewed PDF. If the source refused to help us, we wisely decided not to follow his teaching advice. If – as is likely – the source encouraged us, we felt increasing confidence in his guidance. Just a few minutes have passed and we've made lots of impressive progress. In the distance, we can hear our fellow villagers cheering.

The next obstacle follows this familiar pattern. A fresh task looms threateningly ahead of us. And yet, when we approach it in the right way, it turns out to be perfectly straightforward. To determine whether or not we trust our source, we must now ensure that the magical object has not been **disguised by enchantment**. In other words: does this research really support the source's teaching advice? Does it say what the source claims it says?

Powerful Spells

Of course, breaking a Disguise Spell initially seems intimidating. As villagers, we know precious little about deep magical arts. The PDF we unearthed earlier bristles with obscure terminology and baffling equations. We can barely make out the minuscule font. Although relatively short – few studies run longer than 20 pages – this document unnerves all but the bravest adventurer.

Here, again, the correct approach to the obstacle quickly diminishes it. Almost all psychology studies begin with a one-paragraph summary. To break the Disguise Spell, we chant this magic question: "Does this one-paragraph summary say *exactly* what the source says it does?" He gave us teaching advice and claimed that this study supported it. Does the researchers' own summary confirm that claim?

In Chapter 2, for example, a conference speaker told us that doing calisthenics during mini-breaks helps students learn. When we dig up the peer-reviewed study and look over the one-paragraph summary, we find this:

"We examined the impact of taking exercise breaks, non-exercise breaks, or no breaks on learning among first year Introductory Psychology students. Three 5-minute breaks were equally distributed throughout a 50-minute computer-based video lecture. The exercise breaks group performed a series of callisthenic exercises; the non-exercise breaks group played a computer game; the no breaks group watched the lecture without breaks. Mind-wandering questions measured attention during the lecture. Exercise breaks promoted attention throughout the lecture compared to no breaks and non-exercise breaks, and resulted in superior learning when assessed on immediate and delayed tests. The exercise breaks group also endorsed higher ratings for narrator clarity and perceived understanding than the other two groups. This is the first study to show that exercise breaks promote attention during lecture and improve learning in university students." (Fenesi et al., 2018, p. 261)

This paragraph includes a few odd turns of phrase: "endorsed higher ratings for narrator clarity," for example. Despite those complexities, we can more or less understand what's going on here. We chant our magic question: "Does this one-paragraph summary say *exactly* what the conference speaker claims it does?" Well, he said that "doing classroom calisthenics helps students focus and learn." These researchers asked some students to do calisthenics, and compared their attention and learning with other students who didn't do calisthenics. Sure enough, students who briefly exercised attended better and learned more. That's exactly what the speaker said.

Spoiler alert: like the Kornell study, Fenesi's research on exercise will appear several times on our quest. You might make a mental note of its central points.

At this point, we have several reasons to trust our source. Experts tell us where they get their information; this source did. Experts cite peer-reviewed research;

this source did. Experts limit their claims to precise research findings; this source did. Because he behaves like an expert, we have good reasons to believe he is one.

The quest continues.

Novice Spell-Breaking: Achievable Goals

Let's try a second example. Imagine that a blogger you admire writes a post emphasizing the importance of "achievable goals." This blogger – reasonably – argues that teachers should break assignments down into manageably small chunks. As students complete each chunk, that pattern of success will build motivation. If a daunting assignment demotivates students, teachers can revive their motivation by carefully dividing the assignment into smaller, confidence-building pieces.

That advice sounds so sensible that it might not need research to support it. But this admirable blogger focuses on psychology and neuroscience, and so cites Karakowsky and Mann (2008) to firm up his Big Ask. The presence of that citation, of course, helps us over the Chasm of Self-Doubt. When our shovels strike peer-reviewed PDF gold on Google Scholar, we feel even more faith in his guidance.

So, let's check out the one-paragraph summary to see if it says *exactly* what the source claims it does. By the way, we call those one-paragraph summaries **abstracts**. Here's Karakowsky and Mann's abstract:

> *"The purpose of this theoretical article is to explore the psychological processes underlying employee participation in goal setting. Specifically, it presents a conceptual model that attempts to illustrate the potential pattern of causal self-attributions generated following the performance of participatively set goals. This article addresses two important questions: What are the cognitive consequences for employees who participate in setting their own performance goals? Do employees feel more personally responsible for the outcomes of their job performance if they have participated in the setting of their work goals? Theoretical assertions are summarized in the form of research propositions."* (Karakowsky & Mann, 2008, p. 260)

That very first sentence, alas, makes us feel queasy. Our source made a Big Ask about *students* working on *school assignments*. But, to support that claim, he cited research about *employees* participating in setting *work performance goals*. Of course, the relationship between teachers and students differs markedly from that between employers and employees. Teachers don't pay students. Teachers can't fire students. Employees rarely buy their employers apples, or call them "Mom" by accident. Heck, this study appeared in the *Journal of Leadership & Organizational Studies*. No doubt this journal publishes fine research, but it doesn't specialize in teachers motivating students.

When our source says, "Research shows that students feel more motivated when teachers divide large assignments into smaller, clearly achievable goals," he should cite research showing precisely that. The abstract should say: "We tested two groups of students. One undertook a large academic assignment, with grades and feedback at the conclusion. The other did the same assignment divided up into smaller pieces, with grades and feedback given along the way. This second group reported higher levels of motivation."

When, instead, he cites a conceptual model that attempts to explain why employees potentially feel motivated when they participate in goal setting, we are left with only two possible conclusions:

- Either: no one has directly researched the suggestion that achievable goals motivate students. The source's claim that "research shows" this strategy is effective simply isn't accurate. The source has zealously extrapolated from distantly related research, but he hasn't made a research-based claim.
- Or: someone *has* directly researched the suggestion that achievable goals motivate students. However, the source hasn't succeeded in finding that research, even though he's claiming expertise in this topic – enough expertise to make a Big Ask of teachers.

In either case, we shouldn't trust this source. Like those meddling kids on Scooby-Doo, we have unmasked the reality he tried to disguise.

We might be disappointed by that conclusion because his advice sounds so sensible. But until we find a study that specifically examines the source's suggestion, we can't plausibly call his advice "research-based." And, in any case, we must reluctantly conclude that the source hasn't behaved like an expert.

Advanced Spell-Breaking: Encouraging Students

We've tried to break two Disguise Spells so far: one about calisthenics, the second about achievable goals. We discovered that the calisthenics claim wasn't disguised, so we can trust that source. Alas, we found that the achievable goals claim was disguised, so we can't trust the other source.

In both those cases, we answered our spell-breaking question quickly because the abstract proved relatively easy to read. More often, alas, the abstract will prove something of a challenge. They typically include several technical terms and lumpish acronyms. Their prose lacks Jane Austen's wit and fluidity. Given their complex and jargon-laden sentences, we may have to reread the abstract a few times to make sense of its verbal clutter.

For that reason, when reading an abstract, I find it helpful to focus on three core questions:

1. What did the researchers want to know?
2. What did they do to find out?
3. What did they conclude?

When Goldilocks reads – and rereads – the abstract with these three questions in mind, her confusion will usually clear up enough for her to answer her spell-breaking question. For example, imagine that we attend a conference on classroom management. The keynote speaker champions a "relationships first" approach. One surefire technique – a "magical sentence" – has especially compelling research support. The speaker describes the study in this way:

> *High school students wrote an essay. All students received feedback from their teachers; half of those students got a single extra sentence at the end of that feedback. When researchers compared students' grades at the end of the school year, they found that students who got that extra sentence still scored significantly higher on assignments. (This wasn't "Pygmalion effect"; teachers didn't know which students had gotten the extra sentence.)*

> *This was the extra sentence: "I am giving you this feedback because I believe in you."*

In other words, "research shows" that this one magical sentence helps students learn. When we let our students know that we believe in them, our investment in supportive relationships boosts their academic development.

> Spoiler alert: we'll come back to the word "significantly" – as in, "scored significantly higher" – in Appendix I. That word has two distinct meanings and the potential for confusion grabs our Goldilocks attention.

From one perspective, this advice hardly needs research support. Teachers – some teachers, anyway – have been encouraging students for as long as schools have existed. At the same time, we might be happy to have science behind our long-standing practice. Perhaps we want to tell parents that our encouragement has a firm research basis. Perhaps we have a grouchy colleague who has always insisted that "students must earn my respect before they get my respect" – the right research just might bring him around to a more humane point of view. Or perhaps we simply want to hone our questing skills with an easy case. Time to saddle up.

First, we settle into our Goldilocks balance. Next, we ask the source for the best evidence supporting this (seemingly obvious) suggestion. We are directed across the Chasm of Self-Doubt towards a study: Cohen, Steele, and Ross, 1999. We start digging for this Buried Treasure and Google Scholar locates a PDF in seconds. So far, the keynote speaker is acting like a genuine expert.

To ensure that the research says what the source claims it does, let's review the abstract with our three questions in mind. **What did the researchers want to know? What did they do to find out? What did they conclude?** Of course, we know that the abstract's complexity might test our patience. We also know that our Goldilocks confidence will help us along the way. Take several minutes to read this paragraph a few times, and try to answer those three questions:

> *"Two studies examined the response of Black and White students to critical feedback presented either alone or buffered with additional information to ameliorate its negative effects. Black students who received unbuffered critical feedback responded less favorably than White students both in ratings of the evaluator's bias and in measures of task motivation. By contrast, when the feedback was accompanied both by an invocation of high standards and by an assurance of the student's capacity to reach those standards, Black students responded as positively as White students and both groups reported enhanced identification with relevant skills and careers. This 'wise,' two-faceted intervention proved more effective than buffering criticism either with performance praise (Study 1) or with an invocation of high standards alone (Study 2). The role of stigma in mediating responses to critical feedback, and the implications of our results for mentoring and other teacher-student interactions, are explored."* (Cohen et al., 1999, p. 1302)

In truth, this abstract might test our patience. The language seems needlessly fussy: "buffered," "ameliorate," "identification with relevant skills." With an average of 30 words per sentence, the paragraph requires careful concentration and frequent double takes. But after several readings, we get the gist:

- **What did the researchers want to know?** How do Black and White students respond to critical feedback that is "unbuffered" or "buffered"?
- **What did they do to find out?** They gave some students unbuffered feedback, and other students buffered feedback. Buffered feedback included both an "invocation of high standards" and reassurance that students could meet those

standards. (Presumably the reassurance sounded like that magic sentence: "I believe in you.")

- **What did they conclude?** In the "unbuffered" control group, Black students felt the teachers were biased and they expressed less motivation than White students. In the other group, two-part "buffered" feedback eliminated those differences.

We can now ask the question that breaks the Disguise Spell: does the abstract say exactly what the conference speaker claims it does? That dramatic sound we hear is our trust shattering. Two bizarre omissions have broken the disguise into pieces.

First, the speaker said this research shows what happens to "students" when we emphasize our belief in them. He left out a crucial fact: the study looks at the *differing* reactions of *distinct* student populations. These researchers focused on a concept called **stereotype threat**. They wanted to see if buffering feedback benefits stereotyped students (in this case, Black students) without affecting unstereotyped students (in this case, White students). To emphasize the importance of this focus, they include the words "across the racial divide" in their study's title. Shockingly, our source *simply omitted* the central question investigated by the researchers.

Second, and equally vexing, the speaker left out fully half the definition of "buffered" feedback. The abstract describes buffering as "a two-faceted" intervention: invoking high standards *and* reassuring students that they can meet them. The speaker talked only about the magic reassurance.

- If a friend gives you his chocolate chip cookie recipe and omits half the ingredients, your cookies won't taste as good as his.
- If a doctor says, "Take this medication; it protects you against norovirus," and you discover that taking a *combination of two medications* protects against norovirus, you will feel amazed by his blunder.
- If a speaker says, "You should teach this way because research says so," and omits half of the research-based strategy, your classroom results won't be the same.

Quite plainly, this study does not say what the source claims it does. Not even close. The source has ignored the researchers' core question (the differing responses between Black and White students) and their methodology (a two-step process). The keynote speaker has not acted like a genuine expert.

We might be disappointed that we can't rely on the keynote speaker's guidance – it would have helped us convert our stubborn colleague! However, by leaving out so much vital information, he forfeited our trust entirely. We turn right around and head back to the village.

Spoiler alert: we will return to the "I believe in you" strategy in Chapter 8. Who knows, perhaps we can find research support on our own...

Our Quest So Far

In Part II of this book, we have pursued an audacious endeavor. Although we are novices in both psychology and neuroscience, we have dared to evaluate claims made by seeming experts. To accomplish this mission, we have followed an indirect quest strategy. We admit that we don't know enough about these sciences to appraise this research ourselves. But we do know enough about *expertise* to appraise people making Big Classroom Asks:

- Experts share information enthusiastically and directly. If our source doesn't identify the research basis for his Big Ask, we rightly doubt his expertise.
- Experts care about peer review (although they acknowledge flaws in the system). If our source cites unvetted research without lots of caveats, we rightly doubt his expertise.
- Experts align their claims precisely with the research they cite. If we spot troubling gaps between the abstract our source cited and his Big Ask, we rightly doubt his expertise.

In this chapter's examples, we've seen that the calisthenics claim indeed lines up quite nicely with Fenesi's research. Let the jumping jacks begin! However, the suggestions about achievable goals and encouraging students come from unreliable sources; the research they cite doesn't plausibly support the classroom strategy they champion. Reliable experts don't extrapolate so flippantly. We might ultimately decide to follow either strategy, or both; we hardly need research support to encourage our students. But we shouldn't have these sources as our guides while we do so.

In Part II – by crossing the Chasm of Self-Doubt, digging for Buried Treasure, and breaking the Disguise Spell – we ensured that our source merits the trust we give to experts. In Part III, we take the next audacious quest step. We turn our Goldilocks skepticism from the source to the *research itself*. We want to know: does this research apply to our students, our curriculum, our school? By this point in our journey, we understand that many obstacles will daunt us. But our experience shows us that – strengthened by the right questions and the right mental equilibrium – we can overcome those obstacles with panache. While our steed munches his oats, we survey our map to see what lies ahead.

Intermission I

A Practice Quest: Final Exams

We've covered a lot of map territory in these chapters, so it might be helpful to practice. I'll give you a real-world scenario (an example from my own consulting work) and let you launch your own low-stakes training quest. Here's the setup...

Your school decides to reconsider its policy on final exams. Many colleagues worry about heightened stress levels, lowered motivation levels, and wasted classroom time. Others believe that well-designed exams let well-prepared students consolidate their learning and experience mastery. Which path should your school take?

Wise school administrators decide to ground faculty discussions in research. After a thoughtful search, your principal finds a report that draws on research to arrive at a strong conclusion: *no more final exams.*

Your principal knows your love of quests, so asks you to kick the tires. When you review the report she found, you focus on this paragraph:

We have no evidence showing that exam periods enhance students' learning. In fact, we know from sleep research and memory research that "cramming" is counterproductive. Because students typically cram for the test, exams rarely benefit long-term memory.

This paragraph gets your attention because it concludes with the report's only footnote: "Optimizing distributed practice: Theoretical analysis and practical implications" (Cepeda et al., 2009). With this information, you have enough to launch your quest. As always, your first question is: should your school *trust the source*?

In Appendix IV, I'll tell you my own questly conclusions (see p. 235). But no peeking! Don't read what I've written there until you've explored the chasms and treasure chests and spells. Set out for Google Scholar while you've still got daylight. Let your first practice quest begin!

PART III.
EVALUATING THE
RESEARCH

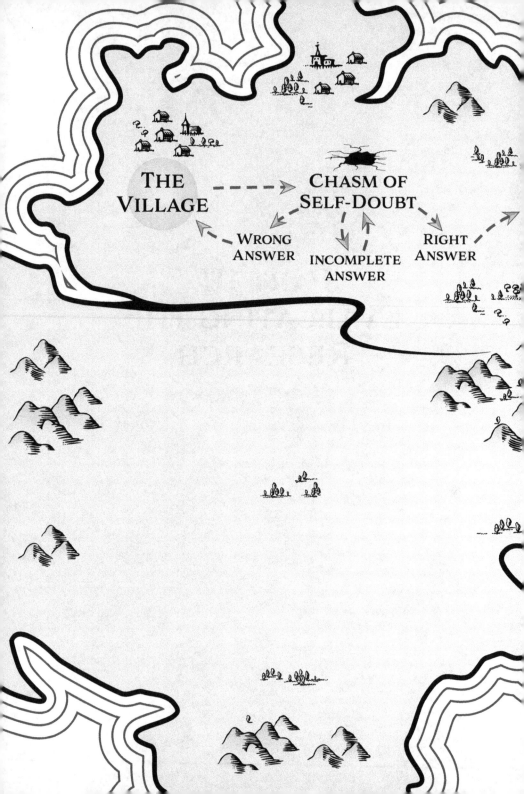

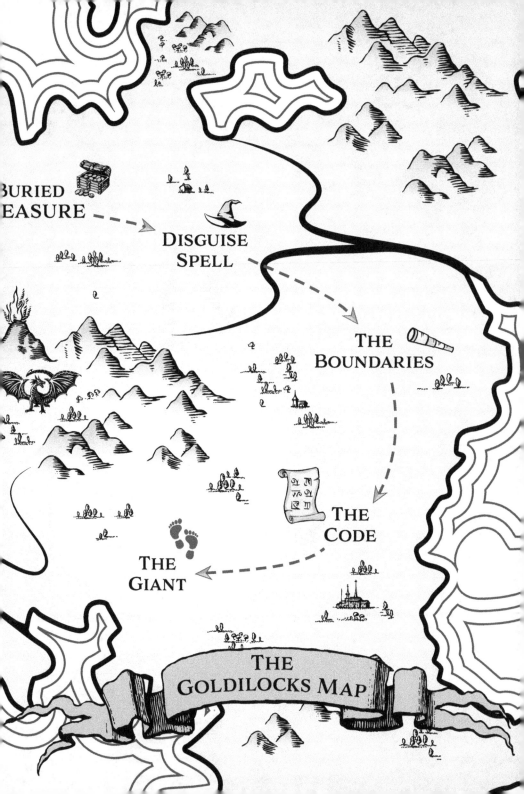

CHAPTER 5.
EXPLORING THE
BOUNDARIES

By now, I hope, you've seen enough evidence to believe that retrieval practice helps people learn. Perhaps you've already got plans to mix retrieval practice into your classroom blend. If that's the case, you might start practicing this strategy yourself.

Now's a good time to pause and think back over the main ideas we've discussed. Try asking yourself the following questions.

- **Chapter 4:** once you've found an abstract on Google Scholar, what three simple questions do you ask yourself to aid your understanding?
- **Chapter 3:** when you look up the source's cited study on Google Scholar, what discovery would help you trust him? Distrust him?
- **Chapter 2:** for an extra challenge, can you draw the decision tree that summed up the chapter? When you ask the source, "What's the best evidence?", how do you respond to his right, wrong, and incomplete answers?

If you struggle with this exercise, you might take some time to review the relevant chapters. As you've seen, each quest step builds on the previous one. The more solid your Goldi-foundation, the more skillfully and nimbly you'll ascend.

As you think over these retrieval practice questions, recall that the chapters behind them pursue a common goal. Before we decide to adopt a new teaching strategy, we should know if we can trust the person who recommends it. That source might know lots of brainy terminology. But, like a car salesman, he could be using it for good or for ill. Now that we have confirmed his trustworthiness, we move to our next substantial goal.

Goldilocks Plus

On our journey so far, we've focused relentlessly on a reasonable middle ground. We listen to new ideas, but aren't gullible about them. We respect cognitive science, but likewise respect our own profession, craft, and experience. Although we live at a cultural moment that valorizes dramatic extremes, we focus – heroically! – on balance and equilibrium.

We should pause at this point to question that position. Why, exactly, does this middle ground deserve our loyalty? Why do we get credit for *not* picking a side? Shouldn't we have the courage of our convictions and fight boldly for whatever team we're on? Here's why: *psychology research is a messy muddle*. No, really. It's a mess and a muddle. Let me explain...

In 2011, the European Organization for Nuclear Research (surprising acronym, CERN) reported that it had measured neutrinos moving faster than the speed of light. If those results held up, they would defy one of Einstein's key predictions: *nothing moves faster than light.* As Geoff Brumfiel noted in *Nature* (2011), "if it stands further scrutiny, the finding would overturn the most fundamental rule of modern physics." Although that sentence sounds polite and measured, Brumfiel was probably thinking: "My God! If even Einstein is wrong, the universe as we know it might be giving way to pandemonium and lawlessness!"

Gamblers rarely make money betting against Einstein, so physics watchers waited anxiously to see if their conceptual models were about to shatter. (Trekkies, however, quivered with anticipatory delight: if neutrinos could travel faster than light, then Warp 8 might be coming soon!)

In 2012, researchers determined that CERN had gotten the timing wrong because – I'm not joking here – *a cable had been loose.* (It seems they needed R2-D2 to fix their hyperdrive.) By the middle of that year, five research teams had conclusively determined that those neutrinos had not violated posted speed-of-light limits (Cho, 2012; Wolchover, 2012). Einstein's predictions remained inviolate and the rest of us could go about our business, confident that only Wookiees and Han Solo regularly make the jump to lightspeed.

The nail-biting drama of these events rested on an unstated assumption: if this *one* CERN experiment truly had sent neutrinos faster than the speed of light, that alone would be enough to upend Einstein's theory. Amazingly, experimental physicists need merely a single contrary finding to throw "the most fundamental rule of modern physics" into disarray.

Well, psychology ain't physics.

In psychology, *all* key findings rest atop a chaotic jumble of contradictory research results. No single research study establishes a broad psychology finding. No single study can shatter it.

Let's take a specific example. As we've seen, dozens – perhaps hundreds – of studies add up to persuade us that retrieval practice enhances learning. We've tested it with young children and adult learners. We've tested it with factual knowledge and physical skills. We've tested it over hours and, yes, months. This technique has more research behind it than almost any study advice offered by cognitive psychology.

And yet, several studies contradict – or at least limit – this advice. Some researchers suggest it has very narrow effects (Wooldridge et al., 2014). Jason Chan's research (2009) suggests it doesn't help right before a test. Some researchers (but not all) find that students with relatively low fluid intelligence learn more from traditional review than from retrieval practice (Minear et al., 2018).

In the world of experimental physics, such contrary results might well upend an entire theory. In the world of psychology, we call those contrary results "a typical Tuesday." Psychologists *expect* that thorough research into any topic will produce a wide range of results: confirmations, disconfirmations, and shoulder shrugs.

None of this contradictory research means that we shouldn't recommend retrieval practice to our students. We *should* recommend it, and we should build it into our own teaching. But these studies do highlight an essential point: even though most psychology research supports retrieval practice, we shouldn't be surprised to find that some contradicts or limits it. That's just how psychology works.

Because – say it with me – psychology research is a messy muddle.

More specifically, psychology research always produces a heap of contradictory results because it focuses largely on *humans*. We're a contradictory lot. When psychologists measure human cognition and behavior, they can indeed calculate averages based on those measurements. And yet, because humans differ so much from one another, an exact mathematical average just doesn't apply to many of us.

Todd Rose (2015) offers this helpful example. Automobile makers would, presumably, prefer to design their cars with fixed parts. It would be much cheaper to build seats that don't move, side-view mirrors that don't swivel, temperature settings that never vary. Yet GM and Mazda can't follow this cost-saving strategy because *people are so different*. Each driver prefers a unique arrangement of knobs, angles, and temperatures. (If you share a car, you feel my pain.) No one arrangement fits the average driver, because the "average driver" exists only in some calculation – not in real life.

When researchers summarize a conclusion – "Retrieval practice works!" – that summary in fact stands in for a more complex statement: "Retrieval practice works for most people learning most things, most of the time." However, Goldilocks knows that psychology research is a messy muddle. Retrieval practice *does* work in *these* circumstances, but *doesn't* work in *other* circumstances. To succeed on our quest, we want to find the limits within which retrieval practice works.

In psychology lingo, we're looking for **boundary conditions**. When the source offers research showing that "retrieval practice works," we want to know the boundaries within which it works:

- Does it work with 11th graders *and* second graders?
- Does it work for people studying fractions *and* others studying the history of the Silk Road? How about others rehearsing ballet?
- Does it work for students with diagnosed learning differences?
- Does it work in American *and* Korean cultural conditions?
- Does it work in a Montessori school, a KIPP academy, *and* a webinar?
- Does it work for loud/funny/performative teachers *and* quiet/subtle/parental teachers?

Goldilocks embraces the reasonable middle ground because, when we apply the complexities of psychology research to the complexities of teaching, we always find meaningful nuances.

In Chapter 3, for example, Nate Kornell's research (2009) told us that students learn more when they review one deck of 20 flashcards than when they review four decks of five flashcards. Given our respect for expertise, we start by trusting Kornell's findings. At the same time, we note that he worked with students learning vocabulary at the University of California, Los Angeles.

Let's speculate about boundaries:

- If I teach foreign languages, then my students might require a great many flashcards to develop their vocabulary. The sheer bulk of index cards might run past an outer limit that Kornell's research doesn't explore.
- If I teach first graders, then I might not want them practicing too many math facts at once. Perhaps they've got five sums to practice, not 20.
- If I teach in a markedly different setting – perhaps I teach swimming at a summer camp – I just don't see how flashcards will help.
- As you contemplate your own teaching world, you might immediately recognize that, despite this research finding, one deck of 20 just doesn't make sense for your students.

That is: Kornell's psychology research has given him information appropriate to one context, whereas my teaching experience gives me information appropriate to a markedly different one. He's not wrong. I'm not wrong. His (psychology) wisdom doesn't automatically apply to my (teaching) world because we operate in such different settings. And, unlike some ardent advocates of branded teaching methodologies, Goldilocks *can* handle that truth.

> Famous words: speaking of educational innovations, the noted scholar Dylan Wiliam says, "Everything works somewhere. Nothing works everywhere." I agree with the second half of that statement. I'm a little wary of the first half.

In Part II of this book, we repeatedly asked ourselves if we could trust the source. Here in Part III, we focus on a different question. Now that we *do* trust the source, we still need to know if the research he cites reasonably fits within our boundaries. Does that research apply to *these* students learning *our* curriculum in *this* cultural context? To answer those questions, we explore the boundaries of the research cited by our source.

Exploring the Boundaries: Participants

We start out wanting to know if the source's recommendation works with *our students*. In Chapter 4, for instance, we reviewed a research abstract about mid-lecture exercise breaks. Sure enough, they helped students focus and learn. But wait a minute: breaks helped *those students* focus and learn. Now we want to know: do those students plausibly resemble ours?

We have faced some daunting obstacles so far on our quest. The abstract's dense prose might have left us woozy. This obstacle, however, couldn't be simpler to overcome. All psychology research includes an easy-to-locate section describing the people who took part in it. That section typically comes under the heading "**participants**," but it might be called "**subjects**" or some other obviously related term.

> A note on structure: Appendix III briskly summarizes all the different parts of a study – abstract, participants, and so forth. If you want a handy overview or review, you can always look there.

Because we already looked up the study on Google Scholar, we have a PDF handy. We can quickly skim through it, spot the "participants" section, and scan its few short sentences. We will immediately find all the pertinent demographic information about the participants: their age, gender, socioeconomic status, race, ethnicity – and often many other variables.

For instance, the participants section of that study about mid-lecture exercise goes like this:

"77 undergraduate students at McMaster University enrolled in an Introductory Psychology course (78% females; age M ± SD = 18.7 ± 1.4 years; 18–22 yrs old) were recruited from an online recruitment portal and were pre-screened for prior exposure to lecture content. Only participants without prior exposure to the lecture content could enlist in the study. The study was conducted at McMaster University. All participants provided informed consent (study approved by McMaster Research Ethics Board, # 2014 131) and were compensated with course credit for their participation." (Fenesi et al., 2018, p. 262)

That's it. That's the entire participants section. (OK, I left out a distracting sentence about methodology. But that's all.)

These few sentences give us helpful and clear information. This research team, led by Barbara Fenesi, worked with undergraduates enrolled in a psychology course at McMaster University. Most were women, a few were men. The mean age was just under 19 and the standard deviation around that age was about one and a half years. (Once you've explored Appendix I, all this talk of **means** and **standard deviations** will make more sense.) We know that the students hadn't attended a lecture covering this same content before.

With this information, we can draw some reasonable conclusions. Obviously, these students are older than K-12 students. They care enough about education to attend college. They've had enough academic success to get into a highly ranked Canadian university. Odds are that most of them received most of their educational training in a Western cultural context. (We don't know that, but it strikes me as a reasonable inference to draw.)

We don't know what percentage had diagnosed learning differences. We don't know about their socioeconomic status (typically abbreviated SES). We don't know their IQs. We don't know about their racial or ethnic self-identification.

We read this brief section because we wanted to know if these participants are "reasonable proxies" for our students. But who decides if McMaster undergrads resemble our own classes enough for this research to be helpful? *We do.* We teachers determine if these boundaries include our students. Yes, we value researcher expertise, and we evaluate it through the lens of our own experience.

What does that evaluation process sound like? When I compare the students I teach with those who participated in Fenesi's study, I can certainly spot differences between them. My 10th graders don't have as many years under their belts as these college students do. Unlike Fenesi's students, mine rarely hear me lecture; when

I do present lots of information, I include interactive questioning. ("So, in this sentence, is the word 'giggling' a *gerund or a participle?*") In Fenesi's study, women outnumbered men 4:1. My classes have as many girls as boys.

In my view, however, those differences don't add up to much. Fenesi's research suggests that when my students get restless or lethargic – as they certainly do – I can take a quick exercise break to calm them down or wake them up. I don't see why an age difference of a few years, or the gender ratio, would change that conclusion. Are my particular students within these particular boundaries? In this teacher's view, indeed they are.

In other circumstances, however, I might draw quite different conclusions. For instance, when I teach *acting*, my students spend the lesson on their feet rehearsing scenes. In that setting, they simply don't need to take a physical break to rebalance their energy. The lesson itself provides all the cardio they need.

Yes, my acting classes demographically resemble my English classes: the same age groups, the same gender parity. But the *content* of the theater lesson itself means that I don't typically have the classroom problem that Fenesi's research is solving. The boundary conditions that apply to this research – students sitting through a lecture – don't include my acting classes.

In other cases, cultural dynamics might place my students outside Fenesi's boundaries. If, for instance, I taught in a business school, I imagine that the coat-and-tie ethos might make such sweatin'-to-the-oldies antics seem absurd and counterproductive. If I taught in a non-Western context, cultural norms might encourage students to sit still and take notes during lengthy lectures. For me to violate that norm might disturb and upset my students, not soothe and benefit them.

At this point you might be asking yourself, "Do *my* students fit within Fenesi's boundary conditions?" Only you can answer that question. The answer will depend on many factors: your students' age, your lesson content, the school's teaching philosophy, the broader cultural context, and doubtless many others.

In fact, your own personality probably matters as well. As a high school teacher, I have no problem with asking my students to get up and move around. They grumble, then tell me how much better they feel. However, as a consultant who leads teacher PD workshops, I would honestly feel uncomfortable asking other adults to "drop and give me twenty." As I tell my workshop participants, I trust them to manage their own energy levels. Whenever they need to get up and move around, they can do so; coffee and snacks are in the corner!

Yet I know plenty of workshop leaders who don't share my discomfort. They regularly get teachers on their feet; I wouldn't be surprised to see square dancing at some of the conferences I attend. To take one example, I've presented with

John Almarode, associate professor of education at James Madison University. His workshops include lots of interactive movement, which both he and the attendees obviously enjoy. This movement strategy works for Dr. Almarode because it matches his exuberant personality. He feels comfortable doing it; he revels in it. I don't think that strategy would work for me when I'm teaching adults because I'd feel like a fraud. It's just not my thing.

In this case, we've stumbled across a rarely discussed boundary, an unnamed participant: *the teacher*. When Fenesi ran her study with those McMaster undergrads, the professor who led the calisthenics presumably felt comfortable doing so. The technique worked for those students in part because they sensed their teacher's comfort with it. If, instead, the students picked up on the teacher's obvious discomfort, then the project might have collapsed under the weight of the unacknowledged awkwardness.

To repeat: who gets to decide whether the boundaries include our own context? *You do.*

Great Power, Great Responsibility

Let's try a few more examples.

As we explore research boundaries, we most often find that the psychology research has been done with college undergraduates enrolled in psychology courses. (Psychology professors more or less require their students to participate.) For that reason, we routinely ask ourselves the following Goldilocks question: "In this specific case, are college students a good stand in for *our* students?"

For instance, the motivation researcher Aneeta Rattan has explored a counterintuitive proposal (Rattan et al., 2012). She identified college students who felt intimidated by math homework and divided them into two groups:

- She reassured Group A that their professor would *not* call on them during class (in order, presumably, not to embarrass them). Likewise, to minimize students' frustration, the professor would give them *less* demanding homework than other students.
- She told Group B that the professor would call on them *more often* in class (in order, presumably, to be sure they understood the material). Likewise, to give students much-needed extra practice, the professor would give them more demanding homework than others.

As I think about the motivational results of these interventions, I would incline to the following predictions:

- Group A would see their professor as a sympathetic soul. Because she recognized their math anxiety and took concrete steps to alleviate it, I imagine these students would feel more at ease in the class. The likely result: enhanced motivation.
- Group B, on the other hand, might assume that the professor cared more about math than about students. Weighed down by the extra homework demands, stressed at the thought of being called on often, they would tremble all the more at the sight of math equations. The likely result: decreased motivation.

And yet, Rattan's team found the opposite result. Students in Group A inferred that the professor assumed they couldn't learn math. They felt *demotivated* by her implied doubts. Group B, on the other hand, inferred that the professor believed all students could learn math, with the right amount of support and practice. They felt inspired *and motivated* by her conviction.

Because of Rattan's study, when I talk with teachers about motivation I make two Big Asks. First, to keep track of their understanding, we'll tell struggling students that we'll call on them more in class. Second, to give them the extra practice they need, they'll receive more challenging homework than some of their peers. After all, we have good psychology research to support this counterintuitive strategy.

Once, when I was speaking at a school in Texas, I got pushback from an experienced third grade teacher. "That technique might work with older students," she observed, "but I just don't think it will motivate my kiddos at all. Extra homework will feel like a punishment, not like encouragement. Being called on when they're unsure of the answer will be threatening, not inspiring. I'm not going to do that."

In other words, this teacher drew on her considerable experience to argue that her own students lay outside Rattan's boundary conditions. To check the teacher's logic, let's look up the participants section in Rattan's study:

> *"Fifty-four students at a competitive private university on the West coast participated for pay (26 males, 28 females; 8 African-Americans, 15 Asian-Americans, 21 European-Americans/Whites, 6 Latino-Americans, 2 Native Americans, 2 Biracial; mean age=20.2, SD=2.36)."* (Rattan et al., 2012, p. 735)

Sure enough, Rattan's 20-year-olds are considerably older than your average third grader.

This teacher's objection intrigued me. I didn't know of – and couldn't find – any research testing this strategy with younger students. When I reached out to

Dr. Rattan, she said that, not being a developmental psychologist, she didn't want to speculate about third graders (A. Rattan, personal communication, 2018). Quite reasonably, she noted that the best way to answer the question would be to research it directly.

Pro tip: notice that Rattan does what, according to Chapter 4, experts do. She refuses to extrapolate too far beyond the research – even when it's her own research.

I can think of important reasons why third graders and college students might process academic motivation differently:

- Third graders are at least 10 years younger than college students. Eight-year-olds might interpret an adult's stern demands quite differently from 18-year-olds. Perhaps they haven't yet developed the perspective to interpret additional academic work as an opportunity, not a punishment.
- Rattan's participants, we can see, attended a "competitive private university on the West coast [of the US]." Given that Rattan herself worked at Stanford, we might have a good guess about its identity. I suspect that your average Stanford undergraduate has experienced higher levels of academic success and motivation than your average third grader. Motivation strategies that work with Olympic athletes might not work with Little League players. So too, motivation strategies that work with Stanford undergrads might not work with grammar school children.

In this case, we have powerful conflicting voices. Research done with Stanford students leads to one conclusion. Experience teaching eight-year-olds leads to a different conclusion. Resolving this conflict calls for a Goldilocks perspective. After all, we respect the researcher's insights *and* the teacher's experience. Because we know that psychology research is a messy muddle, and because we know to look for boundary conditions, we can reasonably decide that these third graders aren't within the boundaries of that research. In this case, *the experienced teacher gets to make that call*.

If you, too, have years of experience teaching third grade, you might make a different call altogether. Perhaps your school champions a culture of error: a classroom climate that encourages students to make as many public mistakes as possible (Lemov, 2015). Perhaps your students have heard since kindergarten that the right kind of hard work makes learning possible, and so take on challenging math homework quite amiably (Watson, 2019). For these reasons, you're inclined to give this strategy a try. Just as Rattan's research doesn't override this Texan teacher's experience, so too her experience doesn't override yours.

At this moment, we should recall the Spider-Man mantra that with great power comes great responsibility. (How Spider-Man found his way into a book about Questing Goldilocks is anyone's guess.) Yes, we get to decide if our students fall outside the boundary conditions of Rattan's study. But that freedom requires us first to give Rattan's insight and research their due. My teacherly instincts might tell me that the tough-math-love strategy won't help with my third graders, but Rattan's scrupulous work should at least prompt me to ask some hard questions about my assumptions. In other words: yes, we get to decide – but only if we're first willing to explore the possibility that we might be wrong.

To get some practice in exploring the boundaries, look over the following four descriptions. Ask yourself, "Are these participants reasonable proxies for the students I teach?"

1. *"A sample of 111 sixth graders (51 boys, 60 girls, mean age = 11.42 years, SD = 0.49) individually participated at their school with the permission of their parents and school authorities. Information about parental occupation was collected from school administration and used to determine participants' socioeconomic status (SES; see Croizet & Claire, 1998). Thirty-one percent of the participants were of high SES, 22% were of intermediate SES, and 46% were of low SES (for 2% of the participants, this information was unavailable). Participants were randomly assigned to one of three conditions: difficulty with reframing, difficulty without reframing, or standard."* (Autin & Croizet, 2012, p. 611)

These sixth graders might seem like a good proxy for K-12 students overall. They're roughly in the middle of that age range, are close to being gender-balanced, and are distributed – albeit not evenly – across social classes. Certainly they offer a good place to start. That general truth, however, doesn't necessarily determine your answer. If you teach children with autism, for example, you might well want to rely on research that matches your student population more precisely.

Your students might, or might not, fall within the boundaries of these other studies as well:

2. *"The participants were 168 entering university freshmen from the division of social sciences at a university in Hong Kong."* (Hong et al., 1999, p. 593)

These researchers worked with college students in Hong Kong specifically to look at a cultural blend of British and Chinese educational philosophy and systems. If that blend doesn't match your student body, then this research might not be useful to you.

3. *"Participants in this study consisted of sixth- and seventh-grade students who were attending a middle school in an affluent community in the Northeast. During the year 2000, the median annual family income in this region was reported to be almost $102,000; the highest national median income ever recorded by the U.S. Census is $40,816 (U.S. Census Bureau, 1999). Of the total sample of 302 students, 168 were sixth graders, and 134 were in the seventh grade, with mean ages of 11.8 and 12.8 years, respectively. Most students (92%) were of European American background; of the rest, 1.5% were African American, 1.5% were Hispanic American, 3% were Asian American, and 2% were of other ethnic backgrounds."* (Luthar & Becker, 2002, pp. 1595–1596)

In this study, Luthar and Becker deliberately focus on academic difficulties among very wealthy families. The study title says it all: "Privileged but pressured? A study of affluent youth." This study presumably helps us understand a relatively small slice of the student population; its sample's demographics don't much resemble society overall. Of course, those facts don't diminish the importance of this research. But they do limit its applicability.

4. *"Twenty-four 4-year-old children (M=4 years 6 months; range=4 years 1 month to 5 years 1 month; 12 boys) acted out several scenarios."* (Cimpian et al., 2007, p. 314)

The fourth study, clearly, works with children at the very beginning of their educational career. If you teach college – heck, if you teach seventh grade – you might not think that four-year-olds can offer you much guidance on working with your students. If you teach kindergarten, however, you're probably delighted to find a study that takes your students seriously.

As you can see, participant profiles in psychology research can vary dramatically.

The students' level of expertise should matter in our decisions as well. In a recent study (Izquierdo et al., 2016), researchers championed a specialized method for teaching linear algebra to college students – specifically, students double-majoring in "business management and administration/engineering of technology and communication services." The researchers might conclude that this innovative method helps their participants learn this complex topic.

However, that finding wouldn't automatically suggest that we should teach math novices in this innovative way. After all, anyone who knows enough math to study linear algebra has already achieved extraordinary understanding of intricate mathematical concepts. (In this case, the students are pursuing simultaneous majors in two polysyllabic disciplines.) Math novices – even math novices in their 20s – almost certainly benefit from different pedagogical strategies than math experts.

When we explore the boundaries, we occasionally stumble across surprising variables. I once read a study about the effect of stimulants – Ritalin, Provigil, caffeine – on chess playing (Franke et al., 2017). When I looked for boundary conditions, I noted a surprising detail: the participants' IQs averaged 125. In other words, they had higher IQs than 97% of the population. Unless I taught at an extraordinarily exclusive chess school, I wouldn't extrapolate from this population to my own.

As you can see from this quick exercise, the participants section gives us immensely practical information as we contemplate research-based teaching guidance. Our trustworthy source gave us research showing that his suggestions work *somewhere*. These few sentences help us discover if those Big Asks might work with our students *right here*.

Out of Bounds

Chapter 1 includes these sentences:

> *"Goldilocks rarely believes 'always'; she rarely believes 'never.' She prefers 'most of the time, but with some important exceptions.' And she straight-up loves 'under these specific circumstances, but not those circumstances.'"*

Now that we've spent several pages exploring boundary conditions, the logic behind those sentences should make even more sense. Retrieval practice works "most of the time, but with some important exceptions." Mid-class exercise breaks help students learn "under these specific circumstances, but not those."

Occasionally, however, Goldilocks finds a "never" she can embrace. Here goes:

> *Never change your teaching based on research into **non-human animals**.*

Researchers might find that rats solve mazes faster after they've had the right amount of sleep. Perhaps chimps do better on logic puzzles when they listen to soothing music. You might read a newspaper story saying that pigeons cooperate more selflessly after jazzercise.

These research findings offer psychologists and neuroscientists lots of important insights. In truth, many core discoveries about human cognition began with animal research. If you want profound insight into emotions, for instance, you could start with Frans de Waal's amazing book *Mama's Last Hug: Animal Emotions and What They Tell Us About Ourselves* (2019). Paul Howard-Jones's book *Evolution of the Learning Brain: Or How You Got To Be So Smart* (2018) explains how neurobiological evolution allows learning. (Believe it or not, even single-celled organisms like *E. coli* learn.) Eric Kandel won his Nobel Prize for memory research into *Aplysia californica*, more commonly known as Mediterranean sea slugs (Kandel, 2006). Much of psychology, and practically all of neuroscience, wouldn't exist without research into non-human animals.

And, yes, when teachers swap stories at the end of an exasperating day, we occasionally compare our students to animals. They swarmed over those pizza boxes like *famished rats*. When the bell rang for recess, they shrieked like *giddy monkeys*. When jazzercising, they looked like *antic pigeons*. This griping helps us let off steam, but the comparisons should not delude us. Although they occasionally act like rats, monkeys, and pigeons, our students *aren't* rats, monkeys, or pigeons. The boundary conditions on that research don't remotely extend to our classrooms.

This point merits emphasis because teachers and schools occasionally do rely on animal research to make teaching decisions. Those decisions, now deeply embedded in our profession, harm students. The best-known example is **enriched environments**.

For several decades now, neuroscientists have explored brain growth in rats. Specifically, they want to know if and how the environment influences their neural development. To answer that question, researchers raise rats in two distinct ecosystems.

Some rats endure **impoverished** environments. Their cages include food and water, and maybe a few outdated magazines of the kind you find in doctors' offices. These rats have their basic biological needs met, but otherwise live quite drab lives. Luckier rats live in **enriched** environments. In addition to food and water, they get running wheels and mazes and toys. They probably get HBO and ESPN and the rat equivalent of a Sony Playstation. Compared with their impoverished colleagues, these rats live grand and fulfilling lives.

After raising rats in these distinct ecosystems for several months, researchers check out their brains. Sure enough, if Templeton One enjoyed an enriched environment, his brain developed more than the brain of Templeton Two, who made do with basic cable in the impoverished environment. In his fascinating book *The Brain that Changes Itself* (2007), Norman Doidge summarizes the early research in this field:

"Mark Rosenzweig of the University of California at Berkeley [studied] rats in stimulating and nonstimulating environments, and in postmortem exams he found that the brains of the stimulated rats had more neurotransmitters, were heavier, and had better blood supply than those from the less stimulating environments." (Doidge, 2007, p. 35)

Those results sound spectacular. Simply by upgrading from basic cable to premium, these rats got brains that were better, stronger, and faster. Steve Austin wishes his transformation into the Six Million Dollar Man had been that easy.

These discoveries quite literally helped transform neuroscience. For decades, brain researchers had believed that, after early development, brains didn't change. Santiago Ramón y Cajal, a towering founder of the discipline, reluctantly concluded in 1913 that "in adult [brain] centers the nerve paths are something fixed, ended, immutable. Everything may die, nothing may be regenerated" (quoted in Doidge, 2007, p. 249). Contradicting this founding father, Rosenzweig's rats showed that brains can and do change. Neuroplasticity – as you recall from Chapter 2 – is now known to be entirely commonplace.

Rosenzweig's research might seem inspiring for brain-focused teachers. On a professional development day, a speaker might explain the benefits of an enriched environment and urge us to the obvious conclusion: we must enrich our own classrooms and corridors. The livelier the students' physical world, the more neural growth they'll experience. The quickest strategy to boost neurotransmitter production might be engaging posters on the wall.

This "brain-based" advice has, in fact, won the day. Generations of teachers have been exhorted to "enrich the school environment" with elaborate decoration. Grade-school teacher evaluations often include stern requirements that walls and bulletin boards glow with festive, inspiring energy.

Alas, this entire argument rests on the striking belief that our students fall within the boundary conditions of Rosenzweig's research. As teachers, we shouldn't rely on research into rat brains when we "enrich their environments." We should rely on research into student brains when we decorate their classrooms.

Researchers have, in fact, studied this question from several angles now. Two researchers in Portugal have compared working memory and visual attention in an undecorated setting – basically an empty library carrel – with those cognitive capacities in a highly decorated setting – the same carrel with lots of photos. And they've tested this question with students aged 8-12, high school students, and older adults (Rodrigues & Pandeirada, 2018, 2019, 2020). No matter the effect enriched environments had on rat brains, Rodrigues and Pandeirada's photographs ended up muddling and distracting human beings trying to accomplish mental tasks. Yes, decorations made it *less likely* that students could learn.

Other researchers have moved from cognitive tasks in library carrels to students in classrooms. Anna Fisher's research team, for instance, took kindergarteners to an alternate classroom for six weeks of science lessons: volcanoes, bugs, plate tectonics, and so forth (Fisher et al., 2014). Half the students learned in a room decorated with "science posters, maps, the children's own artwork provided by their teacher" (p. 1364); the other classroom contained visual information pertinent to the lesson. The result of this research?

"Children were more distracted by the visual environment, spent more time off task, and demonstrated smaller learning gains when the walls were highly decorated than when the decorations were removed." (p. 1362)

So much for enriched rats.

Of course, teachers have good reasons to decorate classrooms: to make them feel homey and welcoming, to highlight students' work, to introduce fresh personality to generic beige spaces. At the same time, we should remember that "enriching the environment" does not enhance students' neurogenesis; taken to extremes, it measurably interferes with learning.

Alas, this problem isn't simply ancient history. A science news website recently summarized a press release warning readers about dangerous lighting conditions: "Spending too much time in dimly lit rooms and offices may actually change the brain's structure and hurt one's ability to remember and learn, indicates groundbreaking research by neuroscientists" (Michigan State University, 2018). The obvious teaching implication: we must keep classrooms Klieg-light bright, lest we harm our students' "ability to remember and learn."

You can predict where this adventure leads: to reach this conclusion, researchers studied Nile grass rats. You might join me in wondering: exactly how much time do Nile grass rats spend in their offices? (You may also have quivered when you read the words "actually change the brain's structure." As we know, breathless claims about changing brains often signal hyperbole.)

A teacher's quest map focuses exclusively on research into people. Non-human subjects, although important to other sciences, never count within our kingdom's boundaries.

Twitter alert: the research sleuth James Heathers has created a humorous Twitter account: @justsaysinmice. If a source makes a dramatic claim – "We've found a potential cure for lumbago!" – Heathers responds with two curt words: "In mice." If you're on Twitter, he's worth a follow.

This chapter began with a surprising claim: psychology research is a messy muddle. Researchers regularly get contradictory results, in part because we need to test each finding in so many different circumstances.

As we've seen here in Chapter 5, we teachers can use this insight to further our quest. Unless the research participants plausibly match our own students, we should hesitate to follow the source's advice too closely. And, as we'll see in Chapter 6 and beyond, this insight helps us refine our understanding of research. We need to know not only who the participants were, but also *exactly what they did...*

CHAPTER 6.
CRACKING THE CODE

Our quest so far has produced many surprises – none more unexpected than its simplicity. Our fellow villagers assumed we would face fearsome dragons and daunting knights. So far, no obstacle (except, perhaps, the turgid abstract) has given us much difficulty.

- "Mr. Source: can you share with me the best research supporting your recommendation?" *"Why, sure. Here it is."*
- "Google Scholar: was this research peer-reviewed?" *"Why, yes, indeed it was. And you get a bonus PDF just for asking!"*
- "Abstract: did the source summarize you accurately?" *"Why, yes, indeed he did."*
- "Participants section: do my students fit within your boundary conditions?" *"Why, yes, they do."*

Unless we get dodgy answers along the way, the early portion of the quest requires 15 minutes (give or take). Goldilocks dressed for battle, but is out for an afternoon stroll instead.

Yet here, at the opening of Chapter 6, we arrive at a genuine challenge. We discover an unnerving truth: the research we're reviewing almost certainly relies on a secret code. Our heroic task? We must *decipher that code.*

Familiar Problems

Why, exactly, do we need to crack a code? Why was the study encoded in the first place? You guessed it: because psychology research is a messy muddle. Here's the story...

All specialized fields require insider terminology. When bakers banter with bakers, when trout fishers trade stories with trout fishers, when badminton champions chat with badminton champions, they rely on words and phrases that baffle outsiders. Contractors have their soffits, traffic engineers have their bollards, lawyers have their *res judicata*. All specialists talk this way. Including teachers.

Often, these obscure terms represent physical objects. When I study anatomy, I can distinguish among the spleen, the pancreas, and the gall bladder. When I study neuroscience, I know the differences among Broca's area, the corpus callosum, and the ventral tegmental area. I can prod those distinct regions with my scalpel. This one is *right here*. That other one is *right there*.

In psychology research, however, definitions create irksome challenges. Because psychology describes mental activity, I can't name all the parts with the precision that an anatomist would require. For instance, I have a hunchy sense of what *attention* is, but how exactly do I define it? I can't tap on it, the way I can tap a bollard or an inferior parietal lobule.

As a result, even basic cognitive behaviors require elaborate descriptions and result in highly technical debates. What are the differences among **self-control**, **self-regulation**, **inhibition**, and **willpower**? How, exactly, do we define **executive function**? Are **stress** and **anxiety** the same thing? How about **emotions** and **feelings**?

These debates can lead to daunting complexities. One case vexes me in particular...

If I had to pick only one psychology topic to discuss with teachers, that topic would be **working memory**. This short-term mental processing system (typically) combines new information with ideas already stored in long-term memory. Whenever students learn in school, their learning requires working memory. It's that important.

How, precisely, do we define this all-important cognitive capacity? My own definition goes like this: "Working memory is a short-term cognitive capacity that *selects*, *holds*, *reorganizes*, and *combines* information from multiple sources." When I explain it this way, teachers can easily see its importance and understand the various working-memory strategies that help students learn (Watson, 2017).

How do *psychologists* define working memory? Fasten your seat belts.

The well-known working memory scholar Nelson Cowan has surveyed the relevant literature (2017), coming up with *nine* meaningfully different definitions. His list even includes something called "long-term working memory," a puzzling phrase given that – just two paragraphs ago! – I defined working memory as a *short-term* cognitive capacity. If we can't define even this most essential of mental functions, imagine the debates that rage over more nuanced psychology topics.

For that reason, sources and researchers must discuss their ideas with an insider's code: a shorthand lingo. They study **attentional blink** or **prior misconceptions** or **retrieval-induced forgetting** or the **expertise-reversal effect**. They champion **metacognition** or **dual coding** or **active listening** or **differentiation** or **maker spaces**. They lament **entity theorists** or **stereotype threat** or **toxic stress**. In every case, these phrases stand in for much more precisely defined concepts, each of which must be measured with exactitude and described at length.

When researchers write their studies, when sources explain that research, when websites summarize these conclusions, they all rely on these shorthand words and phrases to communicate their main ideas.

As classroom teachers, we can recognize the usefulness of these tidy phrases. And yet, we also need to know *exactly* what teaching strategy has research support. Only then can we decide if a specific suggestion makes sense in our own classrooms. Perhaps, for example, research shows that metacognition helps students learn. But what metacognitive activity did these students undertake? If I don't know the answer to that question, then I can't decide if it makes sense for my own students. (The blogger Greg Ashman frequently laments the definitional fogginess that surrounds metacognition (Ashman, 2018).)

Hence, we need to crack the code. Because boundary conditions always matter, no one research study captures every classroom application of any one strategy. Just as we look at the participants to see if a teaching strategy applies to our students, so too we must find out exactly what teaching technique is summarized in the handy code phrase.

This chapter's missions are to decipher the code. We want to understand:

1. Precisely what the participants did, and
2. The researchers' definition of improvement, benefit, or success.

Happily, the last five chapters have prepared us well for this challenge. Because we started by asking all the right questions, we have already gathered essential background knowledge. If we had tried to crack the code when we first departed the village, its complexity might well have defeated us. Now we have a fighting chance.

To understand the importance of this quest step, let's start with a compelling example: a study on the benefits of wearing a parachute when jumping out of a plane or helicopter (Yeh et al., 2018). In this study, researchers found that parachutes provided *no benefit* in preventing death or major traumatic injury. In other words: people wearing a parachute experienced the same rate of injury or death as those not wearing one.

Before we follow this study's implied advice – "don't bother with parachutes" – we should decipher the code to understand *exactly* what the participants did. A bit of Goldi-sleuthing turns up this relevant information: participants jumped from an average of 0.6 meters (that's a hair under 2 feet); the airplanes and helicopters from which they jumped were traveling at an average speed of 0.0 kilometers/hour. In other words, parachutes provide no benefit *to people jumping from stationary aircraft, parked on the ground.*

If we had simply relied on the headlines – "parachutes don't help!" – our misapplication of this research could have led to dreadful consequences. So too, teachers need to know *precisely* what researchers did before we accept their Big Ask in our classrooms.

Cracking the Code: Sages on Stages and Guides on Sides

To explore this process in detail, let's consider a more realistic example. The field of education loves a good debate, and few edu-debates rage hotter than the battle between **low-structure** and **high-structure** pedagogy.

In one corner, high-structure advocates believe that – as the experts in the room – teachers should explain concepts to students directly, precisely, and clearly. We should tailor practice exercises that hone and connect specific skills. Depending on your own teaching philosophy, you might call this approach **direct instruction** or – more dismissively – "sage on the stage." Lots of other monikers, complimentary and otherwise, echo through teaching conferences.

In the other corner, low-structure advocates argue that students learn by building their own models of understanding. Teachers should – as much as possible – stand back and let students figure things out for themselves. Students should practice not by getting the answer from the teacher, or even getting the answer that the teacher expects. Instead, they learn by struggling through multiple mistakes to discover correct answers (and deeper understanding). Inaccurately called constructivism, this approach might also be called **problem-based learning** or **project-based learning** or **inquiry learning**. Those who dismiss "sage on the stage" instruction typically laud teachers who act as a "guide on the side."

Having quested this far along our journey, we have strong reasons to step back from this battle. Because we know that psychology research is a messy muddle, we know that the best teaching choice for the lesson I'm teaching right now will depend on *boundary conditions.*

In the first place, the participants: how old are these students? What am I teaching them? What cultural expectations do they have about the teacher's and students' respective responsibilities? Crucially: *how much do they already know about the topic?* Because we spent lots of time in Chapter 5 exploring boundaries, we won't follow research that doesn't align persuasively with our students and our classrooms.

In the second place, what do all those coded phrases mean? What exactly does direct instruction entail? What *precisely* is the difference between problem-based and project-based teaching? What did the researchers actually *do* with students that led to their claim that one school of pedagogy should rule? Although "sage" and "guide" act as customary shorthands, they don't tell us what to do with sufficient precision. As always, we need to decipher the code before we make a recommendation to our fellow villagers.

Earlier quest obstacles have been easily overcome because each one came with a straightforward solution. How can you be sure that the source summarized the research accurately? *Read the abstract.* How can you know that the research applies to our students? *Check out the participants section.* To arrive at those useful answers, you diligently followed narrow instructions.

As you attempt to decipher the code, however, you have to follow a subtler, more nuanced path. Vexingly, the key to the code might be tucked into many different places throughout the study. You can, I promise, find it eventually. But be realistic about this task – you'll need all your Goldilocks stubbornness and lots of mental flexibility.

Start by returning to the abstract. The first time you read the abstract, you did so with a specific question in mind: *do I trust the source?* You wanted to know if his description of the research matched the researchers' own summary of their work.

Now that you trust the source – you wouldn't be at this step if you didn't – you have a different question for the abstract: *does it narrowly define the key terms? Does it help you decipher the code?* If yes, then you've got an answer pronto.

Back in Chapter 2, a source told us that mid-lecture exercise promotes learning. In Chapter 5, we confirmed that participants in Barbara Fenesi's study – college students – more or less match our own. Now we want to know: what, *exactly*, did Fenesi have these students do? What does she consider to be "mid-lecture exercise"? When we reread the abstract, we find that the participants "performed a series of calisthenic exercises" during three five-minute breaks (Fenesi et al., 2018, p. 261). That simple description suggests plausible expectations: jumping jacks, running in place, vigorous stretching – something like that. Of course we want to understand Fenesi's intervention more specifically. After all, if she considers feisty thumb-wrestling as calisthenics, we might need to rethink our interest in her research. But in this case, Fenesi's abstract gives us a helpful head start on codebreaking.

Truthfully, an abstract rarely defines a study's terms fully. It usually sticks with the secret code. Simple limitations on the abstract's word count almost always prevent a researcher from getting too specific in defining her terms. At the same time, reviewing the abstract offers multiple benefits.

First, the abstract – by definition – contains the study's core ideas. The more fully we understand the abstract, the more substantially we prepare ourselves for the codebreaking task ahead. Second, the abstract almost certainly introduces a few vital abbreviations. "Vital" may sound like an odd adjective to describe abbreviations, but trust me: researchers *love* abbreviations. Nothing gives them greater joy than to compose a sentence like this: "This EF, whose neural substrate is the dlPFC, facilitates successful performance on the WCST." If you don't keep track of the abbreviations, you'll never know what they're talking about.

Some abbreviations show up frequently: EF for **executive function**, dlPFC for **dorsolateral prefrontal cortex**, and so forth. In other cases, you have to stay sharp to notice that WCST stands for **Wisconsin Card-Sorting Task**.

> Pro tip: whenever I spot a new letter combination, I circle it and the words that it abbreviates. When I come back to the study later and try to remember what an acronym stands for, I don't have to search through every parenthesis. I simply look back over my circles.

Let's imagine that we're contemplating adopting a project-pedagogy philosophy for our primary school. A consultant finds an impressively large and persuasive study (Bando et al., 2019). Researchers in South America ran 10 field studies, which included over 17,000 (!) pre-kindergarten-through-fourth-grade students. Their conclusion? Compared with traditional pedagogy, inquiry- and problem-based pedagogy increases students' learning of math and science. Given the extraordinary size and depth of this research, our consultant strongly encourages us to adopt **inquiry- and problem-based pedagogy**. (Unsurprisingly, that phrase has an acronym: IPP.)

This information comes to us with quest steps pre-completed:

- *The source's best evidence?* That study of 17,000 students in South America.
- *Peer-reviewed?* Houston, we might have a problem. Let's come back to this question…
- *The abstract matches the advice?* Indeed.
- *Participants match our students?* Quite nicely, thank you.

The topic of peer review prompted hesitation above. We find that the consultant's best evidence appears not in a scholarly journal, but as a report from a non-profit research organization in the US: the National Bureau of Economic Research (NBER). Because such reports rarely face peer review, we have every right to ask hard questions.

After extended scrutiny, however, our skepticism might abate. The NBER has a long history of doing scholarly work, is supervised by professors from well-established universities, and boasts lots of Nobel Prize winners in its ranks. Yes, we might continue to worry that this research was done by economists, not education scholars. We might reasonably fret over the lack of peer review. We might want further evidence to trust its claims. But, unlike the vocabulary teaching example that we considered in Chapter 3, this "best evidence" isn't a Word document "published" in a hard-to-locate journal, uploaded to the internet by scholars who don't answer emails. We decide to relax our peer review requirement in this case.

Relaxing a rule: in Chapter 3, when we dug for buried treasure, we championed the importance of peer review. Given this NBER example, we can soften that insistence a bit. If you come across research by a well-established foundation or research organization – the Brookings Institution, the Education Endowment Foundation, the Fordham Institute – you can make reasonable judgments about its reliability. No doubt you'll click around on the organization's website to verify its credentials; no doubt you'll look for conspicuous bias. If the organization passes muster, you can give its research a respectful read.

Equally important: you might also come across an unpublished MA or PhD thesis when you search. These documents haven't been peer-reviewed but – in most cases – they've received lots of critical scrutiny. They're often worth a look, if only as a place from which to launch a Chapter 8 quest.

Because we moved through those early quest steps relatively easily, we might doubt the need to decipher this code. Let's be frank: it's not much of a code. We might already have rough definitions of direct instruction and project-based learning clearly in mind. Any teaching practice that fits in a high-structure classroom – say, direct instruction – almost certainly will be banned in a low-structure classroom, where independent investigation and discovery guide the day. Sages ain't guides, and guides ain't sages. Why waste valuable quest time decoding words already written in plain English?

Alas, because psychology is a messy muddle, this quest stage can't be skipped. If so important a concept as *working memory* can vex definitional categories, then substantial pedagogical strategies might well defy our understanding of them. We really must confirm specifics. To do so, we now home in on this question: what do the phrases "inquiry- and problem-based pedagogy" and "traditional pedagogy" mean in this particular study?

Certainly Bando's abstract provides a useful starting place. According to its definition, "IPP creates active problem-solving opportunities in settings that provide meaning to the child. Students learn by collaboratively solving real-life problems, developing explanations, and communicating ideas" (Bando et al., 2019, p. 1). That all sounds comfortably within guide (not sage) norms, so we feel increasingly comfortable with our rough-n-ready definitions.

To crack this code precisely, however, we need some more specifics: what does "active" mean in that abstract? What specific parameters shape the "collaborative" work? What counts as "communicating"? Equally important, the abstract doesn't define – or even mention – traditional pedagogy. We shouldn't reject such pedagogy until we know exactly what it is.

Because we couldn't fully crack the cipher simply by reading the abstract, we must delve further into the study. New vistas of possibility open before us.

When a researcher writes the study's **procedures** section, she wants to explain her step-by-step protocol with absolute – even gruesome – precision. If she gets it right, a total stranger could read this section and replicate the study flawlessly.

For instance, if study participants answered questions on a computer, the researcher will typically name the *size of computer monitor* she used. (No, I'm not joking: see Seabrooke et al., 2019). She will identify the *font* in which the question appeared. In all likelihood, she'll include the size of the font, and perhaps even the distance from the table that the chair was placed. (Still not joking.) Whereas the abstract remains, well, *abstract*, the procedures section gets lots of dirt on its hands.

This commitment to thorough precision streamlines your sleuthing mission. Because the researcher has promised to reveal all, you should be able to find the cipher she used. You have high hopes that her detailed description will help you crack the secret code.

Of course, as she piles detail on top of detail, the researcher both simplifies and complicates your mission. You know that the key to the code lies somewhere in this treasure trove. Almost certainly she will share – probably overshare – the precise definition of the shorthand terms you want to understand. But where, among details about computer monitors and font sizes, will you find the information you need?

For this reason, this quest stage encourages *artful* skimming. Yes, you could pore over each lovingly crafted sentence describing, perhaps, the methods used to sort participants into random groups. No doubt other researchers read such methods with giddy glee. You might feel intrigued by those details, but your quest requires you to concentrate on cracking the code. So, remind yourself: *don't get lured into side quests*. Eyes on the prize.

Happily, Team Bando reveal their code almost immediately. As they define it, "traditional pedagogy" relies on "lecturing with passive listening" (p. 2). They go on to expand the abstract's definition of IPP:

> *"IPP creates active problem-solving opportunities in settings that provide meaning to the child. Students learn by collaboratively solving authentic, real-life problems, developing explanations, and communicating ideas. They are taught to search for information from different sources, both text-based resources and by gathering their own data, and to develop problem-solving skills by collaboratively engaging in investigations." (p. 2)*

At this point, we're inclined to relax our definitional vigilance. These shorthand phrases – traditional instruction, IPP – mean exactly what we thought. Tradition-bound sages dispense knowledge to passive students; IPP-inspired guides encourage active engagement with and independent creation of knowledge. Not much of a code, really. Although we're wearing armor, we'd like to lean back in a Barcalounger and crack open a cold one.

The researchers' next sentence, however, jolts us out of our comfortable confidence: "When done well, IPP includes elements of explicit instruction and scaffolding" (Bando et al., 2019, p. 3). Wait just a minute. Our prior understanding of these terms pits sages against guides. These South American researchers, however, envisage their cheerful cooperation:

> *"[In IPP], teachers facilitate learning by guiding students through a series of steps and explicitly relating learning to students' prior knowledge and experiences. Teachers guide learners through complex tasks with explicit instructions that are relevant to the problem at hand. They provide structure and scaffolding that help students not only carry out specific activities, but also comprehend why they are doing those activities and how they are related to the set of core concepts that they are exploring."* (pp. 3–4)

That paragraph repeatedly uses the verb "guide." And yet, this guide undertakes lots of sage-like functions. "Explicit instruction and scaffolding," obviously, come from sages who "explicitly [relate] learning to students' prior knowledge," give "explicit instructions," "provide structure," and "help students … carry out specific activities."

The researchers' classroom examples highlight the frank inadequacy of our familiar definitions. For instance, Bando's team describes a fourth-grade anatomy unit undertaken in the spirit of IPP:

"Teachers pose research questions and guide students through the formulation and testing of hypotheses to explore the questions. One research question might be: What do bones help people do? Students then research facts about bones from texts and other sources from which they devise hypotheses. One such hypothesis is that calcium strengthens bones. Students might then soak chicken bones in vinegar for different lengths of time to extract different amounts of calcium, concluding that the more calcium a bone loses, the more it will bend." (p. 3)

This unit clearly enacts inquiry principles. Students undertake independent research to understand an authentically interesting topic: what's cooler to a fourth grader than bones? As a research project, they even get to soak bones in something stinky and them *bend* them. You can already hear cries of "Gross!" and "Whoa!" as you imagine nine-year-olds marveling at pliable chicken limbs.

At the same time, the unit obviously requires substantial direct instruction and explanation. Fourth graders might generate the hypothesis that "calcium strengthens bones," but they no doubt require all sorts of sage-like coaching to get there. The vinegar-soaking experiment, we can be sure, did not come from a nine-year-old. A biology teaching colleague assures me that, without highly structured teacherly explanations, the students won't usefully connect the bendy-bone experiment with the unit's starting question: "What do bones help people do?"

When we initially set out on this quest, our school's faculty clearly understood direct instruction and project pedagogy to be distinct and competing philosophies. Using this study, our consultant encouraged us to prefer the latter and reject the former. However, when we crack the code, we discover that the researchers actually *combined* guiding and saging into a flexible and coherent system. This study doesn't encourage us to choose one approach over the other. Instead, it suggests we unite them sensibly.

The researchers' example of traditional pedagogy reinforces this conviction. Whereas the IPP anatomy lesson had students undertaking meaningful independent cognitive work, the traditional lesson had quite a different feel: "students copy facts about bone tissues and the names of the 206 bones of the human skeleton that teachers have written on the blackboard into notebooks" (p. 3). Whatever label we apply to this lesson plan, "direct instruction" doesn't fit. I have yet to meet any teacher – traditional or progressive – who thinks nine-year-olds should *copy down the names of 206 bones.* It seems some teachers do work this way. But no one who informs teaching practice with cognitive research would find support for such an approach.

Bando's research shouldn't discourage our school from using direct instruction, because the researchers didn't study direct instruction. Even in a field rich with brand names, I don't think anyone has claimed the "copy 206 facts into your notebook" pedagogy as their own. If you've read *Hard Times* by Charles Dickens, you might call it the "Gradgrind method." *Of course* students who copy the names of 206 bones learn less than students who – with sagely guidance – explore meaningful questions about human anatomy. Who would seriously argue otherwise?

If we had relied on our rough-n-ready understanding of direct instruction and project pedagogy, we would cheerfully have agreed with our consultants' recommendation. This huge study (again: 17,000 students!) showed quite clearly that A works much better than B. However, when we sleuth our way through the procedures, we discover that *A and B don't mean what we thought they meant.* We had understood inquiry learning and project learning to forbid direct instruction. These researchers, in contrast with our prior understanding, found that a nuanced combination of both works better than repetitious drudgery.

This study might ultimately inspire us to update our pedagogy. But, now that we know its code, we won't make the same changes the consultant recommended. Our students will benefit from our scrupulous work.

Cracking the Code: Training Executive Functions

Gosh, that was hard work. To get more familiar and comfortable with this process, let's consider a second hypothetical.

At a recent conference, a speaker lists multiple "research-based" strategies for *helping struggling readers.* Because several of your third graders read well below grade level, you're delighted to hear the speaker's list. It would be great to have fresh teaching strategies – especially those supported by science.

At the same time, you're surprised by one suggestion: "train students' executive function." Experience tells you that executive function resists tidy definition. Clearly EF matters in school. Just as clearly, that broad category includes several distinct cognitive functions: prioritizing, inhibiting, task-switching. Heck, most definitions include working memory as one executive function. We need to know: when the speaker says that EF training helps struggling readers, does he plan to train all of those functions? Just a few? One?

Time to saddle up:

- You ask the speaker for the best research support for this claim. She cites Kelly Cartwright's 2020 study in *Cognitive Development.* (Boom: chasm crossed.)
- You go to Google Scholar and discover that, indeed, Cartwright's research has been peer-reviewed. While there, you snag a PDF. (Boom: treasure unearthed.)
- You read the abstract to ensure that the speaker summarized Cartwright's research accurately. Sure enough, the speaker's claims tidily align with it. (Boom: no disguise found.)

- You quickly scan the PDF for the participants section. As a third grade teacher, you're delighted to discover that Cartwright's team worked with second to fifth graders. (Boom: boundaries explored.)

Because you followed these well-defined quest steps, you needed 15 minutes (give or take) to verify the source's credibility and determine that your students fit within the study's boundaries. To confirm this strategy's alignment with your school and curriculum, you now need to crack the code. In the first place: what did the students do? What does Cartwright's *executive function intervention* entail, precisely? Equally important, what sort of executive function got the love? You know that this category embraces a long list of interrelated skills. Which one(s) were trained?

Unsurprisingly, Cartwright's abstract doesn't define executive function training precisely. Thus, you gallop forward into the procedures section, determined not to be distracted by tempting side quests. After skimming past several fascinating-but-off-topic paragraphs, you stumble upon a section helpfully labeled **intervention**. Tiny celebration bells ring in your head as you realize that you've found the cipher.

In Cartwright's intervention, students undertook a word-sorting exercise, once a week for five weeks. Each student received a set of 12 words: e.g., cup, bread, can, box, cake, bag, cookie, bucket, corn, beans, crate, banana. A student first sorted those words into two groups according to the *sound they begin with*. If he's on his game, his list looks like this:

/k/ sounds	/b/ sounds
Cup	Bread
Can	Box
Cake	Bag
Cookie	Bucket
Corn	Beans
Crate	Banana

Then, the student re-sorted those words into two different groups according to the *meaning of the word*:

Foods	Containers
Bread	Cup
Cake	Can
Cookie	Box
Corn	Bag
Beans	Bucket
Banana	Crate

For a final step, the student completed a fill-in-the-blank matrix exercise (Figure 10). The student's goal: fill in the blank box with a word so the matrix has two of everything – two /b/ sounds, two /k/ sounds, two foods, two containers. As you can see, the matrix already has two /b/ sounds, so the student should choose a second /k/ word. Likewise, the matrix has two containers, so it needs one more food. Searching for a /k/ word that names a food, the student perhaps chose "cookie" or "cake."

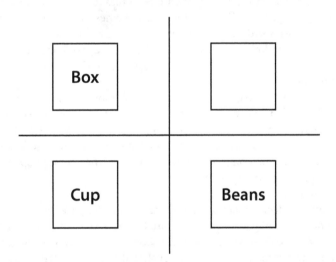

Figure 10. (Source: Cartwright et al., 2020)

Voila: your artful skimming has led to spectacular success. Were a grouchily dubious colleague to ask exactly what this so-called "EF training" included, you could smile winningly and answer in detail. You might bust out a matrix and invite your colleague to try.

Your sleuthing also revealed other essential snippets of code. You started this quest phase a bit uncertain about executive function. You'd really like to know: which part of EF gets trained? As you rummaged around in Cartwright's code, you found the answer: **cognitive flexibility**.

More specifically, Cartwright has a tongue-twister of an answer. To read effectively, in English especially, students must be cognitively flexible about *spelling and sound*. The letter "c" might indicate a hard /k/ sound (like "crate") or a sibilant /s/ sound (like "celery").

Students must also be cognitively flexible about the *meanings* that words have. The word "can," for instance, could be a noun or a verb. In either case, it includes wildly different meanings: "Because I don't really like fruit, I got canned from my job canning peaches. Now what can I do?"

Because readers must use cognitive flexibility *simultaneously* with letters (graphemes), sounds (phonemes), and meanings (semantics), Cartwright studied **graphophonological-semantic cognitive flexibility**. Naturally, this mouthful gets the acronym GSF.

Let me say that again. Cartwright's students had to sort words based on their sounds and spelling: that's flexibility with graphemes and with phonemes. And they had to re-sort words based on their meanings: that's semantic flexibility. Putting all that together, students practiced their graphophonological-semantic cognitive flexibility. Because skillful reading requires GSF, this training helped them read better.

As you can see, this segment of the quest took more Goldilocks stubbornness than the others. You had to skim past irrelevancies, and page back-n-forth to translate obscure acronyms. The result, however, repays all your effort. You know quite specifically how Cartwright trained the students' EF. You also know that the training focused narrowly on cognitive flexibility, specifically graphophonological-semantic cognitive flexibility (GSF).

This knowledge creates power.

First, you can decide whether Cartwright's training paradigm fits within the boundary conditions of your own classroom. In search of a boundary condition for this suggestion, I spoke with a blind student about using this GSF training paradigm with Braille. After some discussion, he concluded that the matrix segment would complicate it beyond usefulness. Because that matrix exercise spreads information out in space, he thought it would make the task too difficult for struggling Braille readers (B. Peters, personal communication, September 2020). (By the way, if you have experience teaching students to read Braille, you might thoughtfully disagree with this student's analysis. I've never taught anyone this skill, and so defer to others' expertise.)

That is: this exercise might help some struggling readers, but it might not help all of them.

Second, you can prevent mission creep. Imagine, for instance, that a colleague attended the same conference you did, and heard the speaker's advice that "training executive function helps struggling readers." Your colleague, plausibly enough, notes that many children's games improve EF. For that reason, he proposes that struggling readers should play "Mother May I" and "Simon Says" more often. Doing so would boost EF and thereby – research says! – improve their reading.

Because you've deciphered the code, however, you quickly spot the flaw in this otherwise delicious suggestion. Mother May I certainly trains EF, but it trains a *specific* EF: **inhibition**. Children must wait to do something until they have asked for and received explicit permission. Cartwright's research does *not* show that *inhibition* helps reading. That's a different EF altogether.

Yes, we urgently want our students to develop inhibition, and can arrange sessions of Mother May I to promote it. But we shouldn't do so to help uncertain readers. Unless your optimistic colleague can create a GSF version of Mother May I, he can't say that his proposal has research support.

More to the point: unless he can create a GSF version of Mother May I, your struggling readers *probably won't benefit from his teaching suggestion.* Because you have undertaken your perilous quest, you can save your students from his well-intentioned misunderstanding. And you can rescue your colleagues from wasting their time. They might not know they should thank you, but indeed they should.

You worked hard to crack this code. That work benefits your students and your colleagues. Villagers send a congratulatory raven, promising warm grog.

Cracking the Code: Defining Success

Typically, we read a study because we believe its teaching suggestion might work.

So far in this chapter, we've been questing to define that teaching suggestion:

- Exactly what kind of curriculum helps South American students learn math and science? *A judicious combination of direct instruction and independent investigation.*
- Exactly what kind of EF intervention helps struggling readers? *A word-sorting task that enhances graphophonological-semantic flexibility.*

To truly believe that these methodologies work, we also need to decode the researchers' definition of **work**. How, precisely, do we know that one method produced better results than another? What did they measure? What counts as success?

Because the procedures section spells out the researchers' methodology so precisely, it always answers this question. Yes, the wealth of information might briefly obscure the answer. But the researchers will certainly highlight their definition of success, and probably repeat it several times.

We might even find an initial answer in the abstract. According to Cartwright's abstract, "the reading-specific EF intervention produced *medium to large effects* on *reading-specific and domain-general EF skills* as well as on *researcher-administered and school-administered reading comprehension measures*" (Cartwright et al., 2020, p. 2, emphasis added). Like many sentences in an abstract, this 25-word humdinger might exhaust its readers. But once we've read it a few times, we can see that the researchers measured success in several ways. They tested the students' *general* EF skills and their *reading-specific* EF skills, and found "medium to large effects." Both the researchers and the school gave follow-up reading comprehension tests; those also demonstrated students' improvement. Clearly, Cartwright's team gives us *lots* of reasons to believe their intervention worked.

Bando's study of IPP in South America (2019) requires a bit more sleuthing. After reviewing the abstract and hunting about in the main body of the paper, we discover that the team looked at students' standardized math and science test scores both *seven months later* and *four years later*. While the specific results – reported in standard deviations – don't feel intuitive to non-stats majors, the decision to use test scores makes sense: it's probably the best way to compare students from so many school systems. Honestly, the fact that they found significant results *years* later should boost our confidence in their methodology. If nothing else, the researchers demonstrated admirable patience.

> Spoiler alert: you might need to brave the **results** section to answer this question. We'll discuss strategies for doing so in the next chapter. The odds are good, however, that you'll hear about the headline definition of "works" much earlier.

Once again, cracking this code gives us power. Now we know how researchers define success, we can ask several common-sense questions:

Common-Sense Question #1

Did the researchers measure something meaningful? Do we care about the definition enough to accept the Big Ask?

Several years ago, I read about a study showing that "outdoor education works!" Because I've devoted years of my life to summer camps – I was a camper and counselor for ages, and go back every July to dunk myself in the lake – I was *delighted* to find this research. I conjured a clear vision in my head: when I spoke with school leaders about starting outdoor-education programs, I could cite this study to support my Big Ask. Already I could smell pine on the breeze.

When Goldilocks and I armored up for our quest, alas, we barely made it out of the village. The study included a great many obvious flaws. For instance, to show that outdoor education works, the researchers asked several teachers and students. All of them said that they liked having class outdoors. That was the researchers' definition of "success" – *100% of the participants said they liked it.*

On the one hand, we should be glad that the students and teachers liked it. (Of course, we're not surprised they liked it. They *chose* to attend or work at an outdoor school.) On the other hand, to believe that this pedagogical model *works*, we'd like some more substantive evidence. For instance, we would love to know that, compared with students who attended indoor school, these students...

- Learned more about biology, and the sciences generally, or
- Developed greater leadership skills and empathy, or
- Reported lower stress and greater self-esteem, or
- Demonstrated less anti-social behavior in the summer following school, or...

...or almost any measurable quality beyond "they liked it." Presumably we don't want to upend our school system without meaningful evidence of greater benefits.

Common-Sense Question #2

Does the study's definition of success fit our school's need?

Imagine for a moment that our middle school – concerned about our students' sloth – has decided to prioritize physical fitness this year. As our faculty meet to brainstorm fitness-enhancing ideas, a colleague reminds us that **mindful meditation** has lots of science behind it: "Research shows that mindfulness offers profound benefits to the brain!" Brief web sleuthing finds lots of supporting evidence. For instance, our athletic director easily conjures up a study by Doss and Bloom (2018) showing lots of potential benefits to mindfulness. Because mindfulness is good, we should add it to our daily schedule.

Sober contemplation reminds us: we don't want research showing that mindfulness offers lots of *potential* benefits. We want research showing that it *truly* yields a *particular* benefit: enhancing physical fitness. A quick scan of Doss and Bloom's abstract reveals several mismatches:

- The researchers didn't measure mindfulness's effects on physical fitness. Instead, they measured its effects on stress, perfectionism, and anxiety.
- They didn't get consistently good results. Even within the researchers' definition of success, some students did – and others did not – get the benefits they hoped to see.

- Doss and Bloom ran this study with "gifted" students – hence their interest in anxiety and perfectionism. Unless our middle school has an unusual profile, our student body at large probably doesn't fit within those specific boundaries.

These mini-quest results don't mean that Doss and Bloom ran a flawed or unimportant study. If we ran a gifted program and worried about our students' anxiety and perfectionism, we'd fall on this study like peckish hyenas.

But at this moment, we don't need research on stressed-out gifted students; we seek research showing that mindfulness training *enhances physical fitness in middle schoolers*. We might reasonably hypothesize that reduced perfectionism increases fitness. But this study doesn't reach that conclusion. It doesn't even ask that question. Doss and Bloom measure success quite differently. Because we took the time to crack their code, we can refocus our search in more productive directions.

Common-Sense Question #3

How long did the benefits last?

Like teachers, psychology researchers have lots to do. Except in unusual circumstances, they can't devote months and months to a single experiment. For that reason, study design often prioritizes immediate results. The science communication expert Neil Lewis even worries that, because tenure decisions rely on the volume of published research, psychologists feel tempted to run many quick studies rather than a few long-term ones (Lewis & Watson, 2020).

For example, a researcher might want to know if a specific note-taking technique improves learning. She has students use that technique to take notes on a lecture, and then, say, 30 minutes later, tests them on the content of that lecture. Next, she compares their scores to test results for students who used a more traditional note-taking format. The result: the novel note-taking technique *resulted in higher average scores*. Success!

Like the Doss and Bloom study, this fictional study design doesn't earn demerits. The researcher had a specific question and organized a perfectly plausible study to arrive at one answer. At the same time, we should note crucial limits on its conclusion. We can't say that the students who used the new technique learned more; we can say that they learned more *as measured by a test 30 minutes later*. If we were to test those same students a week later or a month later, we might arrive at completely different results.

This caveat doesn't result merely from a persnickety nature. In psychology, sadly, short-term learning – as revealed by an *immediate* test – does not reliably predict long-term learning – as revealed by a *delayed* test. In a 2015 masterpiece of a review article, Nick Soderstrom sums up this paradox nicely:

> *"The primary goal of instruction should be to facilitate long-term learning – that is, to create relatively permanent changes in comprehension, understanding, and skill … . During the instruction or training process, however, what we can observe and measure is performance, which is often an unreliable index of whether the relatively long-term changes that constitute learning have taken place."* (Soderstrom & Bjork, 2015, p. 176)

Alas, Soderstrom notes, "[long-term] *learning* can occur even when no discernible changes in [short-term] *performance* are observed. More recently, the converse has also been shown – specifically, that improvements in [short-term] performance can fail to yield significant [long-term] learning" (Soderstrom & Bjork, 2015, p. 176).

A specific example clarifies this point. Back in Chapter 2, we looked briefly at a study about the spacing effect (Rohrer & Taylor, 2006). In that research, students who spaced their practice out did relatively well (64%) on a quiz one month later. Students who did all their practice at once remembered much less (32%). In the long term, spacing leads to more learning than massing.

Spacing vs. Massing in Mathematics Learning

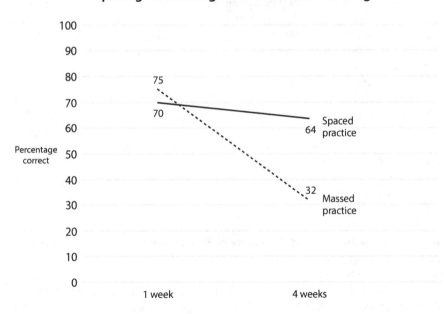

Figure 11. (Source: Rohrer & Taylor, 2006)

Notice, however, a big surprise in Figure 11. When Rohrer and Taylor tested students relatively quickly – a week later, not a month later – they got strikingly different results. Both groups had roughly the same score: 70% for the spaced-practice group and 75% for the massed-practice group. In other words: if we look only at short-term performance, we might conclude that both strategies work equally well – or even that practicing all at once is slightly superior. As Soderstrom and Bjork warned (2015), improvements in week-later performance failed to predict month-later learning.

When we decipher the researchers' definition of success, therefore, we should check the duration of that success. Although we don't expect all studies to gather data for four years (hats off to Bando's research team in South America!), we do expect changes to last for meaningful periods of time. We agree to Big Asks only if they create enduring improvements.

Not Bad News, *Good* News

Two chapters ago, the news that psychology research is a messy muddle might well have felt disappointing. Whereas other scientific branches expect predictable consistency, psychology sloshes about in puzzling uncertainty.

This surprising truth does create perils when we bring research into classrooms. Sources – sometimes confused, sometimes unscrupulous – can exploit these subtleties to overhype their suggestions. Colleagues – enthusiastic but unschooled in psychology's nuances – can fall for ineffective advice. Perils lurk in these shadows.

And yet, this understanding gives teachers real power.

In the first place, this muddle just makes sense. In the past, you might have wondered why some research shows that stress is good for your learning, and other research shows that it's bad. Answer: those contradictory research claims depend on the definition of "good," "bad," "learning," "stress," and "you." The stress of cold water might impair your learning if you're a rat trying to learn a water maze (Hölscher, 1999). The stress of public speaking might boost your learning if you're a college student trying to remember emotion-laden words (Smeets et al., 2009). Boundary conditions always matter.

Your cynical friends say, "You can find research 'proving' anything." Now that you understand this research field more richly, you respond: "Studies always vary based on the participants and precise definitions. That variety isn't a weakness; it accurately reflects human complexity."

In the second place, this understanding lets us align our teaching practice with the most appropriate research. Teaching strategies that work for college students might not work with our students. An example: we might hear a podcast about the benefits of **generative learning strategies**. Given all the evidence behind the podcaster's claim – and given his obvious confidence – we might be tempted to start right away.

If instead we start thinking about boundary conditions, we will be grateful to happen across a study by Garvin Brod (2020). Brod looks for evidence of *different* generative learning strategies ("the code") and the quality of that evidence for *different* age groups ("the participants"). As Figure 12 highlights, we simply can't know if we should – broadly speaking – "use generative learning strategies for our students." Instead, we can answer narrower questions. Should we use *concept mapping* with university students? According to Brod, the evidence is favorable. Should we use drawing with *primary and middle-school* students? Evidence there is unfavorable.

Evidence on the Effectiveness of Generative Learning Strategies in Different Age Groups				
	University students	Secondary-school students	Fourth/fifth-grade students	Below fourth-grade students
Concept mapping	Favorable	Favorable	Favorable	Insufficient
Explaining	Favorable	Favorable	Mixed	Mixed
Predicting	Favorable	Favorable	Favorable	Favorable
Questioning	Favorable	Mixed	Mixed	Unfavorable
Testing	Favorable	Favorable	Favorable	Favorable
Drawing	Favorable	Favorable	Unfavorable	Unfavorable

Figure 12. (Source: Brod, 2020)

Because psychology research offers a richly chaotic cornucopia, we know to focus on specific participants. We take time to decode particular definitions. The result: our students benefit from optimal teaching strategies. Goldilocks couldn't be happier.

Question: in Chapter 4, we "broke the disguise." Here in Chapter 6, we've been "cracking the code." What's the difference?

Short answer: disguise = bad; code = good.

More precisely: disguise = almost always bad; code = utterly normal.

That is: sources should not disguise a study by claiming it supports their Big Ask if it doesn't. If we have to break their disguise, we usually stop trusting them.

However, researchers almost always write with some coded shorthand. Research's complex nuances require handy catchphrases and abbreviations. These ciphers don't raise our doubts; they pique our curiosity.

CHAPTER 7.
FACING THE GIANT

As we look back over our quest so far, we can and should feel genuine pride. We left the village as research neophytes. Now that we've crossed chasms, broken spells, and cracked codes, we have the look of grizzled veterans. Well-fed hobbits might eye us warily, or accidentally call us "Aragorn."

In Part II, early quest obstacles gave way before us quite easily. (Digging up buried treasure sounded laborious until we found Google Scholar.) Here in Part III, more recent obstacles – especially the researchers' mysterious cipher – posed greater challenges. Now our quest moves from potentially difficult to potentially dangerous: it's time to face the Giant. Although our knees might be knocking, we approach **the researcher** herself to ask bold questions.

Back in Chapter 4, we dared to ask: "Does the research say what the *source* says it said?" Here in Chapter 7, we ask a considerably more audacious version of that question: "Does the research say what the *researcher* says it said?"

Needless to say, this question requires the greatest dose of Goldilocks humility. Researchers have, obviously, devoted months of thought and sweat to this research. They fought for funding and scrounged research subjects and went through an infuriatingly slow peer-review process. They know their work – and the business of research – better than we ever will.

For that reason, we start this portion of our quest assuming that they have done their work well. (I call this section "facing the Giant," not "slaying the Giant," because it's rare to find slay-worthy flaws.)

At the same time, researchers publish their research *in order that others be able to examine it critically.* They are not infallible prophets revealing sacred scrolls. They offer tentative conclusions based on specific theories, methodologies, and experimental results. They've written all that down so that anyone – yes, including us – can check for themselves. So, we can both respect their expertise and ask hard questions at the same time.

In fact, asking hard questions is a form of respect for their expertise. In my experience, researchers often respond enthusiastically when I ask about methods and choices: "You've read this really carefully. I'm glad it piqued your interest. Now, to answer your question…"

At the same time, we should acknowledge an important truth: researchers are people too. After investing so much time and cognitive effort in gathering meaningful results, they really, *really* want their findings to have important implications. We can't blame them for presenting their research in the best light possible. They're not supposed to – in fact, they're typically required to include a **limitations** section in their study. But, humans being humans, we all feel tempted to err on the side of making our work look good.

Facing the Giant, we ask three respectful questions:

1. Does the control group inspire confidence?
2. Do the most important numbers add up?
3. Does a teacher's perspective offer additional – even contradictory – interpretations of this study?

Almost certainly, we'll get reassuring answers to our questions. In those rare cases when we don't, this perilous path will have been worth the risk.

Taking Control

Most psychology research works in a predictable way. For example: a memory researcher gathers fifth graders together and randomly sorts them into two groups. The first group – typically called the **experimental group** or **treatment group** – studies for a photosynthesis test using *retrieval practice*. The second group – the **control group** or **comparison group** – studies simply by *rereading the textbook*. When those two groups take the subsequent photosynthesis test, the researcher compares their average scores. If she discovers a meaningfully large (a.k.a., statistically significant) difference between their averages, she can conclude that the retrieval practice helped. (Theoretically it might have hurt, but that's rare for retrieval practice.)

Crucially, the researcher wants to isolate the variable in question. As much as possible, the *only* substantial difference between the two groups should be the retrieval practice. The experimental group and the control group should – on average – resemble each other eerily.

If, for instance, the experimental group comprised seventh graders while the control group comprised fifth graders, that difference alone muddles the memory researcher's conclusion. In that case, the retrieval practice might explain why the experimental group learned more. But the *age difference* might also matter.

Imagine all the ways that comparison groups and experimental groups could meaningfully differ:

- They could attend different schools.
- They could come from different countries.
- They could learn about photosynthesis in different ways. One group might have watched a video, while the others did a lab.
- They could have studied for different amounts of time.
- Their gender mix, or SES composition, or cultural backgrounds could be meaningfully different.
- They could have different learning profiles – say, ADHD diagnoses.
- They could take the photosynthesis test under different conditions. If one room were cool and quiet, and the other hot and noisy, those environmental differences could influence test scores.

We call these potential alternative explanations **confounding variables**, or **confounds**. Because any of these confounds could explain why one group learned more than the other, they would make the results less persuasive. If we find enough confounds on our quest, we tell our fellow villagers not to follow this set of recommendations.

Researchers go to remarkable lengths to design good controls and avoid confounds. For example: one research team, led by Jay Greene, wanted to show that *attending live theater* enhances students' tolerance of other people, and their ability to consider another person's point of view (Greene et al., 2018). That's a bold hypothesis. Just imagine the difficulties in creating a plausible control for *attending live theater*.

Greene might have had control group participants *read* the same play that the experimental group *attended*. Sadly, that plan would create many troubling confounds. Students who read a play must figure out the characters' motivations as they go along. Students who watch a production get the substantial benefit of the actors' choices, the director's interpretations, the set designer's insights, and so forth.

Perhaps, to avoid those confounds, Greene might have had the control group watch a *movie* version of the play. A movie adaptation, like a live production, includes actors', director's, and designers' interpretations. However, students who attend live theater often have a meaningfully unusual experience. They leave the school campus. They file into an unfamiliar theater. They fall silent with anticipation when the lights dramatically dim.

You can see the problems that Team Greene faces.

To escape this fix, Greene came up with an impressively elaborate procedure. In his study, both the control group and the experimental group took the same busses to the same building on a nearby college campus. The experimental group turned left into one theater to see a live production of *Romeo and Juliet*; the control group turned right into another theater to see the Baz Luhrmann film *William Shakespeare's Romeo + Juliet*.

Having contemplated Greene's elaborate control-group plans, we might still have quibbles. Luhrmann's film, after all, offers an unusual take on this classic love story. Perhaps differences in the directors' interpretations might create a confound. But we doubtless feel reassured that Greene did everything reasonably possible to isolate the variable that interests him: watching live theater. His intricate steps persuade us to befriend, not doubt, this Giant. (If you're curious, by the way: Greene has indeed found that attending *live* theater results in lots of social-emotional benefits.)

As we arrive at this quest stage, therefore, we start to look for confounds. Specifically, we should study the control group and ask ourselves: "Is this group a plausible match for the experimental group?"

The procedures section should describe these control groups in detail. As always, we might find the minutiae mind-numbing. But once we sort through the long sentences and the inscrutable acronyms – we're so glad we circled them! – we can readily compare these groups to one another. If we discover confounds, we dare give the Giant the side-eye.

Let's try this hypothetical. Having read Chapter 6, we recognize the vital importance of working memory. All school learning requires working memory, and our students don't have much of it. (Truthfully, although we ourselves have more than they do, we rarely have enough.) For that reason, we feel an adrenaline rush when our district launches a research-based initiative to *increase students' working-memory capacity*.

After that adrenaline high subsides, we decide to investigate the research behind this district initiative.

As experienced heroes, we move briskly through early quest stages. We locate the supporting study, confirm peer review, double-check the abstract, and unpack the researcher's definition of success. Sure enough, she increased working memory! When we decipher the code, we learn *exactly* what she did to achieve this miracle. Participants undertook a highly specialized series of physical exercises, thoughtfully designed to boost working memory. For the sake of thoroughness, let's bestow an acronym on that specialized series of exercises: SSE.

Our adventure has gone remarkably smoothly: no goblins, no avalanches, no trap doors. Experience tells us that, when we approach the Giant, she will answer our respectful questions quite chummily.

Because the study labels the experimental group and the control group quite clearly, we can easily compare them. In fact, this study includes two control groups – a research paradigm that boosts our confidence even higher. A quick scan reveals that the participants in these groups match each other nicely.

Alas, details suddenly turn gruesome:

- Participants in the experimental group undertook SSEs over **two** sessions: the first lasted **two hours**, and the second lasted **two-and-a-half hours**.
- Participants in the first control group sat still and listened to a **two-hour** lecture. **Once.**
- Participants in the second control group did an alternative, non-SSE exercise. For **one hour. Once.**

We have to ask: did the difference in working memory scores result from the SSEs that participants undertook? Or from the exercise *duration*? Or from the *number* of *sessions* they attended? We simply can't answer that question, because the researcher's study design doesn't allow us to know.

Did I just see you give the Giant the stink eye? I won't tell on you. I did too.

This alarming discovery invites different responses:

- We might jump ahead to Chapter 8 and look for other research confirming the benefits of SSEs.
- We might, respectfully but firmly, conclude this quest with a hard pass.

Whichever response we pick, we should not simply go ahead with this "research-based" district initiative. Our quest clearly shows that the initiative does not rest on *plausibly designed* research. Although we feel disappointment that we can't enhance working memory, we also feel relief that we haven't wasted our students' time.

As both the *attend live theater* and *enhance working memory* examples show, teachers on a quest can make well-informed decisions about nuanced methodological details. By decoding essential terminology and scrutinizing the control group, we find crucial information. As informed consumers, we can draw discerning conclusions.

To hone these informed consumer skills, we should devote especial skepticism to one control group paradigm: **business as usual**. In a business-as-usual control group, researchers compare the experimental group to students or schools who didn't change their typical routine. In other words, researchers compare students who did *something special* to students who did *nothing new*. This control group strategy invites an obvious concern: maybe the novel teaching technique helped, or maybe a simple change in routine caused the improvement. With a business-as-usual control group, we rarely know if students did better because they did something *special*, or because they did *anything at all*.

A study about the benefits of mindfulness illustrates this problem. Researchers hypothesized – sensibly – that mindful meditation might help students whose anxiety vexed their school performance. They instructed a group of students (the experimental group) in meditation, starting an hour before school. After eight weeks of controlled breathing and mindful attention, these students did moderately better on tests of emotional and psychosocial health. Crucially, they did better on those tests than the business-as-usual control group: other students whose experience at school didn't change at all.

Sadly, this control group doesn't allow us to draw strong conclusions, because it doesn't isolate the variable. The *only* difference between the two groups should be the key intervention: in this case, the mindful meditation. Alas, these two groups differ conspicuously. Did the students benefit from the mindfulness? Or, from waking up early to get to school? Or, from extra adult attention? Would they have gotten the same benefit from, say, *calisthenics* before school, or *drum lessons* before school, or a *paper route* before school? We don't know because we can't know. The control group design foils our inquiries.

This problem vexes system-wide studies as well. One education group (not the same one discussed in Chapter 6) wanted to show that a research-inspired *inquiry curriculum* could improve science learning. In an ambitious study, they provided several school districts with carefully developed curricular materials. To ensure that teachers deployed this inquiry approach correctly, the researchers provided several professional development trainings. Sure enough, their inquiry curriculum produced impressive results. Over the span of a few years, students learned a *few extra months' worth* of science. That's amazing.

When Goldilocks peers at the control group, alas, she finds a business-as-usual paradigm. Those students made extra months of progress *compared with students in schools that got nothing*. Their teachers did not get an alternative research-based curriculum. They did not get extra training. They got bupkis – except, perhaps, that "why do those other school districts get the shiny new toys?" feeling.

We might, as these researchers did, conclude that the inquiry curriculum helped the students learn more. We might just as reasonably conclude that inquiry teachers felt re-energized by the jazzy curriculum and crisp textbooks. Rejuvenated by district-level attention, they dove into their work with renewed vigor and enthusiasm. With a business-as-usual control group, we have no way to know which explanation truly matters.

Useful phrase: if the researchers eschew a business-as-usual control group, we call that an **active control group**. Goldilocks really likes active controls, and always hopes to see that phrase in a study.

Of course, Goldilocks resists the word "never," as in "never trust a business-as-usual control group." At times, researchers use this approach quite reasonably: e.g., when they compare students to themselves. In this case, the experimental group and the control group resemble each other not *eerily* but *precisely*.

A recent example demonstrates this exception. Earlier chapters in this book have championed the benefits of *retrieval practice* and of *spacing*. Memory researchers, led by Jessica Janes (Janes et al., 2020), wondered what would happen if students combined those strategies. (As we know, researchers typically abbreviate long descriptions into convenient shorthand phrases; Janes's team encodes this combination with the phrase *successive relearning*.) Her team instructed students in an advanced biopsychology course to study some concepts using successive relearning. Those students reviewed other course concepts "as they normally would" (Janes et al., 2020, p. 1123): i.e., business as usual. Sure enough, on the final exam, students consistently remembered *successively relearned* concepts better than *studied-as-usual* concepts.

The phrase "business as usual" might have worried us when we first saw it in the abstract. However, the procedures section easily relieves our fears. Janes compared the efficacy of Study Method A (successive relearning) and Study Method B ("as they normally would") *within the same student*. That is: each student tried two equally plausible study strategies, and benefited more from A than from B. (We know that Method B was plausible because it got these students into an advanced college course.) In this case, a business-as-usual control group compared two viable study strategies within the same population. That research method makes perfect sense.

This exception reinforces a principle that has guided us since Chapter 1. On our quest, we do not apply inflexible rules with absolute, unquestioning rigor. Instead, we respect researchers' expertise, respect our own experience, and combine both with a dollop of open-hearted common sense.

- We've seen that Word documents uploaded to the web might not be peer-reviewed. But we've also seen they might be. We're extra-skeptical, but not robotically strict.
- We know peer review might confirm that a study has met baseline research standards. But we know that peer review is a buggy process. It can't weed out all flawed studies; it might needlessly reject good ones. And we also know that some foundations and thinktanks produce admirable work outside the peer-review system.
- We understand that neuroscience research might be a sketchy source's smokescreen, or might be a fascinating introduction to on-point psychology research.
- Here we see that a business-as-usual control group raises urgent questions. But it does not automatically disqualify research. Using our judgment, we can *both* set that mindfulness-before-school study aside *and* embrace successive relearning. That's not hypocrisy; that's wisdom.

Because we found disqualifying control groups when we read these few studies, we know that this question merits the time we took to ask it. Of course, in most cases, we will discover thoughtfully designed control groups, à la Greene. When that happens, we return to the Giant and respectfully ask our second question.

Check the Numbers, Check Your Gut

Imagine you were to ask me how well my Advanced Placement students did on the English literature exam. I could, no doubt, spin you an inspiring yarn. "My students grew as thinkers, as writers, as scholars. Although independent and feisty, they learned to work imaginatively and harmoniously together. Nobel prize winners pleaded to be interpreted by these budding professors. I'm just so *proud* of them."

Yes, you say, but what was *their average exam score*?

At this moment, all my airy rhetoric fails me. If you insist that I give you a frank number, I have a much harder time dazzling you with verbiage.

So, too, in a study. Researchers can use abstract or enthusiastic sentences to highlight their positive findings. But at the end of the day, the numbers are the numbers. If we look at the right numbers and ask the right questions, we might gain revelatory insights.

Alas, the average study features an appalling collection of numbers, graphs, tables, charts, and mysterious mathematical squiggles and abbreviations. The **results** section, where we find the numbers we seek, contains literal pages of indecipherable statistical incantations. For that reason, this Goldilocks guidance deserves emphasis: *we should not read the results section*. Let me say that again:

we should not read the results section. Instead – once again – we practice artful skimming. All the work we've done up to this point shows us how.

With the detailed knowledge accumulated on our quest so far, we can formulate a straightforward summary of the study's key claims. For example:

- Cartwright argues that the right kind of executive function training helps struggling readers, compared with readers who didn't get that training.
- Janes's research shows that successive relearning helps students remember concepts better than their typical study strategies do.
- Fenesi's study suggests that students who take quick exercise breaks during lectures learn more than students who remain still.

In these quick mental summaries, we focus on the researchers' main argument and the boundaries of their experimental and control groups.

Having conjured that research precis, we now know what we're skimming for. As we leaf through the results section, we *don't* need to interpret tables comparing demographics about the participants. We *don't* need to understand how researchers calculated the Bonferroni coefficient. We *don't* need to understand why they chose Unpronounceable Stats Method A instead of Unpronounceable Stats Method B. (The USMA vs. USMB debate will rage on quite nicely without us.)

We *do* need to locate the table or the graph that focuses precisely on the research question we just summarized. That is:

- Cartwright's study should have a graph comparing reading comprehension scores for students who did, and who didn't, get EF training.
- Fenesi's results section will include a table comparing attention measures for students who moved and students who didn't.

Both studies, of course, will offer a tidal wave of other charts, graphs, and equations. Because we're artfully skimming, however, we float past those without a second glance. Undistracted by those side quests, we focus keenly on charts of essential information.

An example: a tweet recommends a new method to teach *rules for multiplying exponents*. Because your students always struggle with these rules – powers of products, powers of fractions – you eagerly suit up for a quest. Within minutes, you've dug up the study, matched its participants with yours, deciphered its code to understand its exponential insights, and verified an active control group. So far, so good.

To check the numbers, you summarize the study briskly: "This research team says that students who practice the cool new method learn exponent multiplication rules better than those who learn the boring old way."

Now you skim the results section for the chart/graph that reports that information. Sure enough, you spot the table summarizing the core data. Take a moment to study this table and come to your own conclusions. (No peeking: don't read what I've written below until you've got a firm opinion.)

	Cool New Method	Boring Old Method
Number of students tested	14	13
Score on low-difficulty problems	77%	86%
Score on medium-difficulty problems	68%	46%
Score on high-difficulty problems	62%	75%

Figure 13

What do you notice? What do you wonder? Me, I wonder a lot.

As I look at this table, I can clearly see that – on the medium-difficulty problems – the Cool New Method (CNM) helped students learn more than the Boring Old Method (BOM). But when I look at scores on the low-difficulty and high-difficulty problems, I'm much less sanguine. Right there in black and white, I can see that they scored higher after the BOM than the CNM.

Honestly, what gives?

This table highlights key differences between researchers' thinking and teachers' thinking. This research team, I suspect, went through this (entirely correct) thought process:

> *We measured three outcomes. In one outcome, students learned statistically significantly more. In the other two, the two methods did not result in a statistically significant difference. So, it helped in one case and didn't hurt in the others. We have a modest winner!*

In other words: the difference between 68% and 46% is statistically significant. But the much smaller differences (77% vs. 86%, and 62% vs. 75%) don't meet the relevant statistical threshold. Those differences, unlike those for the medium-difficulty problems, might have resulted from *chance or error*. For these reasons, researchers needn't worry too much about the lower scores for CNM in those two categories.

Good news! If this talk of **statistical significance** sounds daunting, fear not. We'll explore the topic more deeply in Appendix I.

As non-researchers, we can have some confidence that this thought process fits within research norms. After all, if it violated standards, then this study (almost certainly) wouldn't have made it through peer review.

At the same time, I suspect we teachers respond to this data table with the hero's immortal cry: *Oh come on!* We had thought that this CNM would help our struggling students. It turns out that it probably helps them about a third of the time, and might very well muddle them the rest of the time. (OK, fine, those other results don't "meet the relevant statistical threshold." But we have to admit that they look *really bad*.) Now that we've seen the numbers, we're deeply unlikely to accept the tweep's Big Ask.

By summarizing the core variables and scanning the PDF for the right table, we've successfully challenged the Giant.

We might likewise find a graph that raises our suspicions. A researcher recently published a graph showing how interest in dinosaurs changes by age group. (It's possible I made up "interest in dinosaurs" as the topic of this graph.)

What do you notice? What do you wonder?

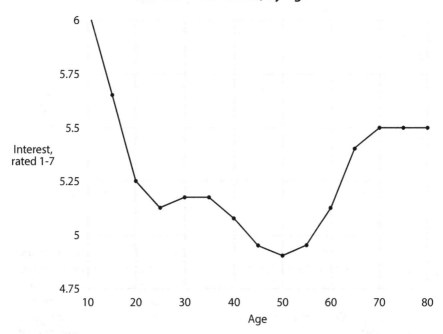

Figure 14

As novice questers, we might notice a shocking trend. Interest in dinosaurs craters in our teen years, and only starts to recover as we enter our 60s. Not until we boast eight or nine decades do we refocus on T. rex and her awe-inspiring cousins. What could account for this tragic loss of perspective?

Expert questers might instead wonder: what's going on with the y-axis? Why the narrow range? Participants who filled out these surveys rated their Triceratops love on a scale of *one to seven*. We have to ask: honey, who shrunk the scale?

If we present this graph with a one-to-seven y-axis – which, by the way, the researchers also did – we get a dramatically different impression of the data.

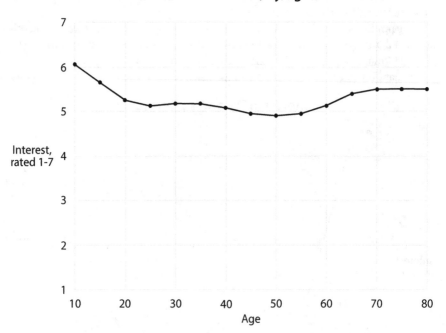

Figure 15

In this version, dino-interest doesn't crater in our teen years. It ticks down. It modulates. It relaxes. Depending on the topic actually being surveyed, that one-point difference might influence important school decisions. But its dramatic exaggeration in the first version doesn't clarify our decision-making process; it distorts that process.

The first graph might seem preferable because it reveals the data with greater precision, and because it packs a much bigger emotional punch. Something dramatic is happening between 10 and 20. But researchers deviate from professional norms when they cue big emotions. Studies should present numbers neutrally and let us decide if we're wowed. Attempts to force the wow worry Goldilocks.

This general topic – how numbers can deceive – gets lots of popular attention. If you'd like to explore further, Edward Tufte's books – starting with *The Visual Display of Quantitative Information* (2001) – make for fascinating reading.

In my experience, the two strategies we've explored here hit the Goldilocks sweet spot. We can ask and answer these questions readily. We find transgressions rarely, but often enough to make the investigation worthwhile. And, we don't get distracted by more side quests than we can handle. If a study puts too positive a spin on a table, or monkeys with a y-axis, those surprises should weigh heavily in our analysis.

Bigger Pictures, Bigger Doubts

We began this chapter knowing that the researcher's skill and experience merit our deference. She knows this field and this study much better than we ever will, and only rarely will we spot divots that trouble us. Occasionally an implausible control group will raise doubts. Quite rarely we will spot overly optimistic interpretations of data. For the most part, however, we accept that the researcher has done her work expertly and professionally. After all, she's a Giant!

As a final respectful question in this chapter, we reassert our own teacherly confidence. After all, Goldilocks strives for balance. Yes, the researcher's knowledge and skill deserve our regard. At the same time, our classroom experience and professional knowledge do as well. We get a voice here too.

For that reason, we can take a step back, survey the bigger picture, and ask ourselves: "Yes, but does this all make classroom sense?" We know this research rather well by now. Given our facility with the abstract, our knowledge of the participants, our many-layered understanding of the procedures, and our focused reading of the results, do we think the whole argument holds together? From a *researcher's* perspective, those parts clearly cohere. Do they from a *classroom teacher's* perspective?

For instance: Fenesi's research (2018) suggests that mid-lecture exercise breaks help students pay attention. Does that conclusion make sense based on my classroom experience? Indeed it does.

Rattan's research (2012) suggests that higher levels of challenge, framed correctly, might motivate struggling students. For my high school classroom, I find her research persuasive. One of my greatest teaching successes – helping an "unteachable" student learn lots o' grammar – came after I followed this advice.

As we saw in Chapter 5, however, an experienced third grade teacher thought that Rattan's participants didn't match her own well enough to take the advice. As long as this teacher gave the research-informed perspective a respectful hearing, I think she gets to make that call. After all: I'm not teaching those students, *she is.*

A final example helpfully contrasts a psychologist's and a teacher's perspectives.

As we contemplate using technology for teaching and learning, one specific question has received outsized attention: should students take lecture notes longhand, or on laptops? This question inspires surprising passion in many teachers. As it turns out, that passion aligns with the best-known "research-based" answer.

In 2014, two Princeton psychologists concluded that handwritten notes result in superior learning (Mueller & Oppenheimer, 2014). Their study's clever title – "The pen is mightier than the keyboard: Advantages of longhand over laptop note taking" – might explain its unusual fame. With near unanimity, our profession has embraced their conclusion: handwritten notes rule.

Mueller and Oppenheimer's careful research doesn't just answer this specific question. It offers a sensible mechanism to explain why handwriting helps more than keyboarding. In essence, Mueller and Oppenheimer found that two key variables interact in a complex balance.

First, unsurprisingly, the number of words that students write matters. Predictably, students who *wrote more words* in their notes remembered information better than others who *wrote fewer words.*

This result suggests an intriguing possibility. Because people can type faster than they can write, laptop note-takers should be able to write more words – and therefore get higher scores – than hand-writers. What explains the reversal?

Mueller and Oppenheimer found that a second variable mattered more. That variable: students' fidelity to the lecturer's original words. Students who *reworded* the lecture's ideas as they wrote remembered information better than others who *merely transcribed* the lecture *verbatim.* This finding makes sense, because students who reorganize the lecture's ideas into their own words are thereby *thinking harder* about the lecture than those who just transcribe it.

This second variable explains why the laptop's benefit paradoxically turns into a burden. Because laptop note-takers can write more words, they can transcribe lectures. Their simple transcription minimizes cognitive processing, and thereby dulls long-term memory formation. On the other hand, because hand-writers can't write fast enough to transcribe, they must go through the mental effort of rewording. That extra mental effort enhances memory – and offsets the benefits that laptop users might have gotten from all their extra words.

Voila: handwritten notes help more than laptop notes.

This investigation demonstrates again the remarkable insights that detailed research can yield. Mueller and Oppenheimer went beyond a simple verdict:

"Handwritten notes win!" Instead, they carefully charted the competing forces – number of words, degree of rewording – that influence their conclusion.

This two-variable conclusion, however, leads to a tempting possibility. Imagine that we could teach laptop note-takers to reword their notes in the same way that hand-writers reword their notes. Those trained students would get both advantages. That is: they would get the benefit of writing extra words *and* the benefit of rewording. Given a double boost, trained laptop note-takers should crush the competition.

Mueller and Oppenheimer spotted this possibility and tested this hypothesis. In a second run of their experiment, they had one student group take notes by hand, a second group take laptop notes, and a third group get extra instructions before they took laptop notes. The instructions went like this:

> *"We're doing a study about how information is conveyed in the classroom. We'd like you to take notes on a lecture, just like you would in class. People who take class notes on laptops when they expect to be tested on the material later tend to transcribe what they're hearing without thinking about it much. Please try not to do this as you take notes today. Take notes in your own words and don't just write down word-for-word what the speaker is saying."*
> (Mueller & Oppenheimer, 2014, p. 1162)

Alas, Mueller and Oppenheimer found that these instructions produced no meaningful changes. Despite this good advice, laptop note-takers promptly fell back into old habits and copied the lecturer's words verbatim. They did no better than the laptop students who got no instructions, and worse than the hand-writers. Conclusion: the pen is indeed mightier than the keyboard.

We can see that, from a research perspective, Mueller and Oppenheimer have done precise and thoughtful work here. They have active control groups; they have a straightforward study design; they answer an important practical question. Their decision to re-run the study with the "special instructions" group shows their dedication to exploring competing hypotheses.

What happens when we change from a *researcher's* perspective to a *teacher's* perspective? Seen through a teacher's lens, Mueller and Oppenheimer's lesson plan looked like this:

- They worked with students who had an ingrained habit: *transcribing* laptop notes.
- They told those students – once – to change that habit in a cognitively demanding way.
- They did not give the students opportunities to practice the new habit.

- When tested, the students did not change the habit.
- Mueller and Oppenheimer therefore concluded that the students *could not change the habit*, and made a recommendation based on that conclusion.

Let's imagine that we teach our students this way:

- Our chemistry students don't know how to balance chemical equations.
- We tell them – once – how to balance chemical equations.
- We do not let them practice balancing equations.
- When tested on balancing equations, students fail.
- We conclude that students *cannot learn to balance chemical equations*, and so drop the subject from the syllabus.

No. Obviously we don't do any of that.

If we want students to learn something new – balance chemical equations, reword lecture notes on a laptop – we should (at a minimum) do three things:

1. Explain why this new skill is important.
2. Show them, quite specifically, how to do it.
3. Give them several opportunities to practice.

If we don't do some version of those three steps, we can't possibly conclude – as Mueller and Oppenheimer do – that the students can't learn this new skill.

In fact, their conclusion defies common sense. Students can take reworded notes when they write by hand. Presumably, they could – with enough practice – learn to take reworded notes on a laptop. That hypothesis hasn't been tested, but it seems wholly plausible. And if students can learn this new skill, then they should get both of the benefits Mueller and Oppenheimer investigated. In turn, they should learn even more than hand-writers.

In other words: this study's conclusion makes sense within the mechanisms of psychology research. Yet from a teacher's perspective, it reaches exactly the wrong conclusion. Goldilocks does not read this study and say, "Close your laptops and take out your pencils!" She says, "Let's build laptop note-taking skills into our curriculum. It will take up some time now, but – gosh – it will help students learn so much more in the future!"

Alas, Mueller and Oppenheimer's conclusion – resting on the assumption that students cannot learn new things – has been widely embraced by teachers, whose job it is to help students learn new things. The result: thousands of students have heard unsupported advice, given confidently by teachers who believe it to be "research-based." Those students might, in fact, have learned less because our profession didn't undertake this quest.

Addendum: if you find yourself thinking, "But wait, the *physical act of handwriting* surely encodes lecture information within kinesthetic neural networks," jump ahead to Appendix IV (see p. 236).

This chapter's quest – ensure that the research shows what the researcher said – might have seemed presumptuous and impossible. Of course, we undertake it deferentially. At the same time, we can ask these few precise and *reasonable* questions:

1. Do the control groups isolate the variable as much as is plausible?
2. Do the key charts, graphs, and tables persuade us?
3. Does the overall approach make sense from a teacherly perspective?

We strongly expect to find encouraging answers to those questions. In those rare cases when we don't, we rightly feel proud to have achieved the rarest of quest accomplishments.

Now, propped against our saddlebags, we sit at sunset by a crackling fire, contemplating our impressive progress. Yesterday, we confirmed the *source's trustworthiness*: chasms and treasure chests and spells. Today, we confirmed the *research's usefulness*: boundaries and codes and giants. If only the cooper from next door could see us now.

With a glint in our eye, we unscroll the quest map to study tomorrow's route. A surprise awaits…

INTERMISSION II

A Practice Quest: Learning with Music

Before we get to that surprise, another chance to practice questing skills might prove beneficial. The example below, in particular, gives you a chance to apply a *teacher's* perspective to a *researcher's* work. Here's the setup...

An education podcast reports on exciting and useful new research: students learn more *when they listen to the right kind of music*. In this case, according to Michael Scullin's research, the "right kind of music" means Beethoven and Chopin. If we put this research to work in our classrooms, the friendly podcaster points out, we'll make learning easier and our schools more musically beautiful.

This research-based Ask has lots to recommend it: time to armor up for your quest. You can be as thorough as you like while you adventure. I suggest you focus specifically on *combining research and classroom perspectives.*

Once again, I'll tell you my conclusions in Appendix IV (see p. 239). Of course, this practice will benefit you more if you sleuth out your own answers before you check in on mine.

PART IV.
THERE AND BACK AGAIN

BURIED
TREASURE
THE PDF

DISGUISE
SPELL
THE ABSTRACT

THE
BOUNDARIES
THE PARTICIPANTS

THE
CODE
THE PROCEDURES

THE
GIANT
THE RESULTS

THE
GOLDILOCKS MAP

CHAPTER 8.
THE IMPROVISATIONAL
QUEST

Up to this point, our quest has followed distinct, *sequential* steps.

- We *first* asked for the source's best evidence; without it, we had nothing to explore.
- We *then* grabbed a peer-reviewed PDF; without it, we didn't know what the researcher said.
- *Next*, we studied the abstract; without understanding its key concepts, we couldn't make much sense of the sections that follow.

And so forth. Although our journey has included surprising pitfalls and treacherous rope bridges, we benefited from the map's consecutive structure. One step finished before the next began.

Now that we have faced the Giant, however, we make an arresting discovery. The path before us branches dramatically. We have several options – each one as tempting and plausible as the other. Some paths lead back to previous chapters, while others wind through unfamiliar realms. No one path can promise success. Happily, by exploring several of them, we practically guarantee a profoundly deeper understanding of our quest.

In this chapter, we'll start with the uppermost path in Figure 16 and work our way down the possibilities. On your own quests, the order probably doesn't matter – as long as you explore most paths. Up until now, you've been questing by numbers. For the rest of your journey, you improvise…

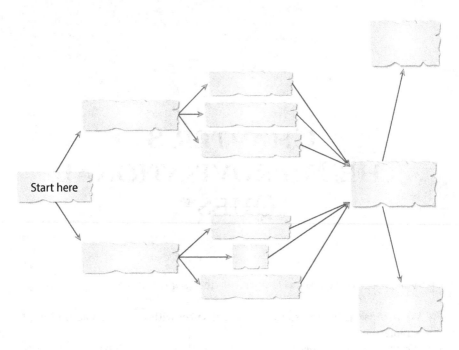

Figure 16

We adopt this new strategy because *we're adopting new goals.*

Up to this point, we have been trying to *reduce* doubts about *one* study. When we saw that it was peer-reviewed, we felt more certain. When we discovered that its participants match our students, we got a confidence boost. When the Giant answered all our questions, her frankness won our trust. With each adventure, we had greater reason to believe.

Starting now, however, we upend that goal. As much as possible, we want to *cultivate doubt.* We will spend this chapter striving – vigorously and inventively – *to undermine our confidence in the teaching strategy we hope to embrace.*

Here's the logic. The study that we have investigated has – up to now – given us compelling reasons to adopt a Big Ask. And yet, because psychology research is a messy muddle, we know that this study could *both* be expertly done *and* be a conspicuous outlier. The researchers could have done everything exactly right and still come up with a flukey result. As Daniel Willingham says in his Twitter bio, "One study is just one study, folks."

Let's consider a sports analogy. Who is the world's best women's tennis player?

Here's one answer: *Roberta Vinci*. "What's that?" you say. "Who? I thought you were going to say that *Serena Williams* is the best women's player. I've never even heard of Roberta Vinci."

"Be that as it may," I respond, "but Vinci defeated Williams (2-6, 6-4, 6-4) at the US Open in 2015." On that one day, under those rare circumstances, Vinci prevailed.

Because sports fans know that quirky things happen, they don't answer "world's best" questions based on *one match*. Instead, they look at lifetime records and cumulative rankings. By these metrics, Williams (and Graf, and Navratilova, and King) all have much better claims to that title. Vinci really did win that one day; nonetheless, she really isn't a good candidate for "world's best."

So, too, we might have spent the last several chapters questing through a Vinci-like outlier study. On that one day, under those rare circumstances, researchers found that – say – retrieval practice harms learning. But that fluke isn't a useful guide for our general teaching practice. We need to see what the bigger picture shows – not just this one study. That is: we need to find the research analog for Williams's lifetime records and cumulative rankings.

And so, we start improvisationally questing to discover contradictory evidence. We look within this cave, beyond that crag, behind that troglodyte. If we search energetically and *can't find compelling research to deter us*, then and only then do we truly believe we've found research gold.

Our desire to cultivate doubt explains the new quest structure. We try one method to poke holes in our conviction. If that method doesn't work, we go back and try another. And another. If we try several of these strategies and none of them dissuades us, our failure to find persuasive doubts lets us return home with bedrock confidence.

Our quest to cultivate doubt might begin with familiar tools.

Familiar Tools

Since we first started digging in Chapter 3, we've seen that Google Scholar makes seemingly impossible quests surprisingly easy. Whereas at first we used it to reduce doubts, now we can use it to cultivate them.

To do so, we rely on a straightforward strategy. Returning to Google Scholar, we plug in the shorthand code terms from Chapter 6 and inspect the resulting riches. If the study we examined produced flukey results, this search process should reveal the more typical findings.

For instance, Cartwright's research offers us an intriguing strategy to help our struggling readers (2020). Although her polysyllabic code phrase – "graphophonological-semantic cognitive flexibility" – might have alarmed us at first, her results offered important reassurance. Students who undertook these simple exercises – heck, they even sounded fun – improved as readers. That's HUGE.

Mindful that Cartwright's study is just one study, we return to Google Scholar and start riffing. To keep a search simple, perhaps, we hunt with just two of her code phrases: "semantic cognitive flexibility" and "reading." (We can add the "graphophonological" layer later.)

Sure enough, Google Scholar provides us with countless hits. Now we scan those results for reasons to doubt. We ask ourselves: "Do any of these studies obviously contradict Cartwright's?"

Amusingly, Cartwright's own study appears first on the Google Scholar list. No reasons to doubt here.

The second study boasts this reassuring title: "Cognitive flexibility predicts early reading skills" (Colé et al., 2014). When we click the link and scan the abstract, we find this encouraging news: "[Cognitive flexibility] was found to contribute significant unique variance to passage reading comprehension" (Colé et al., 2014, p. 1). Despite the obscure vocabulary ("unique variance"?), the basic message rings clear: cognitive flexibility helps reading. Cartwright has not offered an obscure outlier argument. Other scholars – even in France! – see that the first contributes to the second.

Because we strive, at this quest stage, to cultivate doubt, we might raise an eyebrow at our next insight. On the first Google Scholar page, amazingly, nine of the 10 studies include Cartwright as a researcher: she's the *first author* on eight. This discovery offers both good and bad news. On the good side, we see that she is a leading figure in this field. Cartwright OWNS this Google Scholar page. On the bad side, this discovery hinders our task. If only one researcher explores this field, we're much less likely to unearth contradictory studies.

Google Scholar didn't raise profound doubts. But we haven't looked enough yet – especially because we do have a substantive question: do other researchers broadly concur with Cartwright? So far, we've found only one additional research team in agreement. Let's go back to the beginning of Figure 16 and restart the process with a second familiar tool: Google itself.

With the freedom of jazz musicians, we now riff our way through various combinations of skeptical search terms. If we discover a potentially doubt-provoking link, we rub our hands, chortle, and explore. We might Google:

- "Cognitive flexibility," "reading," and "controversy."
- "Cognitive flexibility doesn't help reading."
- "Reading myths" and "executive function."

Searches like these – practically *begging* for doubts – lead us to several relevant studies. A quick scan of their abstracts tells us:

- "Individual differences in executive functioning components made differential contributions to early reading achievement. The Working Memory/Cognitive Flexibility factor emerged as the best predictor of reading" (de Abreu, 2014, p. 1).
- "Higher cognitive flexibility and fluid intelligence were associated with better reading comprehension" (Johann et al., 2020, p. 324).
- "Variance in children's sentence reading comprehension was explained by their abilities in the cognitive flexibility tasks" (Søndergaard Knudsen et al., 2018, p. S130).

Wow! We're now up to five research teams who argue that *cognitive flexibility boosts reading* comprehension. Even when we deliberately sought out contradiction, we couldn't find any. Using these two familiar tools, we've had no luck cultivating our now-wilting doubts. Because we have failed to undermine Cartwright's argument – so far, at least – we feel increasingly confident that she might be right.

Of course, these familiar tools occasionally furrow our brows. Let's return to the handwritten notes vs. laptop notes debate.

Imagine that a colleague – brandishing Mueller and Oppenheimer's study (2014) – urges us to champion handwritten notes and banish laptops. (Imagine, too, that we missed their assumption that students can't learn new things.) What happens when we try our Google tools to raise doubts? Can we find contradictory evidence?

Once again, let's start with Familiar Tool #1. The straightforward search terms "pen," "keyboard," and "notes" yield a surprising result. Google Scholar reveals that several scholars tried a **direct replication**: that is, they repeated Mueller and Oppenheimer's procedures as precisely as possible (Morehead et al., 2019). To be thorough, they also included two additional comparison groups. The abstract summarizes their findings:

> *"Some trends suggested longhand superiority; however, performance did not consistently differ between any groups, including a group who did not take notes. ... Based on the present outcomes and other available evidence, concluding which method is superior for improving the functions of note-taking seems premature."* (Morehead et al., 2019, p. 753)

When we tried to cultivate doubt before adopting Cartwright's strategy, we scoured the web and found nada. When we tried to cultivate doubt before adopting a pen-mightier-than-keyboard recommendation, we hit pay dirt immediately. Scholars who tried to replicate Mueller and Oppenheimer's study arrived at contradictory results. Their conclusion: *we don't have enough persuasive evidence to make a recommendation either way.*

Important note: this **non-replication** does not mean that Mueller and Oppenheimer did anything wrong. In experimental psychology, contradictory results happen simply because we're studying human beings.

I do (emphatically) disagree with their assumption that students can't learn. But Mueller and Oppenheimer didn't cheat in any way: they make that assumption quite openly, where you and I can read it and decide for ourselves.

Because we're improvising, we might instead have started with Familiar Tool #2.

Like a Google Scholar search, an old-fashioned Google search also creates substantial doubts about longhand superiority. Those same three search terms ("pen, keyboard, notes") lead to a helpful blog post asking "Is there a clear winner in the note-taking olympics?" (Jarry, 2019). Jarry answers his own question by summarizing contradictory research findings. He insightfully points out that students' note-taking habits often depend on the course content. Given all the relevant boundary conditions, Jarry doubts that any one method will help most students learn most subjects.

Whichever familiar tool we used, then, the time we took hunting for doubt benefits our students.

- With Cartwright's research, our efforts have so far reassured us: Let the GSF planning begin!
- With Mueller and Oppenheimer's, those efforts promptly cautioned us against hasty claims of "research support." For the time being, we should probably admit we don't really know if handwritten notes help more than laptop notes.

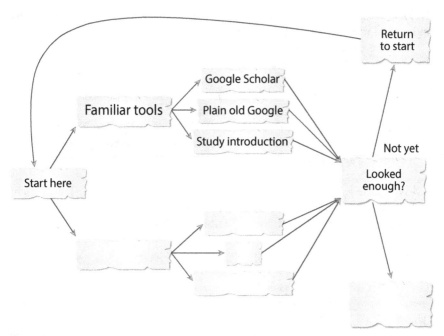

Figure 17

A third familiar tool lurks close at hand. We might be surprised that the researchers themselves can help us contradict their conclusions, but they sometimes do. Here's the story...

Television drama viewers know: fresh episodes typically begin with a brisk storyline recap. A solemn voice intones, "Previously, on *The West Wing*..." Viewers see a rapid montage: CJ belittling Sam, Josh looking foolish in a room full of senators, Toby seething righteously at the President. With that relevant background knowledge fresh in our minds, we can understand the witty banter of the upcoming episode.

Psychology studies begin the same way (except for the witty banter). In the **introduction**, scholars rapidly summarize the background to their research question. It might sound like this:

- Back in the 1970s, Professor A asked *this* question, tried this research method, and got *this* answer.
- In the 80s, Professor B's alternative research method supported A's conclusion.
- Professor C devoted the 90s to exploring boundary conditions identified by B.

163

And so forth. Now that we have all this plot information freshly in mind, we understand why this research team has started its own exploration.

Because psychology research always includes contradictory findings, this storyline recap might well include important doubts:

- Professor Z's study contradicted the A hypothesis; however, subsequent scholarship has questioned the Z method.
- Research Team Gamma used an alternative paradigm to investigate A's question. Their method partially confirmed and partially disconfirmed prevailing hypotheses.

In this way, the study might sow important doubts about itself. We can, quite simply, plug Professor Z's and Team Gamma's opposing studies into Google Scholar. We briskly quest through them, striving to undermine the Big Ask.

For instance: Ayanna Thomas's research team wanted to study an important trade-off. We know that retrieval practice helps students learn; however, retrieval practice exercises might take up class time. If teachers *cover less material* (because they have set some minutes aside for RP quizzes), but students *remember more of it* (because they took the RP quizzes), will the overall effect be more or less learning (Thomas et al., 2020)?

As is customary, Thomas's introduction begins with a review of relevant background research:

> *"Several studies suggest that retrieval practice does confer transfer effects to related information. For example, in a laboratory-based study, Butler (2010) demonstrated that retrieval practice led to better learning and retention of related concepts within the same and in different knowledge domains as compared to study practice."* (Thomas et al., 2020, p. 84)

Drum roll please:

> *"**However**, transfer effects are not always found. In a laboratory experiment using a general biology text, Wooldridge, Bugg, McDaniel, and Liu (2014) found that retrieval practice did not confer an advantage over study practice when participants were assessed on topically related, but not identical information."* (Thomas et al., 2020, p. 84)

Thomas's research ultimately concludes that, yes, retrieval practice helps students even when teachers have less class time to cover material. Before we accept Thomas's conclusion, we strive to cultivate doubt. We could check out Wooldridge's study to see if we ultimately find its concerns persuasive. At a minimum,

Wooldridge's insights could help us use Thomas's findings more insightfully.

In this way, Thomas's introduction helped us skeptically investigate her own conclusions. (Notice, by the way, that the helpful word "however" signaled that usefully contradictory research was near at hand.)

In Chapter 2, I warned against books as references. Although books offer many benefits – obviously! – they don't help Goldilocks determine if the source deeply understands the science behind his Big Ask. Here in Chapter 8, we *love* books. For example: your search for doubts might lead you to *Powerful Teaching* (Agarwal & Bain, 2019), or *Make It Stick* (Brown et al., 2014). These excellent resources offer a usefully broad perspective, perfect for doubt cultivation.

Fair warning: most research questions have a long history, and so this brisk plot recap can go on for pages. Here again, strategic skimming will simplify the quest. We should look for phrases that suggest contradictory or alternative interpretations. If a paragraph begins with "Surprisingly," or "On the other hand," or "In a controversial study," we know that doubt might be flourishing here. Time to start digging!

New Gizmos

We've exhausted our familiar tools with no dubious results. Although tempted to believe we have "looked enough" (on the right side of Figure 17), we know that other tools provide fresh skepticism resources. For that reason, we return to the start and explore our as-of-yet *unfamiliar* tools. These might yield the doubts that have eluded us to this point.

First, we can look for a **meta-analysis** on the topic we've explored.

Because inconsistent research results often bewilder us, we would rejoice to find a mathematical method that unmuddles the psychology muddle. In theory, meta-analysis does just that. Using sophisticated mathemagical processes, meta-analysts combine dozens of studies into grand cumulative equations. By considering all studies that meet relevant criteria, they offer conclusions based on hundreds – even thousands – of participants.

For instance: we've discussed retrieval practice in almost every chapter of *The Goldilocks Map*. As long ago as Chapter 3, I cited several individual studies demonstrating its effectiveness. At that time, you perhaps felt increasingly confident in RP because your source (ahem, *me*) volunteered the research supporting that claim. Here in Chapter 8, however, you might want to scrutinize this Big Ask once again. After all, you've got lots of new tools to dial up your doubts.

A quick online search for "retrieval practice meta-analysis" leads to several tempting hits. The most recent (Adesope et al., 2017) looks at 217 different experiments involving more than *15,000 participants*. Given the extraordinary scope of this meta-analysis, you're no doubt eager to learn its findings. Sure enough, Adesope's team concluded that RP helps students learn. In fact, it helps better than "restudying, and all other comparison conditions" (Adesope et al., 2017, p. 659). In brief: these researchers crunched a daunting heap o' data, and found that this Big Ask has an impressively large research base, indeed.

Meta-analysis can often provide this kind of big-picture overview. For instance, you may know Anders Ericsson's research in the field of **deliberate practice** (Ericsson & Pool, 2017). By studying elite athletes and musicians, Ericsson identified four habits that made them world best at what they do:

- Goals.
- Focus.
- Feedback.
- "Getting out of one's comfort zone" (Ericsson & Pool, 2017, p. 17).

(Malcolm Gladwell popularized this framework by championing "10,000 hours" of practice (Gladwell, 2008), an oversimplification that Ericsson explicitly critiques (Ericsson & Pool, 2017, pp. 109–114).)

For teachers, Ericsson's four habits sound obviously relevant. We want our students to have *goals*; we frequently write learning objectives on the board. We offer them *feedback*, which they tragically overlook. We might turn to Ericsson's research-based suggestions with hungry glee.

Before doing so, in our Goldilocks attempt to cultivate doubt, we search online for "deliberate practice meta-analysis." Click, click, click: we have just what we're looking for. Brooke Macnamara's abstract is unusually easy to read:

> *"More than 20 years ago, researchers proposed that individual differences in performance in such domains as music, sports, and games largely reflect individual differences in amount of deliberate practice. ... This view is a frequent topic of popular-science writing – but is it supported by empirical evidence? To answer this question, we conducted a meta-analysis covering all major domains in which deliberate practice has been investigated. We found that deliberate practice explained 26% of the variance in performance for games, 21% for music, 18% for sports, 4% for education, and less than 1% for professions. We conclude that deliberate practice is important, but not as important as has been argued."* (Macnamara et al., 2014, p. 1608)

Macnamara's conclusions deflate our enthusiasm. Her precise measurement – "percentage variance in performance" – takes a while to explain. But even before we understand it well, we can see that deliberate practice helps a fair bit in games, music, and sports: 26%, 21%, and 18%. In education, however, that number craters: 4%. Deliberate practice might help pole vaulters and pianists, but it doesn't give pupils much of a boost.

Because we looked for reasons to doubt, because we found a relevant meta-analysis, we know that Ericsson's strategies shouldn't be our school's focus – at least not until we get more reassuring data.

A few words of warning: because meta-analysis provides such big-picture clarity, many research enthusiasts take meta-analysis as the final word.

- "We discovered a meta-analysis that shows RP works. We must embrace it fully!"
- "This meta-analysis indicates that deliberate practice offers few benefits. We reject it utterly!"

Sadly, Goldilocks knows, such stark conclusions can't hold.

In the first place, as we've seen before, boundary conditions matter. We might interpret Macnamara's meta-analysis to forbid deliberate practice in schools: it helps a measly 4%. However, if I'm a school's piano teacher or a field hockey coach, I might find deliberate practice research essential to my work. If I lead a school that trains elite musicians, Ericsson's book might be required reading for incoming teachers.

Equally important, my students might not fit the average profile that the meta-analysis investigated. Teachers at a school for special-needs students, for example, won't always learn from research focusing on neurotypical populations. By definition, dyslexic readers benefit from reading instruction strategies that the broader population doesn't need.

In brief: meta-analysis typically includes as many studies as possible. That broad reach necessitates a focus on a population-wide average. The more our students differ from that population average, the less benefit we get from meta-analysis.

Equally important: meta-analysis itself often unearths meaningful boundary conditions. For instance: some teachers like to enliven lessons with stories and videos and jokes. The less intrinsic motivation my students find in the material, the likelier I am to tell a funny Zora Neale Hurston story, or to break into my Godfather voice: "When you look for the direct object, [adopts raspy whisper] *it's important to show respect for the family.*" (Students LOVE it when I do that.)

Researchers call these lively, off-topic asides **seductive details**. We might hypothesize that, because they raise students' interest and alertness, seductive details help them learn. Or, because seductive details briefly distract from the classroom topic at hand, they might impede learning. In the past, I often allowed myself to include seductive details. If I wanted to question my habit, however, I might search for "seductive details meta-analysis." Sure enough, Dr. NarayanKripa Sundararajan's meta-analysis offers introductory guidance. Her abstract's warning: "including seductive details in learning material can hinder learning" (Sundararajan & Adesope, 2020, p. 707). Yikes!

Before I hang up my rasp, however, I should inspect the boundary conditions Sundararajan lists. Yes, her meta-analysis shows that *on average* seductive details impede learning. However, Sundararajan notes that the length of the lesson matters. For short lessons – less than five minutes – my Godfather voice gets in the way. For longer lessons – more than 10 minutes – they have no effect one way or another. Equally important: Sundararajan finds that seductive details distract beginners, but not students already familiar with a concept. So, if I'm teaching a *short* lesson to *beginners*, I should obviously avoid seductive details. In *longer* lessons with *advanced students*, I can tell my Harlem Renaissance stories when needed.

Spoiler alert: unsurprisingly, meta-analysis itself kicks up plenty of controversy (Kvarven et al., 2020; Slavin, 2018). We'll return to meta-analysis in Appendix I. Like almost every fascinating topic, it's complicated.

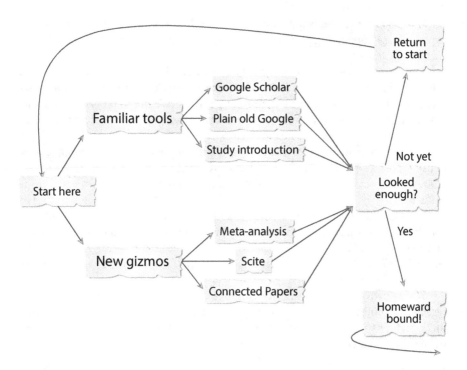

Figure 18

Other new gizmos can help us cultivate doubt as well. Two younger websites, less well-known than the Googles, can boost us along our quest.

First up: Scite.ai. This website targets the doubts that intrigue us. Using artificial intelligence algorithms, it looks to see how many later studies *mention*, *confirm*, or – here's the big one – *contradict* any published research conclusion. Here's an example...

Our skeptical tire-kicking around retrieval practice has so far yielded few doubts. However, we might recall Jason Chan's research suggesting that, less than 24 hours before a test, *retrieval-induced forgetting* inhibits RP's benefits (2009). If Chan's correct, then we should refine the advice we give our students. They will benefit from RP *several* days before a test, but *not the day before*.

Of course, that advice holds only if Chan got it right. Even if he ran his study with professional exactitude, he might have gotten atypical, quirky results. To check Chan's study, more than a decade old by now, we can surf over to Scite. When we plug in his title, we discover that *one* other study disputes his findings, while *seven* other studies support it. That seems like a healthy ratio. (If we want to explore those supporting and disputing studies more minutely, Scite supplies us with handy links.)

If we were experimental physicists at CERN, that one contradictory study might trigger dramatic alarm bells. But because psychology research is a messy muddle, a disconfirmation or two needn't panic us. We might inspect its abstract to see if its boundary conditions match our classroom better than Chan's research. But the fact it exists prompts no special anxiety.

As another example: if we teach in flashcard-intensive courses, we might decide to ask skeptical questions before we follow Kornell's bigger-stack-is-better advice (2009). In this case, Scite finds no contradictory studies, but only two confirming studies.

This meager results page doesn't exactly worry us: after all, no one has yet contradicted his findings. At the same time, we recognize that – at least as measured by Scite – Kornell's conclusion hasn't withstood the same scrutiny as has Chan's. Given Scite's analysis, I would recommend Kornell's strategy, but admit that we have limited research supporting this advice.

An even more recent website conjures a visual representation of relevant research. ConnectedPapers.com creates an intricate spiderweb diagram showing links and relationships among research studies. This visual format allows for flexible and nuanced analysis.

- If the study we enter sits at the middle of the web, it has a central role in the field. If it lurks on the web's periphery, it hasn't gotten much love from fellow researchers.
- If the study has lots of linking lines, it clearly connects to relevant research. If one feeble line connects it to a rich network of studies, it hasn't drawn much from – or contributed much to – the field.
- If a large circle represents the study, it has been cited many times. A small dot reveals its relative obscurity.

For instance, we've seen that a 2006 study by Roediger and Karpicke supports the argument that retrieval practice works. If we search Connected Papers for that study, we find an impressively dense spiderweb (Figure 19).

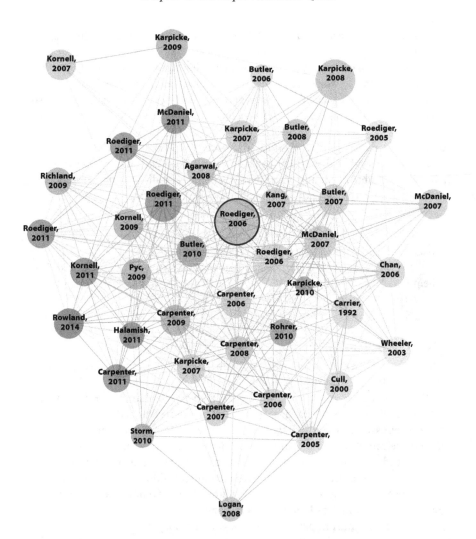

Figure 19. (Source: Connected Papers)

That web gives us additional confidence in the Roediger and Karpicke study, for many reasons:

- Their study sits Charlotte-like at the center of the web. This position highlights the paper's influence in the field.

- The study has been cited almost 1000 times – more than any other paper in this web.
- Because the names Roediger and Karpicke show up frequently in the network, we know that they have published many other relevant studies.
- Happily, many other names appear as well. These researchers aren't solo practitioners exploring an otherwise obscure topic.

As we would expect of a web resource, Connected Papers includes shedloads of information: sortable lists, links to abstracts, and downloadable bibliographies. It invites thoughtful parsing and improvisational noodling. The more time we choose to devote, the more doubts we can explore, and douse.

Watch this space: both Scite and Connected Papers are quite new websites. No doubt, their capacities will expand and morph.

I suspect that other artificial intelligence websites will launch, and help Goldilocks on future quests. Our list of new gizmos may expand powerfully over time.

The Whole Toolshed

So far, we've looked at each tool and gizmo on its own. For a more real-life example, we can try a test case using several in a row.

Earlier along our quest, we examined a strategy to enhance working memory with a specialized series of exercises (SSE). At the time, we worried about implausible control groups, and so declined the district initiative. If, however, the district office insisted, we might launch an improvisational search. Knowing that "one study is just one study," we might discover more persuasive research paradigms done by other researchers. In this case, we're trying to cultivate doubt *about our own doubt*.

Because we're improvising, we can start this adventure along any path. Honestly. At random, let's look for a meta-analysis.

This SSE program hopes to train working memory, so we can simply search for "working memory," "training," and "meta-analysis." Those search terms give us several impressive options. We can scan a few abstracts and see what this statistical method has to tell us.

For the most part, the news isn't good. One research team, for instance, glumly concludes that "working memory training programs appear to produce short-term, specific training effects that do not generalize to measures of 'real-world' cognitive skills." (Melby-Lervåg et al., 2016, p. 512). In other words: SSE might raise scores on specific working memory tests, but probably won't help students learn anything meaningful. Just a bit of web sleuthing using this gizmo heightens our earlier concerns.

We return to Figure 18 and decide – for fun – to try a new gizmo: Scite.ai. When we put the SSE study's information into Scite's search box, we find…nuthin'. Amazingly, it lists zero confirming studies and zero disputing studies, because no one has even tried to replicate its results. Scite also tells us how many studies even *mention* this research. Kornell's study had been mentioned 62 times; Chan's, 100 times. This study: *three times*. Simply put, this study has been mostly ignored. Honestly, our district has given this study more respect than other experts in the field. Once again, our doubts grow stronger.

A visual representation might offer a different perspective, and so we turn to another new gizmo: Connected Papers.

When we searched that website for Roediger and Karpicke's 2006 study, we found it at the center of an impressively dense web (Figure 19). When we search for this SSE study, we find a peculiar result (Figure 20, see the next page). This study floats as a largely disconnected dot, surrounded by several substantial webs. This picture suggests that SSE research makes only tangential connections to well-developed research pools.

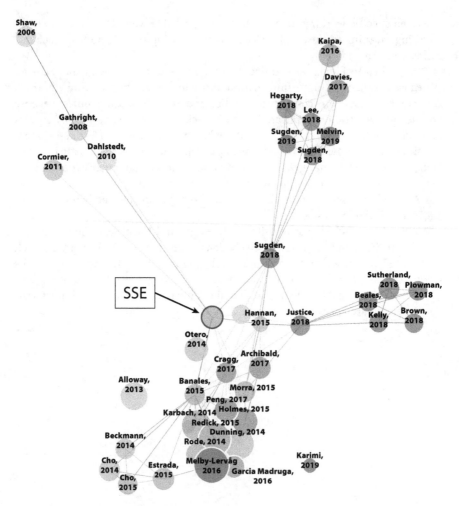

Figure 20. (Source: Connected Papers)

This curious structure prompts a fun improvisational question. We know that the size of each circle represents the number of citations – the bigger the circle, the more seriously other researchers have taken it. We might inspect this peculiar web to consider: what is the largest circle/most respected research within it? That is: of all research related to SSE, what gets the most collegial esteem?

Drum roll, please. That largest circle – at the bottom, in the center – *is the skeptical meta-analysis we found a few paragraphs ago* (Melby-Lervåg et al., 2016).

In other words: the most respected research related to the SSE study throws cold water on training programs like SSE. Our accumulating doubts now gather into an avalanche.

To be thorough, we could continue this improvisational search. It's dimly possible that other tools will turn up *pro*-SSE studies. Or, returning to Figure 18, we might conclude that we have indeed "looked enough." If all three gizmos ramp up and substantiate our doubts, we can quite plausibly turn towards home. Despite that one study, SSE almost certainly does not increase working memory. Let's use our students' time more productively.

As has been so often the case on this quest, *describing* this process takes longer than *undertaking* it. This test case we just did together flew by in a few minutes. You popped over to familiar websites, entered straightforward search terms, skimmed an abstract or two, and reached the obvious conclusion. All the expertise you gained during early adventures made this improvisational process easy, perhaps entertaining.

Despite these glum search results, this point bears repeating. The SSE study should not inform our school-keeping practice. But, more broadly considered, the study itself is not useless or wrongheaded. Researchers developed a hypothesis, tested it one way, and got encouraging answers. Those answers don't yet persuade us. But these findings might ultimately reveal a kernel of useful information. A later research team – inspired by these data – might run another study and home in on a more beneficial strategy. Perhaps, 30 years from now, students will enhance their working memory capacity with an exercise series descended from SSE.

In other words: lots of valuable research doesn't directly help teachers. We can both appreciate initial experiments and decide not to change our teaching because of them.

Rebooting Thwarted Quests

Throughout our journey, we've occasionally arrived at a paradoxical result: *a disappointing success*. That is: we discover that a "research-based" teaching suggestion in fact lacks a plausible research basis.

This discovery counts as a success, because we made sure not to waste our students' time. And yet, we feel disappointed – because we really wanted that Big Ask to have brainy foundations. It matched our classroom experience or our school's philosophy so neatly, we seem to have robbed ourselves by our quest's accomplishment.

At such moments, we can remember an important truth: we don't require psychology or neuroscience research to make school decisions. Our teacherly experience and wisdom have guided us for years, and will continue to do so. Even if we find no research showing that – say – *using students' names frequently* enhances our connection to them, we might decide to adopt that habit because it just sounds so sensible. Research schmesearch.

Of course, Goldilocks grit might instead stiffen our spine and boost our resolve. True enough, the one research study we examined didn't support the Big Ask. It wasn't peer-reviewed, perhaps, or its participants look nothing like our kiddos, or its numbers just didn't add up. And yet, as we have seen, we now have a very particular set of skills, acquired over a long quest: skills that *allow us to discover relevant research on our own*. When our early quest leads to cheerless successes, our three familiar tools and three new gizmos might convert such disappointments to triumphs.

To be clear: we don't have to reboot quests if we don't want to. And, even if we *deeply believe* that a teaching technique must have research support somewhere, Goldilocks warns us that we still might be wrong. That is: we set out on this independent quest hoping for success, but open to the possibility that – surprise! – our beliefs lack the research basis we always assumed they had.

Let's try two examples.

In Chapter 4, a source advised us to offer students this heartwarming reassurance: "I'm giving you this feedback because *I believe in you*." Although that advice sounds both uplifting and sensible, we quickly discovered the source's misdirection. As the abstract revealed (Cohen et al., 1999), the research he cited does not remotely justify that guidance. Our message to fellow villagers: don't trust this source, and don't take his advice.

Although we concluded that quest victoriously – we avoided unsupported advice – that victory strangely doesn't feel like a victory. We really want to reassure our students that we believe in them. We want to encourage our grouchy colleague to do so. We want research to support our long-held beliefs. Although we made the right research call, we felt glum and thwarted as we contemplated riding home.

Rather than return to the village, we could instead relaunch this quest. Tools and gizmos in our saddlebags, we spur our mount back toward the forest.

Contemplating Figure 18, we've got lots of choices. Perhaps, because we already have Cohen's PDF open on our desktop, we might start with a quick review of his introduction. Knowing that introductions recap "the story so far," we hope that this one might identify earlier "I believe in you" research. By power-skimming the PDF, we could locate studies to convince our praise-averse colleague.

Alas, that first attempt at a reboot gets us nowhere. Cohen's highly readable introduction, surprisingly, simply doesn't discuss earlier research on this uplifting language. This path leads to a murky dead end.

Although our first attempt proved a false start, we don't feel discouraged. We have many strategies left to try.

As a next improvisational step, we might romp around in Google Scholar with plausible phrases, hoping to stumble across research gold. For instance: the conference speaker made big promises about the words "I believe in you." That sentence gives us a handy place to start. Sure enough, those very words in a Google Scholar search box yield an impressively on-point result: "*I believe in you!* Measuring the experience of encouragement using the academic encouragement scale" (Wong et al., 2019).

Despite that promising title, this study doesn't *quite* answer our question. It focuses on research methodology: a questionnaire to measure encouragement. At the same time, it does give us vital information: *the name of a scholar who explores this field.* Some strategic Google Scholar clicking brings us to a list of Dr. Y. Joel Wong's research – and to pay dirt: "*You can do it!* An experimental evaluation of an encouragement intervention for female students" (Wong et al., 2020). At long last: *direct research evidence that encouraging words produce measurable results.*

At this point, we can follow several familiar steps:

- By walking the boundaries and cracking the code, we notice important *boundary conditions*: these researchers studied the effect of an email on graduate students.
- When we check Wong's *definitions of success*, we quickly see that they don't much apply to K-12 work. Female PhD candidates who got encouragement from their advisors felt "greater increase in the advisor-advisee rapport, interest in conducting research, and interest in being a professor at a research-intensive university than those in the control condition" (Wong et al., 2020, p. 427). How often do we wonder if third graders want to become professors at research-intensive universities?
- By power-skimming the *introduction*, we find that strangely little research has been done on this topic. As Wong bluntly writes, "research on encouragement remains in infancy" (Wong et al., 2020, p. 428).

For all these reasons, we'll have to use our best Goldilocks judgment before we apply this research conclusion to our own students. Reasonable people – even Mr. Grumpy Colleague – might argue that our students don't fit within Wong's boundaries.

At the same time, these findings offer us tentative backing. A perfectly reasonable hypothesis – "an encouraging email motivates grad students" – does get support from Wong's data. To apply this broad concept to younger students is, indeed, an extrapolation. But these data, *combined with our professional experience,* certainly give us additional reason to proceed. Perhaps the phrase "research-based" would overstate the case. Our school could, however, make the following claim:

> *Here at Goldilocks Academy, we let our students know that we believe in them. Perhaps not surprisingly, that teaching strategy hasn't been researched directly – it seems too obvious to need much study. But the little research we have (with graduate students, believe it or not!) suggests those words matter. And all our experience tells us the same thing.*

> *We know this research field is in its infancy. We're keeping an eye on its growth and development.*

Such a Goldilocks summary honestly encapsulates the on-point research, and explains – wholly plausibly – why we're using our own instincts to go beyond it.

True confession: when I started this "I believe in you" quest, I had no idea I would locate results so quickly. I had assumed much more sleuthing would be required. Amazingly, I had these studies on my desktop in minutes.

Here's a second reboot example.

Because we worry so much about students' stress levels, we were excited about starting a before-school mindfulness program. To our dismay, we realized that the study advocating that program used a business-as-usual control group. We just can't know if the *mindfulness* produced the reported benefits, or if another variable – the early hour, the caring adult attention – did. Wisely but glumly, we ended that adventure.

Rather than stop at this disappointing success, we might quest out on our own. Let's go back to Figure 18 and start improvising:

- A sensible Google Scholar search ("mindfulness," "stress," "middle school") offers up a cornucopia. One likely looking study includes in its title the words "randomized control trial" – a phrase that soothes our control-group concerns (Sibinga et al., 2016).
- If we check Sibinga's study on Scite, we find that it hasn't gotten much direct attention: two confirmations and one (indirect) dispute. Perhaps this study leads nowhere useful?
- A trip to Connected Papers, however, produces a robust web (Figure 21). In fact, Sibinga's mindfulness study directly connects to even more encouraging research – including a meta-analysis about mindfulness programs with youth (Zoogman et al., 2015).

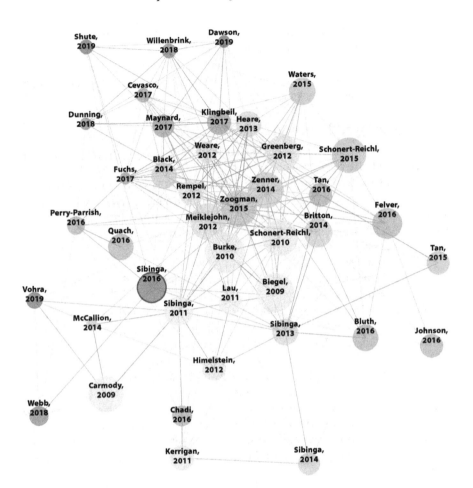

Figure 21. (Source: Connected Papers)

These two studies, of course, require our well-practiced Goldilocks scrutiny. We don't accept them simply because we found them on the 'net. However, our remarkable progress should reassure us. By following these steps and insisting on a just-right balance, we have *both* set aside tempting-but-inadequate research *and* found even better research to take its place.

The result: if Sibinga's study and Zoogman's meta-analysis check out, we'll have a research-based mindfulness program that truly benefits our students.

Of course, some quest reboots heighten rather than dispel our doubts. No matter how vigorously we investigate the SSE program that "trains up working memory," we're likely to find much greater skepticism than we can bear. (If you're curious about this topic, Appendix II has the goods.)

In such cases, Goldilocks knows she has reached the limit. No matter how much we want this idea to have research support, it just doesn't. Disappointed but ultimately persuaded, we head for home.

A Long-Delayed Reunion

As we return over and over to the starting point in Figure 18, we discover an arresting plot twist: *the return of neuroscience.*

Back in Chapter 2, I argued that neuroscience (à la 20th century) *fascinates* teachers but does not *help* teachers. When we launched our quest, we wanted research about mental behavior, a.k.a. psychology (à la 20th century), not neuroanatomy. Here in Chapter 8 – as promised long ago – we welcome neuroscientific tools and perspectives back as a faithful squire.

Why the change of heart?

After so many quest metaphors, a few sports analogies, and a random movie or two, let's try a business analogy...

Because I've read so much about the benefits of mid-class exercise, I decide to build a sweat-while-you-learn website. I create handy demo videos and sample routines and progress charts – all bedazzled with impressive research credentials. If I brand and market this bad boy just right, I'll sell subscriptions by the bushel. No doubt I can retire to a tropical island with my umbrella drinks.

To ensure that my business venture thrives, I decide to run my plan by several pals and gather their constructive criticism. First up, I consult with a teacher friend who now works as a vice-principal. With her combined experience as a teacher and school leader, she can advise me *both* about my website's classroom usefulness *and* about her school's budget priorities. In short, she's got lots of practical experience that can guide me.

Once she has given my project the thumbs up, whom should I consult next? Of course, I could check with another teacher/administrator friend. After decades in the business, I've got loads of them. Truthfully, however, my project probably benefits more from *new and distinct viewpoints.*

- I could check with an IT buddy who knows the perils of scaling up a web business on short notice.
- I might consult an accountant to see if my business strategy creates tax headaches.
- A friend who runs an online decorating site might advise me about the unpredictable world of web commerce.

- A fitness expert could identify a few exercises that might injure – not enliven – the students.

And so forth. Each distinct perspective gives me increasingly beneficial advice. If all these friends greenlight my venture, I can launch it with real confidence.

The same logic applies to our improvisational quest. As we journey down these several paths – familiar tools and new gizmos – we find additional encouragement from each fresh research point of view. If psychology *and* neuroscience *and* endocrinology *and* education research all agree that a Big Ask helps our students, this **converging evidence** makes a teaching suggestion all the more plausible. Unlike Dante, we abandon doubt, not hope.

Let's imagine a brief example.

When we rebooted our mindfulness quest a few pages ago, we found that lots of psychology evidence fills the gap left by that disappointing study. The same Google Scholar search that yielded Sibinga's study also highlights this article: "Mindfulness training reduces stress and amygdala reactivity to fearful faces in middle-school children" (Bauer et al., 2019).

During early quest stages, we would – rightly – have resisted all this talk of neuroanatomy and neurophysiology. "Amygdala reactivity" truly sounds fascinating. But unless students think and learn and behave differently, it doesn't help us to know what their amygdala (or their gracilis, or their dopytocin levels) might be doing.

At this point in the quest, however, we *already* believe that mental behavior changes as a result of mindfulness practice. Sibinga's study and Zoogman's meta-analysis suggest that mindfulness changes thought patterns and behaviors. For the same reason my sweat-while-you-learn website benefits from multiple critical perspectives, so too our quest benefits from different flavors of brain evidence.

When Bauer's research team finds that a *behavioral/psychological* change coincides with an *physiological/neurobiological* change, this additional research perspective does indeed merit our questly interest. Specifically, this study suggests that a mindfulness program both changes students' reported stress levels and enhances connectivity between two relevant brain regions. If the prefrontal cortex (very roughly, a "center of self-control") communicates more effectively with the amygdala (very roughly, a "center of strong negative emotions"), that connection sensibly helps explain stress reduction. In this study, we see that two meaningfully different kinds of "brain science" point in the same direction. Their agreement here gives us additional confidence that a mindfulness program really could benefit our sixth graders.

A fair warning. Chapters 5 through 7 argued that – in Stubborn Goldilocks mode – we really can understand enough about a psychology study to draw strong, even critical, conclusions. Those strategies might apply to neuroscience research. But honestly, they might not. The level of technical complexity in a typical fMRI study could easily defeat the most determined quester. (Once you see the word "voxelwise," you know you're facing a dense forest indeed.) In such cases, relying on a rough-n-ready understanding of the abstract will have to suffice. Because we investigated the psychology research so vigorously, we feel satisfied with an introductory understanding of its neuroscientific confirmation.

When Bauer's abstract notes, "children who received mindfulness training reported lower stress associated with reduced right amygdala activation ... relative to children in the control condition" (Bauer et al., 2019, p. 569), it provides us with useful neuro-reassurance. If we don't understand the technical details behind that statement, we can nonetheless appreciate its importance.

Reliving Quest Stories in the Pub

As we contemplate wrapping up our quest, we imagine meeting friends at the village alehouse – regaling awe-struck neighbors with tales of peril and triumph.

The time that conference keynote speaker said: "You're the first person who asked me for a source on that claim – I'm proud to meet you!"

The time a source quoted the abstract, but left out the words "might not."

The time we unearthed a study whose participants *match our students exactly.*

The time we knew we were right, but couldn't find research that says so.

The time we showed the doubters to be wrong.

The time when – after chapters of patient waiting – we allowed ourselves a glimpse of good old-fashioned *brain research*. Seeing the dorsolateral prefrontal cortex here, the anterior cingulate cortex there, and the neural pathways between them, we cried: "I've got it. Maybe *this* strategy will help motivate my students..."

CHAPTER 9.
EPILOGUE

In January 2020, a teacher tweeted a video of his young students *reading while pedaling exercycles*. (To amuse myself, I'll call this teacher Mr. Adrenaline.)

Edu-Twitter responded with its customary nuance. Many enthusiasts posted heart emojis and celebratory gifs. At least as many critics spat out insults: "foolish," "absurd," "bonkers!" Because of this ferocity – I assume – Adrenaline took his post down soon after. Edu-Twitter moved on to its next battle.

Goldilocks, of course, strives for greater wisdom than Twitter. She wants to be open to new ideas, but not gullible about them. She values others' expertise, and her own as well. Upon seeing this tweet, she summons her steed and dons her armor.

If you saw this video and had your curiosity piqued, you would undertake a quest in your own way. Let me tell you of my own surprising journey…

When I left my village, I started by assuming that exercising *during* reading – a demanding cognitive activity – would interfere with learning. When we divide our attention between two complex tasks – some call it "multitasking"; psychologists call it "foolishness" – we quickly degrade our ability to accomplish either. For this reason, most of us turn down the car radio as we drive to a new destination. On familiar roads, we can manage both car and music, but we need undivided attention when peering out for a new address. Heck, I'm so interested in this topic, I wrote a book about it (Watson, 2017).

Acknowledging my initial skepticism, I nonetheless decided to keep an open mind. After all, if I already know everything about teaching, I have no reason to scan Twitter for new ideas. Sure enough, Adrenaline responded to early criticism with a two-page PDF listing all the sources he relied on before launching this exer-reading initiative. He didn't just dream something up and lob it at his students for no reason: he had *research* behind this plan.

Adrenaline's classroom strategy can indeed point to adjacent research. Broadly speaking, we know that *physical health benefits cognition and learning*. As John Ratey explains in his splendid book *Spark!*, regular aerobic exercise boosts production of brain-derived neurotrophic factor (BDNF) (Ratey & Hagerman, 2008). And BDNF works all sorts of synaptic magic – a beautiful thing for long-term memory formation. As we've discussed repeatedly when questing through Fenesi's mid-lecture exercise study, the right combination of physical activity and teaching enhances learning.

Alas, as I quested along, I found that Adrenaline's research list fell short in two important ways. First, we know that boundary conditions matter. For instance, before we rely on this research, we must ask: what exercise did the students do?

A few of Adrenaline's links reveal articles about stand-biased desks (e.g., Dornhecker et al., 2015). Common sense suggests that *bike riding* while reading could be much more distracting than *standing* while reading. That information about stand-biased desks, although interesting and suggestive, doesn't examine the specific boundary condition that most needs investigation.

Another crucial question about boundary conditions: *when* in the learning process did the exercise take place?

- Ratey's book suggests that exercise *before or after learning* might boost memory.
- Fenesi's research suggests that students benefit when teachers *stop teaching* to let them exercise.
- Adrenaline's strategy, by way of contrast, requires students *to keep reading while exercising*.

This simultaneity creates a split-attention problem that Ratey and Fenesi don't address. And Adrenaline's list doesn't address it, either.

Second, Adrenaline's list includes some famously dodgy claims. Most importantly, he buys into learning styles theories, specifically highlighting the importance of **kinesthetic learning**. As we'll detail in Appendix II, learning styles theory gets no love from neuroscience or psychology research; it should get no love from schools and teachers.

By this point, my quest had accumulated many reasons to doubt this source. If Adrenaline's research basis *doesn't* explore meaningful boundary conditions, and does include dubious claims, I'm inclined (at least for now) to reject this cycle strategy. I'd rather keep my students in chairs – and off exercise equipment – during class.

Of course, Goldilocks reminded me not to embrace that conclusion until I'd cultivated doubt in my doubts. If my handy toolkit revealed contradictory evidence, I might discover that Adrenaline was right all along. If – as frankly seemed likely –

I couldn't find reason to doubt my doubts, that failure would justify my confidence.

At this point, my quest took a surprising turn. Because split attention typically interferes with effective cognition, I had assumed that dividing attention *with exercise* would create the same harmful effect. When I looked for research supporting that belief...I just didn't find very much. That specific question has barely been tested. We can reasonably hypothesize that dividing attention between reading and exercycling will interfere with learning. But I can't back up that claim with direct research, because very little has been done.

Adrenaline doesn't have much on-point research supporting his strategy; I don't have much on-point research rejecting it.

Instead, my tools-n-gizmos revealed a few intriguing studies that almost fit Adrenaline's boundary conditions. Researchers in the Netherlands had students do moderate to vigorous exercise *during* their math and language lessons (Mullender-Wijnsma et al., 2016, 2019). For instance: students multiplied 2 x 4, and jumped up and down eight times as they said the answer. Or, when asked to spell a word, they would squat each time they said a letter. *Two years later*, researchers found that this intervention improved math learning (but not language learning).

I'll be honest: finding an effect two years later is *stunning*.

I have a hypothesis about this result. Notice that the math exercise *directly related to the math content*. When the answer was 8, students jumped eight times. However, the language exercise did not obviously connect to the word spelling. Nothing about squatting while saying "C" differs from squatting while saying "A" or "T." Perhaps – this is my hypothesis – the math exercise helped because it directly reinforced the lesson's meaningful content.

If that hypothesis were correct, then Adrenaline would be right to have students do *particular* exercises during *particular* lessons. Exercycles probably wouldn't help reading, but – hypothetically – jump rope might support learning the times tables.

In any case, I didn't find evidence that persuades me to *start* such a program. But I didn't find on-point evidence that obviously persuades Adrenaline to *stop*. I strongly suspect bike-riding while reading hampers comprehension. That conclusion, in my teacherly judgment, extrapolates quite reasonably from multitasking research. But that's a judgment call, not a settled research conclusion. Unless he asks my opinion, I should leave Adrenaline alone.

This saga end with our final plot twist.

It turns out that, as his name implies, Mr. Adrenaline *teaches physical education*. In other words: he was not a language arts teacher recklessly imperiling his students' understanding of the required curriculum. He was, instead, a PE teacher encouraging students to incorporate cognition with exercise. He strove to *expand* his students' reading time, not diminish it.

A quick glance at Adrenaline's Twitter feed shows admirable PE inventiveness. He has students drum on exercise balls with glow sticks – in the dark! He has them practice field-goal kicks by projecting images of uprights against the gym wall. He organizes calisthenic dances – I don't know what else to call them – to the latest hit music. He is, in brief, the PE teacher I wish I had – and not only because he encouraged his students to read.

For all these reasons, I do not presume to warn Adrenaline against exercycles. I'm in Goldilocks mode. I trust *my* quick survey to know: we don't have a well-developed research answer to this question. *And* I trust *his* PE expertise enough to believe that – as an experienced teacher – he gets to make his own decisions about the research we do have.

I look back on this Adrenaline quest with especial fondness because it included so many twists, surprises, and revelations. I started deeply skeptical; heck, I'm still skeptical enough that I wouldn't use this technique with my students. But once I pushed past that skepticism, I learned that we have surprisingly little research on this important subject. The research we do have suggests that – under exactly the right circumstances – exercise *during* learning just might help. And I'm humbled to see how generous, open-minded teachers can expand classroom possibilities for their students – despite the slings and arrows of Twitter.

The View from Two Hilltops

Riding home from our quest, we pause on a hilltop overlooking our village. From this vantage, we look both forward and back.

Looking forward, we know that – re-entering the village – we still have important work to do. This adventure has persuaded *us* to accept, or reject, a research-based Big Ask. Yet our fellow villagers didn't accompany us on the quest, and might – loudly and grittily – resist our well-informed conclusion. If we learned that an unpopular initiative has lots of research support, or that an uplifting one lacks substance, we might anticipate pitchforks and torches.

At this point, frustration might lead us from our nature's better angels. I myself have been tempted to say, "I did the research; you didn't. You just have to trust me. We're doing this." Yet we halt before we speak such words because of a surprising realization: *we are now the source.* As you recall from Chapter 2, we asked the initial source for his best evidence. If he refused to say ("I can't tell you because you don't have a PhD in neuroscience."), that rebuff alone disqualified him.

Now that we are the source, the same rule applies to us. Our colleagues have little reason to trust our conclusion if we don't share our research and our thought process. We might, in fact, end up replaying a table-top version of the quest to explain our recommendation. (I just table-topped that Adrenaline quest for you.)

Because we have done our work so thoroughly – we decoded ciphers, braved giants, battled orcs – we have everything we need to bring reasonable colleagues along.

From one perspective, that final quest adventure might feel like pointless busywork. After our Herculean labors, who needs it? From a different perspective, this chance to explain our thinking instead lets us train up future questers. Like Yoda training Luke on Dagobah, like General Antiope training Wonder Woman on Themyscira, we create the next generation of champions.

And so as we look forward, we also look back. From our vantage, we can survey an extraordinary journey: an abstract map has turned into gritty experience. Several chapters ago, we neophytes quivered on the verge of a bottomless Chasm of Self-Doubt, hardly daring to ask a simple question. Now we have ventured across this vast research realm: mapping its limits, mastering its language, defying its mages – and arriving at our own conclusions.

Goldilocks might have seemed like an odd persona for a heroic quest, but her insistence on a just-right balance has served us well. We knew when to question a source's claim, and when to defer to researchers' expertise; when to assert our own rights, and when to admit our perilous fallibility. And as a result, we now hold the holy education grail: teaching methods that genuinely help our students learn, develop, grow, and thrive.

As I finish this book, I look back over it from a hilltop of my own. I have tried – over the preceding chapters, and the impending appendices – to map out a clear, accurate, and useful path. As I wrote, I have frequently imagined exasperated voices questioning the choices I've made. Despite those imagined voices, I've drawn this map – with its twists and side-quests and reversals – as best I know how. "All models are wrong," the saying goes. "Some models are useful."

This map might be flawed and torn. My spells might not be letter-perfect. Perhaps I mistook an elf for a goblin, or vice-versa. No matter. Frodo got the ring to Mt. Doom with far less effective guidance. The help he had was enough. May this map-model – however wrong – prove useful.

Here on this hilltop, I hand it forward to you, hoping it inspires you to sally forth. Here's why: *the quest itself matters more than the map.* I genuinely think each one of us can succeed on this adventure.

As teachers, we have wisdom, classroom experience, love of our discipline, and a hard-to-explain optimism about children. As scrupulous scientists, researchers have useful advice – often counterintuitive advice – that can shake up our misguided preconceptions, break through needless limitations, and answer profession-defining questions. When Goldilocks brings our fields together in a just-right balance, she can make learning easier and teaching more effective.

The quest begins. Your steed awaits. You ride at dawn...

PART V.
APPENDICES AND
BEYOND

APPENDIX I.
STATISTICS – OLD
FRIENDS AND NEW

This appendix has two goals.

First: I want to persuade you that statistics seems scary and inscrutable, yet ultimately proves helpful and benevolent.

Second: I want to shift your statistics focus. Most stats discussions center on two measurements: the **p-value** and the **n**. In my view, neither gives teachers especially useful information. Instead, we should focus on a less well-known stats character: **Cohen's d**. We can calculate this number with a simple, easy-to-understand formula. Once we've calculated it, we can use it to make wise and nuanced decisions.

No, really: Cohen's d is GREAT. Once you understand it, it will provide lots of meaningful help.

Out With the Old

When Dunning-Kruger novices first study statistics, they bring a passionate focus to the p-value. "Yes, I read that study. Didn't you notice the p-value of 0.07?" they might say warily.

At the most basic level, the p-value answers this rough question: how likely is it that we would get these results if our hypothesis were wrong? A p-value of 0.50 would mean there's a 50% chance; if $p = 0.05$, there's a 5% chance. In a secret meeting of statistics wizards many decades ago, wise souls decided that we could live with a 5% chance, *but not more*. For that reason, the statistics novice embraces a p of 0.05, but heatedly rejects a p of 0.07. The difference between a 5%

chance and a 7% chance might not seem like much to outsiders. In stats-world, that bright red line divides the wicked from the blessed, dark from light, Sauron from hobbits. Dare to cross it and you'll be banished from Wakanda.

Important note: this description of p-value necessarily simplifies a complex topic. If you want the fuller version, follow the references. Be sure to have strong coffee nearby.

In my work, I don't focus too much on p-values, for two reasons.

First: the research I'm reading has been peer-reviewed. If p-value problems meaningfully undermined the study's conclusion, then effective peer review should have weeded it out. After all, I (almost certainly) know more about teaching 10th graders than the reviewers do; the reviewers (almost certainly) know more about statistics than I do. It's really unlikely that I know enough about stats to overrule a reviewer's informed conclusion (p = 0.0001).

Second: no one really knows what a p-value means.

No, honestly. People who work stats magic for a living have career-on-the-line arguments on this topic. I've given a highly simplified version of a p-value above; a meaningfully more substantial version would stun you into numbness. Here's my thought process: if I can't even understand what a p-value is – heck, if almost no one understands what a p-value is – why should I focus on it?

Just as a sample of the debate, let me quote from Wikipedia's article on p-value: "Important: the probability of observing a result given that some hypothesis is true is *not equivalent* to the probability that a hypothesis is true given that some result has been observed" ("P-value," 2020). Got that?

Few people have spent more time trying to make statistics clear to the public than Nate Silver, founder and editor of FiveThirtyEight. He applies statistical thinking to everything from sports injuries to supreme court nominations, and explains his methodology with enthusiastic openness. Yet his website posted an article entitled "Not even scientists can easily explain p-values" (Aschwanden, 2015). To bolster her claim, Christie Aschwanden quotes Steven Goodman, co-director of a Stanford-based center for upping the quality of scientific investigation:

> "Even after spending his 'entire career' thinking about p-values, he said he could tell me the definition, 'but I cannot tell you what it means, and almost nobody can.' Scientists regularly get it wrong, and so do most textbooks, he said. When Goodman speaks to large audiences of scientists, he often presents correct and incorrect definitions of the p-value, and they 'very

confidently' raise their hand for the wrong answer. 'Almost all of them think it gives some direct information about how likely they are to be wrong, and that's definitely not what a p-value does,' Goodman said." (Aschwanden, 2015)

Goodman has in fact written an oft-cited analysis: "A dirty dozen: Twelve p-value misconceptions" (2008). That's right: *12 misconceptions* for a statistic that people get very fussy about.

Discussions of p-values often include the phrase "statistical significance," as in: "These findings are *statistically significant* at the p = 0.05 level." This turn of phrase, unfortunately, creates genuine confusion – and potential harm. Sources who want to impress teachers often use it accurately but misleadingly.

Take this hypothetical example: "Third graders who used this study method scored *significantly* higher on the subsequent math test, compared to third graders who used traditional methods." Conference speakers often use this phrasing, dramatically punching the second syllable: "sig-NI-ficantly."

Yes, if researchers found a *statistically* significant difference, that dramatic sentence is factually correct. However, most of us interpret that sentence to mean something else entirely: that one group *earned a much higher score* than the other group. I'm here to tell you: *statistical significance does not guarantee meaningfully higher scores.* If enough third graders participated in this study, then the difference between an 80.2 and an 80.3 could be statistically significant. And yet, no eight-year-old will care about that 0.1-point difference. It's statistically significant, yes, but it's not significant.

This verbal flimflam brings us back to Chapter 4's emphasis on spell-breaking. In that quest's adventure, we reviewed the abstract to ensure the source had summarized it correctly. If not, we decided to stop trusting him and wrapped up our quest (or went improvisationally rogue).

Now that we better understand p-values, and recognize the duality in the word "significant," we have another way to break a source's spell. If a PD presenter says that a teaching technique made a "significant difference," we can reasonably ask: "How much difference?" The speaker might not know immediately; if he's citing several studies, the details of each might be fuzzy at that moment. But if he doesn't remember, he should look the information up.

Imagine the speaker gets back to you and says: "The students who took exercise breaks scored 6% higher on the chapter test than the students who didn't. The control group averaged a 78%; the intervention group, an 84%." At this point, you can decide if that trade-off – less time to teach, more time for jumping jacks – is worth 6% to you and your students. I suspect most people will think this difference is both *statistically significant and plain old significant.*

Imagine, instead, the speaker says: "I already told you, it was *sig-NI-ficant.*" Or, the speaker might offer this report: "The experimental group averaged 0.2 points higher on the quiz. That sounds small, but trust me, it was *statistically significant.*" In these cases, the speaker was attempting a disguise spell. Your question has broken it. Celebrate by refusing his Big Ask. Grab a slice of pizza instead.

> To be clear: the speaker might originally have said, "This difference is statistically significant – but in reality, that difference represents only a fraction of a point. Your students won't really notice the difference." In this case, the source has been wholly forthright. No spell; no need to worry.

A second stats topic gets similarly righteous attention, but probably doesn't require it. When researchers report the number of study participants, they use the shorthand "n." If a study includes 72 students, the abstract will say "$n = 72$."

If a colleague wants to critique a study, she might dismiss the p-value. ("Didn't you see that this research includes a p of 0.08? We can't take this Big Ask seriously...") If, however, the p-values all pass muster, she might instead criticize the n: "The n on this research was 26. *Twenty-six!* We can't take such a small study seriously. We certainly shouldn't change our school because of it."

> Christian Bokhove has a humorous guide to embracing or rejecting research, depending on your druthers. You can find it in Appendix IV (p. 240).

Yes, 26 is a small n. But, for two reasons, I don't focus much on the n.

First, we struggle to say what the right n would be. Typically, we draw stronger conclusions from larger studies – that is, studies with a bigger n. We initially focused on that IPP study from South America because it lasted so long, and because it had an n of 17,006. That's huge. For this reason, we can rightly question low-n studies. Except in rare circumstances, teachers don't learn much if a dozen or two students tried out an exciting new study technique. (If *researchers* get a strongly positive result on a small-n study, they *do* learn something valuable: they should repeat the study with hundreds, not handfuls, of participants.)

And yet, critics who rightly question small-n studies rarely tell you what a big enough n would be. If 25 is too small, would 35 change your mind? How about 125? What's the bright line a study needs to cross? Statisticians answer this question with appropriate complexity: "If we have an n of X, we can say Y with Z degree of confidence." As teachers, we just don't have time to crunch those formulas.

Second, a small n would worry us *if the Big Ask relied on just one study*. However, we devoted an entire quest chapter to finding other studies. We scrounged through Google Scholar, rummaged about on Scite and Connected Papers, scoured meta-analyses: all to understand the bigger picture. We're not relying on one study; we've got lots of research behind the Ask.

Meta-analysis proves particularly helpful in persuading n fretters. Meta-analytic formulas weigh large-n studies more than small-n studies. If a small-n study were contradicted by several large-n studies, the meta-analysis would reveal that ugly truth.

In sum, I think teachers have wisely shied away from a statistical perspective because the two most frequently discussed stats topics – p-value and n – don't give us useful information. We rarely need the latter, and hardly understand the former. (No one understands the former.) If we're going to rely on statistics, we need a statistical formula that is *easy to calculate*, and provides us with *obviously useful information*.

In With the New

When teachers look at psychology research, we have a simple question: does this new strategy or program make a *meaningful* difference for *many* students? In a perfect world, we'd like **one number** that answers our two-part question with straightforward clarity.

> Important note: we should think precisely about our definition of "many." I might not teach *many* students on the autism spectrum. But, if I'm looking for research to help those students, I want to be sure that the Big Ask helps *many* of them, not just a few. Even small numbers of students deserve research-informed teaching.

The best candidate for that one number, in my view, is **Cohen's d**. We can readily understand its meaning, easily calculate its value, and sensibly interpret that number.

Understand its Meaning

Let's imagine I run a study on the benefits of *brightly lit classrooms*. I randomly assign students to two groups. The first group watches a lecture in an *unusually bright room* (say, 1000 lux). When they take a quiz on that lecture material a week later, they average 85 out of 100.

The second group watches the same lecture in a *typically lit classroom* (say, 200 lux). Their average score a week later: 75 out of 100. The graph summarizing those results looks like Figure 22.

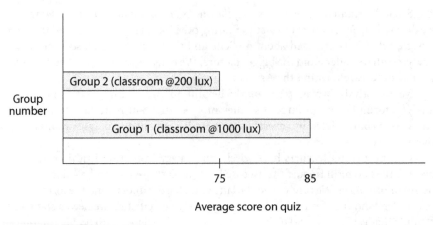

Figure 22

For the time being, we tentatively conclude that bright light enhances learning. Students in the bright room averaged 10 points higher than those in the dark room.

Of course, Figure 22 is correct, but incomplete. Because this graph reports *average* scores, it does not reveal the variety hidden in the average. It's *possible* that all group 1 students scored an 85, and all group 2 students scored a 75. But that result is spectacularly unlikely.

Almost certainly, instead, those numbers spread across a range. In group 2, perhaps, lots of students scored a 75, with some 74s and 76s, and a very few 73s and 77s (Figure 23). Those numbers average out to a 75, but the scores do vary.

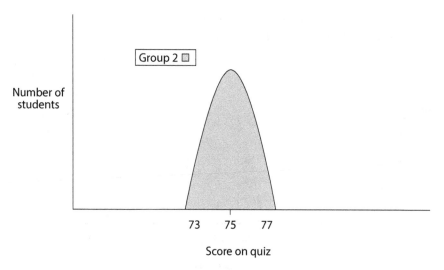

Figure 23

Or, perhaps, the quiz produced a broader range. In this case, lots of students scored a 75, with some 70s and some 80s, and a very few 65s and 85s (Figure 24). Those numbers also average out to a 75 – but we see a lot more breadth around that average.

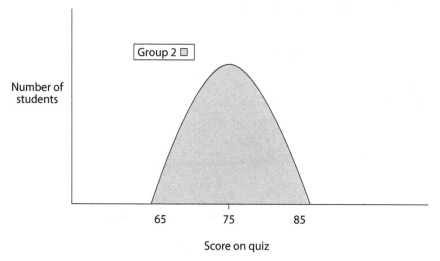

Figure 24

So far, we've seen that the *average score* matters, and that the *range* around that average score matters. Let's put those two concepts together.

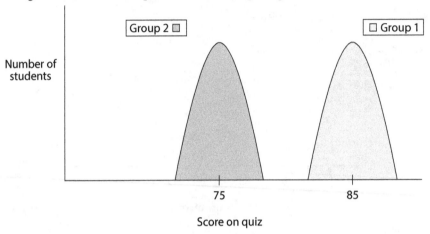

Figure 25

In Figure 25, we graph averages with a very *narrow* range. Because the range is so narrow, the two bell curves don't overlap at all. We easily see that *everyone* in the bright room scored higher than *everyone* in the typical room. With this graph, we feel much higher confidence that bright lights help.

Let's try another version of this graph.

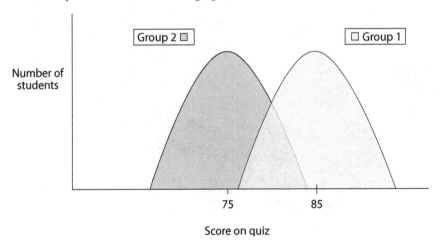

Figure 26

Here in Figure 26, we graph averages with a very broad range. In this case, those two bells overlap a bit. This graph requires a subtler interpretation. Yes: *on average,* students in the typically lit room scored lower than students in the bright room. But: some students defied that pattern. With this graph, our confidence begins to fade.

Our starting question was: does this new strategy or program make a *meaningful* difference for *many* students? When we look at this graph, we arrive at this answer: *the more those two bells overlap, the less meaningful difference we see.*

To deepen this insight, let's start playing around with these two variables.

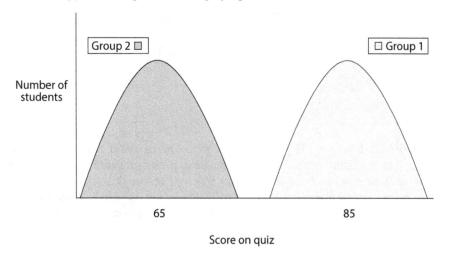

Figure 27

In Figure 27, the *range* remains quite large, but the *averages* have moved further apart. For that reason, the overlap is back to zero. If we had gotten these results, all students in the first group remembered more than all students in the second. Confidence restored.

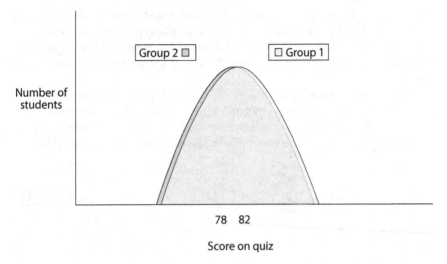

Figure 28

In Figure 28, however, the averages have gotten much closer together, and the overlap is substantial. In this case, we struggle to identify meaningful differences between these groups. Yes, a few students way over on the right clearly benefited from bright lights; a few students on the extreme left obviously languished in typical light. But we have to ask: do those few students add up to the "many" we were hoping for?

Here's the big picture. A mathematical formula that answers this "overlap" question must include two variables:

- The *average* scores; specifically, the *gap* between the average scores.
- The *breadth* of the range; specifically, whether it is *narrow* or *wide*.

If we get the right formula with those variables, we can consistently calculate the overlap. That number, wisely interpreted, lets us know if the Big Ask made a *meaningful* difference for *many* students.

Calculate its Value
Now that we know what this formula means, let's translate it into math. Doing so requires a bit of jargon – but just a little bit. As Goldilocks, we know that determination helps us on our quest. Even if math looks dragon-like to us, we plan to quest ahead.

Step 1: To calculate *the gap between the averages*, we simply subtract one average from the other. Stats folks use the word **mean** for average, and so its abbreviation is M. The first part of our calculation:

$M_1 - M_2$

Again, that's just the *difference* between the averages (means).

Step 2: To calculate the relative *breadth of the range*, we rely on the study itself. In statistics, that variable is called the **standard deviation**. ("Standard deviation," you say. "That's a bizarre name. What gives?" "Just go with it," I say. "Nobody knows.")

Often, the two breadths are roughly the same. To be thorough, we take the average:

$(SD_1 + SD_2)/2$

Again, that's just the *average* breadth of the range (standard deviation).

Step 3: To show the *relationship* between the gap and the relative breadth, we divide the former by the latter:

$$Cohen's\ d = \frac{M_1 - M_2}{Average\ SD}$$

Voila. It's that easy. *Subtract* one number from another. *Find the average* of two other numbers. *Divide.* Feel Goldilocks proud.

Although that math is easy, it might look daunting. To soothe our concerns, let's practice with data from Fenesi's study on mid-lecture exercise. She provides lots of numbers, so we have to pick our way through the results section with discernment. At last, we find that Table 3 presents the data on student learning.

So, let's crunch some numbers.

Step 1: How much did Fenesi's *exercisers* remember, on average, a week later? According to Table 3: 50%. How much did the *non-exercisers* remember? 42%. What's the gap between those averages?

$M_1 - M_2 = 50\% - 42\% = 8\% = .08$

Step 2: What was the standard deviation of the first group? As is customary, Fenesi gives the standard deviation in parenthesis after the mean. When we look there, we find that SD = 0.10. What was the standard deviation of the second group? 0.12. What's the average?

$(SD_1 + SD_2)/2 = (0.10 + 0.12)/2 = 0.11$

Step 3: What's the relationship between those numbers?

$$Cohen's\ d = \frac{M_1 - M_2}{Average\ SD} = \frac{.08}{0.11} = 0.72$$

Scrounge data. Subtract. Average. Divide. Like so many adventures on this quest, it looks scary until you've done it.

Good news! Because Cohen's d answers important questions straightforwardly, researchers increasingly include it in their results section. You might not need to sleuth out numbers and bust out your calculator: Cohen's d might wait for you to find it, tucked quietly away among all those numbers.

Interpret that Number

Our progress report so far. We want to know: does this new strategy or program make a *meaningful* difference for *many* students?

- We understand conceptually why Cohen's d answers that question: it quantifies the relationship between averages and ranges.
- We know how to calculate it.

Now: how do we interpret it? For instance: is Fenesi's 0.72 good or bad? We begin with two easy answers to that question. Then we slather on the nuance.

Cohen himself suggested initial interpretations. A d of 0.20 is **small**; of 0.50 is **medium**; and, unsurprisingly, of 0.80 is **large** (J. Cohen, 1988, pp. 25–27). Given those definitions, we can be impressed with Fenesi's 0.72. That number stands proud at the high end of medium.

With Cohen's initial framework, we could review each study we've quested in this book. For instance, Kornell summarizes his flashcard research with this sentence: "Final test accuracy was significantly higher in the large-stack (i.e. spaced) condition (M=65%, SD=28) than the small-stack (i.e. massed) condition (M=34%, SD=28)" (Kornell, 2009, p. 1307). Once again, we return to our trusty formula.

$$Cohen's\ d = \frac{M_1 - M_2}{Average\ SD} = \frac{0.65 - 0.34}{(0.28 + 0.28)/2} = \frac{0.31}{0.28} = 1.11$$

A d value of 1.11 is – technically speaking – HUGE. In psychology, we rarely see d values higher than 1.0. Although Kornell's flashcard research hasn't been replicated, we feel greater confidence than before.

For a little math-geek fun, let's try one more. We'd like to know: did Cartwright's cognitive flexibility intervention make a *meaningful* difference in *many* students' ability to read? In the GSF study, Table 1 includes a trove of data. We can calculate d values with the gusto that a third grader describes dinosaurs. Just to pick one of many options, how did the students do on a reading comprehension test? Intervention group: 31.03 (5.07). Control group: 29.68 (7.22).

$$Cohen's\ d = \frac{M_1 - M_2}{Average\ SD} = \frac{31.03 - 29.68}{(5.07 + 7.22)/2} = \frac{1.35}{6.15} = 0.22$$

Up until this point, we had felt enthusiastic about graphophonological-semantic cognitive flexibility – even though we struggled to pronounce it. Yet when we calculate a d value that Cohen himself would call "small," we might have to revise that opinion. It seems that Cartwright's intervention did something, but not *much* of something, and not for *many* people.

A second benchmark would also discourage us from focusing on Cartwright's suggestion. In his influential books *Visible Learning* (2009) and *Visible Learning for Teachers* (2012), John Hattie goes all in on meta-analysis. In fact, he synthesizes over 800 meta-analyses: that is, he does *meta*-meta-analysis. (As the humorist Dave Barry says: I do not think I am making this up.) His calculations, of course, lead to many conclusions. Most relevant here, Hattie argues that most educational interventions have *some* effect. We should focus on those that have a *higher than average* effect. As he crunches the numbers, a Cohen's d of 0.40 is average (Hattie, 2012, pp. 15–16). Thus, we should adopt teaching strategies that outstrip that number.

Whether we're using Cohen's standards or Hattie's, Cartwright's 0.22 falls short of the mark. We have to admit: it's looking bad for GSF training.

Both Cohen and Hattie provide helpful starting benchmarks. However, we know by now that nuance and improvisation help us perfect our quest. Several common-sense observations let us interpret Cohen's d more wisely.

For one thing, the *cost* of the Big Ask matters: cost in time and cost in money. Cartwright's training regime doesn't cost any money. As far as we can tell, it's free. And, it takes almost no time. The procedures section suggests that training the teachers took less than an hour. Yes, the students themselves needed class time to do the GSF training; but, the control group took the same amount of time with their regular class work. So, GSF exercises take up *none* of the school's budget, and *no additional* class time.

We might well find an alternative research-based intervention for struggling readers. A painstaking exploration – crossing chasms, breaking spells, facing giants – might confirm its strength. A brisk calculation might reveal a Cohen's d of – let's say – 0.62: almost triple Cartwright's strategy, and well past Hattie's hinge point. At this point we should ask: *what does this hypothetical competitor cost?*

If, like GSF training, it siphons off no school money and no additional student time, it's a clear winner. If, however, this alternative reading program demands scarce resources, we might hesitate.

- If it costs $20 per student, and needs an additional hour a week, our school system might absorb the difference.
- If it costs $1,000 per student and strictly requires five hours a week, we probably respond with a hard pass.

In this second case, Cartwright's less effective and *much less draining* program probably offers the better value.

> A useful web resource: if you want to evaluate *both* the evidence supporting an intervention *and* its cost, the Education Endowment Foundation has a website for you. Surf over to EducationEndowmentFoundation.org.uk and search for "evidence summaries."

As we interpret Cohen's d, common sense also reminds us to focus specifically on the *relevant research field*. We were initially impressed that Fenesi's mid-lecture exercises yielded a d value of 0.72. Generally speaking, Cohen thinks that's warming up on large.

Imagine, however, a competing lab run by Professor Isenef suggested a dramatically different exercise program. When we run those numbers, we find a d value of 0.94. In fact, exercise research might routinely find atypically large d values. *In this specific field*, perhaps 0.72 is embarrassingly low. (This hypothetical isn't true, but it's useful as an example.)

A recent meta-analysis highlights the need to interpret d values within specific fields. For many years, teachers had embraced Carol Dweck's work on **mindset**: the idea that our beliefs about intelligence shape our academic success. That approach has decades of impressive research support (for an overview, see Watson, 2019). In 2018, a substantial meta-analysis seemingly dumped barrels of cold water on Dweck's argument (Sisk et al., 2018). This research team crunched lots of numbers, and found that trying to boost a student's mindset had a trivially small d-value: 0.08. In Cohen's framework, that result falls alarmingly below small. We can hardly see 0.08 from Hattie's hinge point. This meta-analysis – combined with other substantial non-replications (e.g., Ganimian, 2020) – has thrown mindset research into confusion and doubt.

That interpretation, however, makes best sense if we ignore the pertinent research field: student *motivation.*

If you've been in a classroom, you know: motivating students to divide fractions or parse sentences or compare historical eras can daunt the most inspirational sage. Teachers hope keenly to tap our students' intrinsic motivation, but few of my 10th graders ever felt intrinsically motivated to read Shakespeare.

For this reason, we shouldn't simply ask: "Is 0.08 a trivially small d value?" Instead, we need a subtler question: "Measured by Cohen's and Hattie's rough standards, 0.08 seems trivially small. But how does that value stack up to other motivational strategies that we've researched? Within the *narrow field of motivation research,* is 0.08 trivially small, average, or impressive?" After careful searching, we might struggle to locate other motivational strategies that show any benefit whatsoever. A d value of 0.08 might not look like much, unless all the other d values hover at 0.00.

This point resonates especially for one subcategory in Sisk's meta-analysis: **high-risk students.** Typically, high-risk students – for instance, students who have already failed a course – struggle the most with motivation. They have reason to believe they can't succeed, so why should they bother even to try? Sisk's analysis, however, found that growth mindset interventions had a d value of 0.17 for this group. By typical standards, that number would elicit a bored shrug. By translating that number into everyday English, we might discover its real power: "Encouraging students to adopt a growth mindset offers a small motivational benefit, especially for students with the lowest motivation levels." Growth mindset helps – a little bit – the *students who most need the help, and who historically resist it most firmly.* We shouldn't be sneering; we should be putting mindset strategies to work.

This final paragraph, perhaps, reaffirms the promises that opened this appendix. I said at the beginning that we needn't pay attention to p-values or n; sure enough, neither of those commonly cited statistics has appeared in this mindset discussion.

Instead, I promised we could find a number that answered our most pressing question: does the Big Ask meaningfully help many students? By learning about d values, we now have a consistent yardstick to measure clear concepts:

- We know what we want to measure: the *overlap* of the two data ranges.
- We know how to *calculate* that number.
- We know how to *interpret* it with common sense and nuance.

Kornell's flashcards (d = 1.11) seem like a winner. Fenesi's exercises (d = 0.72) as well. Cartwright's GSF training (d = 0.22) at first had us worried. However, we know how to compare that value to other possible interventions. Even in the case of much-maligned mindset, we might conclude that a d of 0.17 ain't much – but it's better than all our other options.

> For an even deeper dive into Cohen's d, check out Thomas Guskey's helpful and readable article (2019).

Sure enough: by focusing on the right topics, Goldilocks finds statistics greatly helpful on her quest.

APPENDIX II.
RECYCLED ORBS

After we have been questing for a while, we should expect this sequel:

A messenger clops into our village, holds up a shiny bauble, and makes catchy wizard-based promises. We inspect the bauble briefly, and answer:

> *Your cousin was here at the last solstice. He offered us the same orb. I think you've put some cheap gild on the runes.*
>
> *The answer was "no grog for you" then. It's "no grog for you" today.*
>
> *The village across the brook stole our wheat last season. You should go talk with them...*

In other words: some edu-suggestions are recycled often enough that we can spot them right away. No need to undertake another quest. Our answer remains the same: a hard pass.

Three orbs get recycled so frequently that they call for special vigilance. You have, almost certainly, been offered one or two. In my classroom years, I saw all three – multiple times.

To understand each orb fully, we should analyze them in three ways:

1. Reasons that this orb is *so tempting* (and – very occasionally – has genuine magical power).
2. Reasons that it's almost certainly not worth quest time.
3. Layers of nuance.

You may be surprised how many of these orbs you have handled.

Orb #1: Different Groups of Learners

With great regularity, teachers hear this promise: "Divide your students into groups *this special way*, and they'll learn better." Despite the popularity of this claim, it's almost never true.

Reasons This Orb is So Tempting

I once directed a production of *The Foreigner*, by Larry Shue. Luckily, I had a spectacular cast: some of the most dedicated and inventive actors I've worked with. Early on in rehearsals, however, I noticed an unusual pattern. The actress playing Betty loved specific, technical feedback:

> **Me:** If you hold your hand flat instead of in a balled fist, the joke will land better. You see why?
>
> **Samantha:** Oh, yes, of course! Let me try...

The actor playing Ellard, however, preferred to stay in character when he got feedback. And, amazingly, he liked getting his notes in movie analogies.

> **Me:** Ellard? Do you remember watching *Star Wars*?
>
> **Brian:** Yes.
>
> **Me:** How did you feel when you first saw Darth Vader?
>
> **Brian** (trembling): I was a little scared. A little bit.
>
> **Me:** Do you think Owen reminds you of Darth Vader when he comes in the living room.
>
> **Brian** (quietly ducking behind a chair, whispering): Yes.

If Samantha heard me talk to Brian, or Brian/Ellard heard my comments to Samantha, they got disoriented. I finally learned to give each one notes on opposite sides of the stage. As long as they were out of earshot, rehearsals went smoothly.

As classroom teachers, we've all had similar experiences. Some students need to repeat what you said in order to understand it. Others like to sit quietly and think a bit. Some want to ask about exceptions to the rule you just described. Others find exceptions baffling until they've mastered the rule. In three words: *students are different.*

This insight might create teaching problems. If I have 25 students in my class, and my students all learn differently, then I might need to have *25 different lesson plans*. The mind boggles. For that reason, we love the idea that we can sort students into specific groups. My "green" thinkers learn this way; my "purple" thinkers learn that way; my "beige" thinkers have their own approach. If I sort my students correctly, I can make three lesson plans, not 25. This strategy *both* helps students in ways appropriate to their "learning style" *and* simplifies my teaching life. Let the sorting begin!

In one important category, this strategy does have research backing. Students with *diagnosed learning differences* have, in almost every case, been evaluated by trained professionals. Students with an ADHD diagnosis really do process stimuli differently. Students with dyslexia really do benefit from specialized reading instruction. Instruction for these students really should be tailored to their cognitive profiles. When we get diagnosis-based recommendations, we should follow them.

In brief: we often *want* to think about students in different learning categories; when our students have a diagnosis, in fact we should.

Reasons the Orb is Not Worth Quest Time

Although the divide-and-teach strategy often feels tempting (and is correct for diagnosed students), it otherwise almost never has research backing. As Daniel Willingham puts it, "Children are more alike than different in terms of how they think and learn" (Willingham, 2009, p. 147). If we want to group students together by "the kind of learner they are," we must remember this essential truth: *we are (almost) all the same kind of learner.*

This tempting orb appears in many, many disguises.

Learning styles theory, for instance, captivated our profession for two decades or so. The idea that *visual* learners differ from *auditory* learners (and *kinesthetic* learners – and, heck, *olfactory* learners) has an intuitive appeal. Other versions of this theory separate *convergent* thinkers from *divergent* thinkers, or *serial* thinkers from *holistic* thinkers. Each version proposes that teachers can divide students into these groups, teach them differently, and thereby help them learn more and better. Mr. Adrenaline held up this orb when championing exercyles.

These theories make testable predictions. When we test those predictions correctly, they simply don't come true. With impressive consistency, well-designed research fails to support learning styles hypotheses. We just don't have evidence to support learning styles theories (Pashler et al., 2008; Willingham, 2018).

As Pashler's review says:

> *"The contrast between the enormous popularity of the learning-styles approach within education and the lack of credible evidence for its utility is, in our opinion, striking and disturbing. If classification of students' learning styles has practical utility, it remains to be demonstrated."* (Pashler et al., 2008, p. 117)

The theory of multiple intelligences also falls in this category. It implies that we can separate "logical-mathematical thinkers" from "musical thinkers" and teach them differently. Although widely admired and frequently translated into teaching Asks, the theory *has not been substantively tested* in psychologically rigorous ways (McGreal, 2013). If you search Google Scholar for "multiple intelligences," the paucity of results will amaze you. This theory has great egalitarian appeal: "We're all intelligent in our own way!" However, the theory of multiple intelligences makes measurable predictions; those predictions have not yet been tested.

This orb has gotten many fresh coats of paint. For instance:

- You'll hear the claim that *boys and girls* think and learn differently, and so we should teach them separately. They don't; we shouldn't. (Eliot, 2009; Hyde, 2005).
- You may hear we should teach people differently based on their *Myers-Briggs personality type.* You might be surprised to hear that many psychologists don't think the Myers-Briggs test measures anything consistently or meaningfully (Pittenger, 1993, 2005). By now, you're not surprised to read that we shouldn't teach people this way. (Practically speaking, we'd need over a dozen different sections for each class. That's a Huge Ask for a theory that has little research support.)
- You might read that we should teach *extroverts and introverts* differently. This claim overlooks a core truth: almost all of us experience both introversion and extroversion, *depending on the circumstances we're in.* (Meet me at a conference, you'll swear I'm an extrovert. Meet me at a party, not so much. Like you, I'm an *ambivert.*)
- I've even heard of a personality profile test dividing people into the four elements: earth, wind, water, fire. Yes, it claims to explain student preferences.
- You often hear that Red Sox fans and Yankees fans think differently. Research into this question is ongoing.

When you next hear a claim – and you almost certainly will – that we should sort *these* students from *those* according to an *under-appreciated-but-crucial mental category,* you can probably decline without a quest. If you choose to quest, remember: we've heard this promise many times before.

Layers of Nuance

To be clear: we sort students by age. We often sort them by their prior knowledge. (Students won't learn much in an Algebra II class if they haven't taken Algebra I.)

In those cases, we're not separating students because third and seventh graders somehow learn differently: "Third graders are *kinesthetic* learners; seventh graders are *holistic* learners." We do so because, practically speaking, maturity and prior knowledge tend to align well by age.

More substantively, Goldilocks can't dismiss several much-beloved educational theories without acknowledging meaningful subtleties. As an example, let's consider *gender differences* as a reason to teach students separately. Here's my argument: "Claims that boys and girls *think and learn differently* don't have enough research support to guide our teaching and school-keeping."

Of course, boys and girls do differ biologically. *Of course*, some of those biological differences include brain differences. (The extent and significance of those brain differences, by the way, prompt ferocious controversy: see Greenberg at al. (2018) and also Rippon (2019).) Yes, *of course*, society treats boys and girls differently; such different treatment surely results in different social behaviors and underlying brain development.

These truths, however, do not add up to show that boys and girls *learn* differently, or *should be taught* differently. Most of the time, when we measure cognitive characteristics relevant to schools, they turn out to be quite small. Yes, boys can throw baseballs farther than girls (d = 1.98, a huge number (Hyde, 2005)). But in most academic categories where gender stereotypes sound meaningful, d values remind us those differences don't add up to much.

Let me return to my core argument: "Claims that boys and girls *think and learn differently* don't have enough research support to guide our teaching and school-keeping." We might educate boys and girls separately for other reasons: heck, some children and their parents might simply prefer such a classroom experience. But we should not overdecorate that simple preference with cognitive science claims about gender differences in learning.

We could replay this detailed back-n-forth about gender differences for those other orbs as well. Learning styles advocates and Myers-Briggs champions, no doubt, have sincere objections to this line of reasoning. If you and your school, open to their arguments, want to quest through the arguments, you have a map to guide you.

If instead you recognize this recycled orb, you might think, "We should beware dramatic promises about different categories of learner." If your village is like mine, you've got lots of other valuable work to do.

Orb #2: Brain Training

We often hear that the brain resembles a muscle. The more we use it, the stronger it grows. That analogy holds in specific circumstances, but – alas – doesn't stretch very far. Many salespeople offer "train your brain like a muscle!" orbs. Resist them.

Reasons This Orb is So Tempting (and – Very Occasionally – has Genuine Magical Power)

We have at least three reasons to look upon this orb optimistically.

First: it's so alluring. Our students often struggle to learn math. Wouldn't it be wonderful if we could help them learn math by doing something less...mathy? If, for instance, *piano lessons* improved math skills, this indirect math instruction would make school easier and more musical.

Second: it's so familiar. Everyone from Lumosity to Tom Brady promises to train your brain. Would the internet lie?

Third: it's obviously (narrowly) true. When students practice writing essays, they write better essays. When they practice the tuba, they toot more tunefully. Voila: they trained their brains.

The first two reasons frequently tempt us. And we might plausibly extrapolate from the third: if tuba practice improves tuba playing, why wouldn't it improve calculus learning?

Reasons the Orb is Almost Certainly Not Worth Quest Time

Because this claim is alluring, familiar, and obviously (narrowly) true, researchers test it frequently. Alas, their results consistently discourage us.

For instance, the claim that music lessons enhance broad cognitive skills gets enthusiastic press. The phrase **domain general** comes in handy during these discussions. It describes a mental faculty that we can use across disciplines. Reading is a domain-general skill, because I can read history and science and philosophy. Patience is domain general, because I can use it at home and the office. When we talk about "brain training," we generally mean domain-general skills. A recent meta-analysis summarizes shedloads of research on domain-general training:

> *"Music training has repeatedly been claimed to positively impact children's cognitive skills and academic achievement (literacy and mathematics). This claim relies on the assumption that engaging in intellectually demanding activities fosters particular domain-general cognitive skills, or even general intelligence. The present meta-analytic review shows that this belief is incorrect. Once the quality of study design is controlled for, the overall effect of music training programs is null."* (Sala & Gobet, 2020, p. 1429)

So too with chess. Even a casual web search leads to articles claiming that chess increases IQ, prevents Alzheimer's, enhances creativity, and grows dendrites(!). I suspect that, in corners of the dark web, I can order chess lessons guaranteed to make me more handsome and improve my singing.

Alas, not so. An improvisational quest quickly unearths individual studies (Jerrim et al., 2016) and meta-analyses (Sala & Gobet, 2017) making that conclusion highly unlikely.

> To be clear: I think schools should offer music lessons and organize chess clubs. We should do so because music and chess enrich our students' lives (they really do!), not because they improve students' domain-general cognitive abilities (they really don't!).

These two examples prepare us for the grim news: most of the time, claims of domain-general cognitive training don't withstand Goldilocks scrutiny. When we want our students to learn more science, we should teach them science. When we want them to get better at collaborating, we should let them practice collaboration. Training in X helps students do X; it rarely helps them do Y, much less do F or G.

And so, back when we first read about SSE training to improve working memory, we probably didn't need to launch our quest. With exasperating frequency, people claim that "playing this video game improves working memory, and thereby helps students learn math!" By now, we can recognize that orb. We've seen it before. It's probably just a polished hunk of glass. No magic here.

Layers of Nuance

Because this claim so often falls short, we might want to dismiss it every time. Alas, Goldilocks knows, we need to keep a balanced perspective. Two cases in particular invite additional scrutiny.

First: *background knowledge always matters*. When we increase our students' relevant knowledge on a topic, they might surprise with what they can do.

Most straightforwardly: background knowledge improves reading and reading comprehension. That claim might sound like an orb: training in X (background knowledge) improves M (reading). But in this case, it makes perfect sense.

For instance: budding readers might use their phonics skills to decode the phrase "Berlin Wall." Unless they have healthy background knowledge of geography, and of 20th century European history, that phrase won't mean much. Yes: context clues can provide valuable insights. And yes: learning factual knowledge about science and history and philosophy and geography makes it likelier that students will read wisely and fluently (Tyner & Kabourek, 2020).

For example: teaching Stephen Crane's *The Red Badge of Courage* to my juniors one year, I was surprised by one student's insightful participation. He had told me frankly that English just wasn't his thing, and hadn't contributed much to our earlier discussions. It turns out: *military history* was his thing. His knowledge about uniforms and regimental formations and weapons opened the text up for his classmates (and me) in entirely unexpected ways. In this case, relevant background knowledge (X) did indeed make him much better at literary analysis (Y). Because relevant background knowledge always matters.

This insight, by the way, should inform our response to claims about **critical thinking**. If we could train students' critical thinking skills, such a domain-general ability would give them a real boost in life. They could think critically about:

- Crane's *The Red Badge of Courage.*
- Get-rich-quick investment promises.
- A new jet engine design.
- Their college options.
- Claims on an internet news site.
- The best features to order for their new laptop computer.

Alas, to think critically *about laptop components*, students need background knowledge about laptop components. That information, in turn, really won't help them make wise investment decisions, or design jet engines. Although claims to train domain-general critical thinking skills sound splendid – who doesn't want students to think critically? – they probably overstate the possibility of doing so. On balance, students benefit more from getting specific, relevant knowledge than from abstract critical-thinking training. After all, the knowledge will almost certainly help them make a wiser decision; the domain-general skill probably doesn't meaningfully exist – at least not in teachable ways (Willingham, 2019).

Let's consider a very local example. By this point in *The Goldilocks Map*, you have read dozens of pages about an exceedingly specific critical thinking skill: evaluating "brain-based" teaching suggestions. Some quest steps, doubtless, seem like domain-general skills. My advice that we ask sources for the "best research," for example, sounds like the first step in many critical thinking paradigms: "evaluate the evidence."

At the same time, the decision tree that followed that domain-general advice requires highly specific knowledge. We might know we *should* evaluate the evidence; unless we've studied this highly specific field, we're unlikely to know why "read this book" or "here's some neuroscience" can't help us evaluate sources effectively. We need background knowledge to use this seemingly general skill.

The same point holds in reverse. Once you've read this book, you will be more qualified than most to think critically about the intersection of psychology, neuroscience, and teaching. Please (please!) do not assume that you're more qualified to think critically about jet engine design. Perhaps the skills outlined on this map transfer to that field; as a non-expert, I don't know. But I highly doubt it.

A second reason that we might look favorably at brain-training orbs is **executive function**.

We've seen that the category "executive function" can be difficult to pin down. Teachers regularly hear the lists (planning, prioritizing, inhibiting, task-switching, etc.), but precise definitions can elude us. We can perhaps understand executive functions most readily by reversing an earlier claim: unlike almost everything else, EFs *do work domain-generally.*

That is: if I'm good at prioritizing (an EF), I can use that skill when I'm doing my biology homework and when I'm rehearsing my lines for the play. If I'm bad at task-switching (an EF) while studying math, I'm probably bad at task-switching while working on my Cub Scout badges. Executive functions help us in almost every cognitive domain.

For that reason: getting better at *inhibiting* makes me better at *inhibiting while playing computer games* and *inhibiting while learning phonics rules.* Practicing graphophonological-semantic flexibility improves my score *on GSF tests* and *on reading tests.*

Because executive functions work domain-generally, effective EF training might work domain-generally. For this reason, we're open to the possibility that:

- Adele Diamond's "Tools of the Mind" curriculum might work as advertised, and enhance students' EF (Diamond & Lee, 2011).
- Cartwright's much-discussed training in cognitive flexibility might improve GSF, and reading.

Of course, we should quest through Diamond's study as we did with Cartwright's. That adventure might find reasons to be skeptical. However, her Big Ask is not obviously implausible, as "brain training" programs typically are.

An exception to the exception: working memory is an executive function, but – unlike other EFs – almost certainly can't be trained. Happily, Goldilocks has the cognitive flexibility required to maintain balance.

Although these nuanced details can disorient us, the headline remains clear: with a few exceptions, brain-training claims don't hold up. We shouldn't let a freshly polished orb distract us.

Orb #3: Authentic 21st Century Transformation

On her balcony, dreaming of Romeo, Juliet laments that names shouldn't matter – but they do. I feel her pain. Big Asks that have uplifting brand names frequently muddle us on our quest.

Reasons This Orb is So Tempting

In a recent study, two scholars surveyed college students to understand their thoughts about teacher **authenticity**. According to their results, authentic teachers are "approachable, passionate, attentive, capable, and knowledgeable" (Johnson & LaBelle, 2017, p. 423). An approachable professor, for instance, admits mistakes, shares personal stories, and makes jokes. The more of these behaviors a teacher demonstrates, the more *approachable* – and therefore *authentic* – she is.

This definition creates a puzzle. Imagine a calculus teacher – let's call him Mr. Escalante – who remains reticent about his home life and rarely tells jokes. Quite authentically, he prefers to focus on his students and his class content, and not on himself and his wit. Let's face it: some people just aren't funny, and they know it. Escalante, oddly, is being *authentic* without being "authentic." That is: he's being true to himself (*authentic*) but not acting in accordance with Johnson and LaBelle's definition ("authentic").

This possibility has grim implications. A conference speaker or a blogger might easily turn Johnson and LaBelle's research into a branded program: "The Authentic Teacher." That program comes with exercises and checklists and scores – and, crucially, is "based on research." However effective and authentic Escalante's teaching, he loses points for not being "authentic" *as defined by the brand.*

Imagine this surreal meeting between Escalante and his principal:

Research-Informed Principal: I need you to be more "authentic." Tell jokes. Share personal anecdotes. It's on the checklist.

Escalante: I *am* being authentic. Jokes and personal anecdotes would be inauthentic. That's just not me.

Research-Informed Principal: No, jokes and personal anecdotes are "authentic." We've got research.

In this case, the loaded word "authentic" makes communication needlessly difficult – and might well hinder effective teaching. Because it has become a brand, "authenticity" loses its commonly understood meaning; the word no longer facilitates understanding, but impedes it.

As far as I know, no one has yet misused Johnson and LaBelle's research this way. (And, to be clear, they don't encourage us to do so.) But uplifting educational brand names regularly create this kind of confusion.

If you read about an Authentic Exploration Curriculum™ or Transformational Teaching Tools® or 21st Century Pedagogy Revolution©, those programs might be authentic, transformational, and pertinent to the 21st century. But they might not. And – here's my complaint – the uplifting brand name *makes our quest harder.* If we explore the research behind Transformational Teaching Tools and find it wanting, we might be accused of being *anti-transformational reactionaries.* If we point out that the Authentic Exploration Curriculum relies on wild misinterpretation of the research it cites, we seem to *oppose authenticity.* Of course, we strongly favor authenticity, and might even welcome transformation. We're simply pointing out that research doesn't support the branded version of those words.

Even seemingly benign words like "engagement" or "relevant" have been amped up in this unhelpful way. Goldilocks might conclude that a curriculum designed by the Center for Interdisciplinary Relevance and Future Engagement doesn't merit our school's time. She doesn't oppose engagement or relevance – but the Center doesn't usefully define the former, and the latter doesn't get any love in the research cited by this source.

This branding happens in reverse as well. Sources encourage us to adopt their program both by branding it inspirationally, and by giving our current practice an ugly moniker. For instance: we might reasonably believe that *learning math facts* helps students by supplying relevant background knowledge. If our source rebrands that strategy as Drill-and-Kill, we suddenly struggle to defend so barbaric a practice. Background knowledge, *good*; killing students, *bad.*

In brief, these orbs tempt us because our *emotions* tempt us. If a source's Big Ask includes a strongly emotive name – uplifting or dismaying – we might react to the *va-va-voom of the brand*, not the *quality and substance of the research.* Such names should prompt us to put extra Goldilocks doubt in our saddlebags.

Reasons it's Almost Certainly a Knock-off

Researchers, typically, are a sober and understated sort. To a fault, they give their research topics bland – even cumbersome – names.

- The "spacing effect" compares the time between practice sessions. It often gets the name "distributed practice." These phrases describe, quite literally, the topic being researched. No bling here.
- "Retrieval practice" emphasizes the benefits of...*practicing by retrieving* ideas from memory, rather than by rereading them in books. The name, quite blandly, says what it is.
- In fact, "retrieval practice" used to be called "the testing effect," because tests are themselves a kind of retrieval. "The testing effect" may be the *worst brand name ever*, because no students and no teachers want anything to do with more testing.

- Competition for worst brand name ever? How about "graphophonological-semantic flexibility"? 'Nuff said.

Because we know that research relies on bland or inscrutable names, we can easily spot hyperbolically rebranded ideas. If a phrase evokes strong emotions, it almost certainly came from the *sales-conscious source*, not from the *data-conscious researcher*.

Layers of Nuance

We can be all but sure that dramatically named programs start with sources more often than researchers. These enticing names certainly raise our skepticism, and certainly make discussion more difficult. But the perky branding should neither reassure us nor utterly dissuade us. A research-based suggestion might *both* have an emotive name *and* help our students. It's possible.

For instance: Brain Gym. This once-popular program gets lots of branding points. It sounds cognitive, and healthy, and cognitively healthy. My hippocampus feels aerobically fitter whenever I say those words in unison. Of course, that strong emotional reaction should make me orb-wary. If I *just love the name*, I need to quest extra cautiously.

In this case, sure enough, the program doesn't withstand much scrutiny. Yes, true, we have seen that fitness generally enhances cognition. We've seen, in Fenesi's research, that even mid-lecture exercise breaks enhance attention and learning. But no: this pricey series of exercises doesn't provide any more "gym" for your "brain" than garden-variety jumping jacks and squats (e.g., Hyatt, 2007).

On the other hand, Diamond might initially get the side-eye for the emotive brand name "Tools of the Mind." In this case, however, we find lots of supporting research. A quick search on Scite, for example, finds three disputing studies and *44 supporting studies*. Diamond's work, in other words, has withstood lots of peer scrutiny. However warily we approached the name, we can feel increasingly confident about her program.

Catchy brand names should alert us, but not scare us off completely.

'Authentic Orbs of the Future that Don't Yet Exist!'

These three categories – groups of learners, brain training, and brand names – capture several of the most common misleading brain promises.

Of course, many more exist. For fun, you might explore the history of "the learning pyramid." Blake Harvard's oft-cited blog post gives a helpful starting place (Harvard, 2017). If you have an afternoon to spare, you might try to find the research basis for statistics about "jobs of the future that don't yet exist." (The last time I tried, I ended up at a World Economic Forum report that cited…a YouTube video called "ShiftHappens." Not making that up, either.)

When you're on the lookout for these three orbs, you will be quicker to spot dubious claims – and might be able to save yourself valuable questing time.

Appendix III.
Study Overview

A handy synopsis of a study's key parts.

Title and Authors

Of course, you'll initially use this information to find the research. Once you have the study itself, you can discover a few useful nuggets tucked away here.

- One of the authors will be designated the **corresponding author**; her email address should be relatively easy to find here. In theory, this title means that she will answer questions you email her. Because of their fantastically busy lives, not all researchers have time to meet this responsibility. In my experience, however, they usually do answer. Often, delighted that a classroom teacher wants to know more about their research, they answer with enthusiasm and gratitude.
- The list of authors typically includes the colleges or universities where they teach. That information occasionally offers useful clues. If the participants section says that "students attended a large Catholic university in the middle west," and all the authors work at Notre Dame in Indiana, odds are good that the participants are Fighting Irish.
- Amid all the reference gobbledygook – page numbers, volume numbers, secret handshakes – you will find a nonsensical string of letters that begins with the initials "d.o.i." Those letters stand for **digital object identifier**, and doi's are *fantastically useful*. You can, for instance, use the doi to find research on Google Scholar, Scite, and Connected Papers. Copy here; paste there; life is easy.

The Abstract

What it is: A one-paragraph summary of the study's central questions, methods, and results.

Other names and forms: The abstract occasionally includes a **general audience summary**, which recaps the study for non-experts. That section can help jumpstart your early investigation of the study. Medical journals often divide the abstract into labeled subsections. They cover the same ground you'd expect.

When to read the abstract: You will probably spend lots of time chilling with the abstract. Early on your quest, when you want to confirm the source's trustworthiness, you read the abstract to understand the study's main questions and conclusions. If, at that moment, you realize that the source summarized it inaccurately, you know not to trust his advice.

Later in your quest, you return to the abstract to ground your investigation. Want to define key terms? The abstract might help. Wondering about participants? Such information might be right there. If ever you feel lost about the study's big picture, the abstract points to true north on its compass.

Important reminders: To write the abstract, researchers boil a few thousand words into one short paragraph. It may well be dense, ponderous, jargony, and, well, abstract. As a newcomer to this research field, we might find it impenetrable and off-putting. As Goldilocks, however, we know our stubbornness will lead to victory. Expect to read the abstract several times. Expect some level of frustration. Trust that, in time, you will indeed master its turgid intricacies.

The Introduction

What it is: The introduction, sensibly enough, gives the background that makes this research question interesting and important. It often tells a story: "One researcher found X to be true. Another team found that Y is an exception. But no one has yet studied if Z is more like X or like Y." Given that background, you now know why this research team is asking Z.

Of course, to explain X and Y and Z, these researchers survey lots (and lots) of earlier studies. You might have the opportunity to read about a dozen or more earlier experiments. If this research question brings together many different research fields, then you can expect a detailed exploration of them all.

Other names and forms: The introduction goes by many aliases: **overview**, perhaps, or **background**. If the research question combines multiple topics, each one might get its own specially labeled introduction. Because you've taken time to understand the abstract, you'll quickly see how and why this introductory material has been organized.

When to read: First, the introduction might help you *crack the code* (in Chapter 6). When you strive to decipher key definitions, you might find that most important terms and phrases were coined by researchers in the past. Like Ebenezer Scrooge, you'll need to consult with those ghosts – in the introduction – to learn essential secrets. In this case, you don't *start* in the introduction, but you might *end up* there.

Second, as a related point, the introduction often creates those abbreviations that delight psychology researchers. If you can't, for the life of you, figure out what ITs and ETs might be, skim the introduction. If you're reading mindset research, you'll probably find that they stand for incremental theorist (IT) and entity theorist (ET). (Reminder: *circle important abbreviations*. You'll thank yourself later.)

Third, the introduction helps as you strive to cultivate doubts (in Chapter 8). A thorough introduction explains the full research background: both the studies that make the hypothesis plausible, and *those that contradict it*. When you set out on that ultimate quest, the introduction may simplify it considerably.

If, for instance, the researchers mention a study contradicting their hypothesis, you can plug it into Scite and Connected Papers. Right away, that information will help you see if the contradictory hypothesis has gotten more traction than the one investigated in this research.

Alternately, you might find that participants in this contradictory study match your students better than the one you're investigating. In either case, simply by surveying the introduction, you have quickly learned that your students will benefit from a different teaching strategy.

Important reminders: In most cases, *strategic skimming* yields optimal results in the introduction.

- If you're struggling to crack the code, scan the introduction quite purposefully for the key words you want defined.
- If you seek out contradictory studies, look for language suggesting opposition: "however," "did not confirm," "on the other hand," "surprisingly," "counter-example." Study authors typically signal this disconfirmation quite clearly.

Just possibly, however, you might fall in love with the topic you're researching. Fenesi's study on mid-lecture exercise (Fenesi et al., 2018), for instance, might intrigue and fascinate you. If so, her introduction – boasting something like two dozen references to earlier research – gives you a thorough, annotated overview of relevant research in the field. You can think of it as a reading list: one to explore at your leisure once this quest has ended.

To be clear: most of us don't have the time to chase down every study cited in an introduction. Our Goldilocks has her eyes on the prize, and – unlike Red Riding Hood – won't be lured off the path.

The Study

What it is: Now that the researchers have provided appropriate background, they offer all the gory specifics for the current research. This broad heading covers many sub-topics to follow: participants, procedure, results, etc.

Other names and forms: Like the introduction, this section has many different monikers. They all sound like what they mean, so common sense tells you what you need to know.

When to read: This brief section provides helpful signage in case of confusion. Not sure how this research fits into the question asked in the abstract? Puzzled about the relationship between this stage of the study and the one described two pages later? Check out this short paragraph. If, however, you clearly understand where you stand in your quest, you won't need to spend much time here.

Helpful note: Some studies include several different experiments. Imagine, for instance, that researchers want to explore boundary conditions for their idea. They might first test their Big Ask with a *few college students*. If that first attempt goes well, they might then try a second round with *many high school students*. Perhaps a third version tries the same concept using *reading passages instead of math problems*. By studying older and younger students, by studying STEM and humanities materials, researchers potentially expand the usefulness of their suggestion. The PDF will introduce each attempt ("Study #2") by discussing its place in the broader investigation.

In other cases, researchers work with impressive diligence to *disprove their own hypotheses*. They run one study and find that their method helped students learn. They then conjure up another explanation for their result – one which would contradict their hypothesis – and devise a study specifically to test that alternative explanation. Some researchers repeat this process three or four times. Only when they can't find any other way to explain their results do they admit they believe their own argument. Here again, the headings remind you where you are in the broader argument.

Just for fun: one of my favorite research studies follows this "trying to prove ourselves wrong" process. Lindsey Richland hypothesizes that **pretesting** can help students learn – even when they get questions wrong on the pretest. Her first experiment supports that hypothesis. She then tries *four different ways* to contradict her own findings. Only when all those attempts fail does she admit that her hypothesis was correct all along (Richland et al., 2009).

Participants

What it is: With its winning simplicity, the participants section makes Goldilocks smile. In this straightforward paragraph, you'll find relevant information about the people studied by researchers.

Other names and forms: Sometimes called **subjects**.

When to read: This section helps us recognize crucial boundary conditions. If the participants look like our students, we feel more confident applying these suggestions to our classrooms. If I teach dyslexic second graders in Iceland, and the research looks at reading strategies to help college students master math terminology in Korea, those accumulating differences suggest that this study – however well done – doesn't apply to my students.

Important reminders: We might be tempted to focus narrowly on the students' age. If the participants attend the same grade that I teach, that match feels persuasive. Of course, other variables matter. If I teach in a military academy, research done in a Waldorf school might not apply – even if the participants match my students' ages. Differences in culture or socioeconomic status or diagnosis or curriculum might, in your reasonable opinion, mean that this research doesn't apply in your classroom.

Note too: participants sections often note the number of students who drop out of the study. "Dropout" sounds suspicious, but – in small numbers – is perfectly normal. Students get sick; they don't complete the exercises correctly. Computers malfunction. If the study has made it past peer review, the dropout rate probably isn't a concern.

Most participants take part in research studies because, well, they have to. Psychology courses more or less require their students to "volunteer." (If they don't, they have to write an extra paper.) In some cases, researchers pay participants. These practices might both sound sketchy, but you needn't worry – as long as the research has been vetted by an ethics panel: an Institutional Review Board (IRB).

Finally: whenever possible, participants should be sorted into groups *randomly*. Keep an eye out for indications that researchers followed this procedure.

Procedures

What it is: An exhaustively detailed, step-by-step description of the study. This section describes everything from – say – the computer game students played to the tests used to measure their reaction times.

Other names and forms: This section might be called **methods**. Depending on the study's complexity, it could have many subsections.

When to read: When cracking the code, start here.

Important reminders: First, skim, skim, skim. You do not need to know every detail. You need enough information to translate this research into your classroom's circumstances. Doubtless you'll find yourself going back and forth as you sleuth out key terms. You should not, however, try to master intricate specifics.

Second, Chapter 6 encourages you to understand the researchers' **definitions of success**. Often, they use standardized tests to measure reading comprehension, or attentional blink, or motivation. Those tests will be described here in the procedures section.

I rarely spend much time sifting through these descriptions. After all, scholars who create such tests certainly know more about these subjects than I do. At times, however, I do note obvious concerns. For instance, researchers occasionally create their own tests to measure abstract cognitive functions (working memory, self-regulation, generosity). If that test hasn't been vetted by other experts, I do wonder how much to rely on its validity. In some cases, a research study consists entirely of asking *one question* (e.g., Schlosser et al., 2019). Such a study might point in a useful direction. But I wouldn't draw strong conclusions from a single study with a single question.

Results

What it is: The most extravagant display of statistics minutiae ever gathered into one document.

Other names and forms: Maximus Tedius Purgatorius.

When to read: In Chapter 7, Goldilocks checked key charts and graphs to ensure that the researchers' conclusions sound right. In Appendix I, she calculated Cohen's d to ensure that the Big Ask had a meaningful effect – not just a statistically significant one. In both cases, she braved the results section.

Important strategies: To discover the most important **charts and graphs**, study the description underneath them. A study might have several data tables, each more puzzling and statistically abstruse than the last. *Don't get bogged down.* Hunt scrupulously for the one or two diagrams that report headline results.

- *Does mid-lecture exercise help students learn more?* Look for the graph that compares test scores for exercisers and sloths.
- *Does graphophonological-semantic EF training improve reading scores?* Look for the chart listing pre- and post-training scores in the control group and the study group.
- *Does a specific mindfulness routine reduce stress?* The study probably has a graph showing stress levels for those who did, and those who didn't, meditate mindfully.

In some rare cases, the correct graph or chart jumps out at you right away. Most of the time, you have to reject several false leads before you find the most helpful one.

Next up: **Cohen's d-values** require *basic math*, but demand *next-level sleuthing.* As you know from Appendix I, that simple formula requires two sensible variables: the average ("mean") and the breadth of the curve ("standard deviation"). Logic suggests that these variables will stand out from the text, because researchers report them in a consistent shorthand: for example, (M = 7.26, SD = 0.43). (Yes, the shorthand is typically in parentheses.)

Alas, the results section typically includes hundreds of numbers and formulas, studded with Greek letters and obscure symbols. Even more vexing, that section regularly calculates means and standard deviations by the fistful. You will see those parenthetical data in paragraph after paragraph. Which d-value should you calculate?

Here again, look for the headline result. You don't need to know the d-values confirming that the control group and the experimental group match each other well. (Yes, psychologists calculate that number. And many, many more.) Scan the results section until you find the paragraphs that report essential information.

One tip may simplify this process. The charts and graphs you've been analyzing have numbers. For instance, the Janes study on successive relearning reports its headline numbers in Figure 5 and Figure 6 (Janes et al., 2020). By looking directly at those figures, or in the paragraphs nearby, you have a higher chance of finding the information needed to calculate Cohen's d. This trick doesn't always work, but it certainly shortens your quest when it does.

Discussion

What it is: A narrative review of the whole study, starting with the introduction and reveling in the results.

Other names and forms: If a study includes several different experiments, each one will conclude with its own mini-discussion. The overall document will then conclude with a grand summary discussion.

When to read: The discussion section, in theory, brings all the study's pieces together into a coherent whole. If at any time you feel lost, you might give it a read to clarify connections and establish priorities.

- You're trying to crack the code. The procedures section doesn't define key terms explicitly, and the introduction's dash through dozens of studies has left you woozy. Try the discussion section. With its straightforward narrative, it might clear up confusion generated by those earlier passages.
- After meticulous skimming, you haven't located key data from the results section. Alas, you can't check the numbers, or check your gut, or calculate Cohen's d. You can, however, leaf through the discussion section to see if it presents that information more straightforwardly.

Important reminders: Because the discussion section brings together everything that has come before, it often repeats earlier passages at length – sometimes verbatim. If you've read earlier sections with great care, you might find this one (ahem) repetitive. If so, I suggest a positive reframe: "I'd rather feel vexed because *I know this already* than vexed because *I have no idea what's going on*." This note-to-self has gotten me through many a discussion section.

Limitations

What it is: Required humility. Good scientific method requires researchers to state, boldly, both what they can reasonably conclude *and what they can't*.

- A study on retrieval practice might note that it measured success by testing students one hour later. For that reason, it can't determine if its benefits last longer than an hour.
- Fenesi's study might state that its conclusions about mid-lecture exercise don't necessarily apply to pre- or post-lecture exercise.
- Cartwright's limitations section might emphasize that graphophonological-semantic EF training benefits early readers, but hasn't yet been tested on older readers.

When to read: The limitations section often includes relevant boundary conditions – as in the examples described above. For that reason, this section helps questers explore the boundaries and crack the code.

Important reminders: This section often emphasizes research methodology, and so focuses on topics that don't immediately further our quest. For that reason, we should give it a strategic skim, but not expect that it always provides us with great riches.

Gifted Thoughtbots

A final note on study organization. You have seen that these sections often have different names; in truth, they might even come in a different order. What gives?

Researchers publish in dozens – heck, hundreds – of journals. A quick scan of this book's reference section reveals the breadth of possibilities: from *Review of Educational Research* to *Educational Psychology Review*; from *Gifted Education International* to *European Neuropsychopharmacology* to *Seminars in Hematology*. Alas, each journal has its own house style. Researchers have to reorganize and rewrite their findings each time they submit them to a new journal. Trust me: however frustrated we feel having to sort through the structural muddle, researchers feel vastly more frustrated that they have to go through this needless reorganizing process.

As has so often been the case, your Goldilocks grit will guide you through the muddle. You might have found a journal that calls participants "Thotbots" and tucks that section into the limitations section, which it calls "causes for circumspection". No matter. Because you understand the core meaning and function of these sections, you can translate this journal's quirky style and discover the information you need.

Even more vexing, a few journals place the narrative elements – abstract, introduction, discussion – up front and tuck the nitty-gritty – participants, procedures, results – in the back. For reasons I struggle to imagine, they format those later sections in even tinier font. The implied message: "Nothing to see here. Move along." Of course, our quest requires us to spend lots of time scouring these sections. Don't be dissuaded by the six-point font. If Goldilocks can calculate a d value, she can zoom in on a PDF to make that essential information legible.

When you first left the village, this document was an inscrutable tome. Now, you pick your way through it with wizardly aplomb. After all her questing, Goldilocks has got this balance just right.

Appendix IV.
The Back of the Book

In preceding chapters, several topics have required extra space or explanation. Here, at last, we take up those topics again.

From Chapter 2: When to Consider Neuroscience Research

Chapter 2 (see p. 60) argues that – when we ask for the source's best evidence – we should only rarely accept neuroanatomy/physiology as an answer. Knowing the function of the gracilis doesn't help soccer players score; knowing the neural pathways connecting the thalamus with the visual cortex doesn't help teachers teach.

This emphatic advice matters because such misdirection happens all too frequently. Sources ask us to change our teaching, but offer no *direct* evidence that their Big Ask benefits mental behavior: learning, attention, motivation, and so forth. Until we see psychology research, we shouldn't be persuaded by the neuroscience.

Because Goldilocks always looks for balance, we should open this embargo slightly. To explain the narrow exception, I'll offer an example, and then the rule behind it.

Example: Middle School, High School, and Teenagers

Why are teenagers so wonderfully, maddeningly adolescent? One answer: brain function.

Let's step back and look at the big neural picture. As we age, our brains develop in many ways: connections form, connections break, connections deepen. Along vast neural networks, signals travel in both electrical and chemical forms. When we're young, electrical signals travel along "uninsulated wires." The result: slow and disorganized messages. As we get older, our brains "insulate" those wires by coating them with fat – more politely called **myelin sheathing**. Thus, brain maturation includes the process of **myelination**: very roughly, more myelin = "more mature."

This maturation process doesn't happen uniformly across the brain. Regions myelinate on predictable schedules. Babies first need to *perceive* the world, and so their *perceptual centers* – vision, audition – myelinate first. When it comes time to start *moving*, their motor cortex myelinates. And so forth.

The ability to regulate our own emotions depends on a crucial neural balance. Emotional impulses, both positive and negative, arise from distinct and recognizable neural networks. (As a convenient shorthand, let's oversimplify those regions to the **amygdala** and the **nucleus accumbens**.) Self-control networks, in turn, live in a different brain neighborhood. (Shorthand, the **prefrontal cortex**.) If the amygdala ("negative emotions") and the nucleus accumbens ("positive emotions") myelinate faster than the prefrontal cortex ("self-regulation"), that imbalance would result in recognizable behaviors: risk-taking, emotional outbursts, unpredictability, and so forth.

You guessed it: that's what happens during adolescence.

As children grow, their amygdala and nucleus accumbens myelinate faster than their prefrontal cortex. In automotive terms, their vehicle has a powerful engine and weak brakes. That developmental imbalance reaches its peak during the teen years. In the twenties, happily, prefrontal cortical myelination starts to catch up, so that adults have neural brakes appropriate to their emotional engines. (This brisk summary draws on a vast research pool (Blakemore, 2018; Casey et al., 2011; Gogtay et al., 2004; Medina, 2018; Spear, 2010; Steinberg, 2014). By now you're not surprised to read that these paragraphs offer a highly simplified version of a staggeringly complex process. Myelin, for instance, is only one part of the story.)

We don't get mad at infants who aren't walking; their motor cortex hasn't yet myelinated. Instead, we design a world where their age-appropriate crawling is safe: a world that also encourages them to stand and walk when appropriate. We know babies' development takes time. We keep them safe along the way.

We shouldn't get mad at teenagers who don't maintain consistent emotional balance; their prefrontal cortex hasn't fully myelinated. Instead, we should design a world where their age-appropriately inappropriate behavior is safe: a world that also fosters their maturation and emotional balance. We know teens' emotional development takes time. We keep them safe along the way.

When middle and high school teachers and leaders think about our students, we benefit from this broad neurobiological understanding of adolescence. As we contemplate our school-keeping systems, disciplinary policies, and classroom expectations, we'll do so more wisely if we keep this "imbalance hypothesis" in mind. In other words: yes, discussion of adolescent neurophysiology can give us an important – even vital – perspective. We're grateful to get this information from the source.

At the same time, we should watch out when sources jump too quickly from neuroscience to definitive policy recommendations. We want to hear some discussion of behavioral (psychology) research as well. That is:

- A source might say, "Think about your school's discipline policies with this myelin imbalance in mind." This general advice draws sensibly on neuroscience.
- A source might say, "With the imbalance hypothesis in mind, we developed a hypothesis about an innovative disciplinary policy. When we tested it in three schools, we got encouraging results. I recommend it to you as well." This advice starts generally with neuroscience, then moves to a specific hypothesis *which it tests at the behavioral level* – that's psychology.
- A source might instead say, "Because of the imbalance hypothesis, we developed the Awesome Discipline Program™. You should buy it." This advice starts generally with neuroscience, then pole-vaults over psychology to land on commerce. At this moment, Goldilocks slams on her adult brakes and insists on seeing some behavioral research as well.

In brief: neuroscience as useful background? Yes! Neuroscience to insist on classroom specifics? Whoa!

The Rule Behind the Example
Our willingness to *start* with neuroscience research depends on the genre of the source's advice. Often, sources give us specific, practical, immediate classroom advice:

- Never cold-call.
- Use individual whiteboards.
- Greet students by name at the door.
- Replace review with retrieval practice.
- Interrupt lectures with brief exercise sessions.
- If your students struggle to read, train their cognitive flexibility.
- Spread homework problems on a topic over longer periods of time.

In these cases, they are saying – in effect – "*do (or don't do) this thing.*" Here's the Goldilocks Rule, Part I: when a source says "*do this thing*," **we must see behavioral/**

psychology research. Sources may not tell us to change a specific teaching practice without research into that practice.

On the other hand, sources sometimes offer us broad conceptual frameworks rather than specific advice. They are saying – in effect – *"think this way."*

- How should we design a high school disciplinary program? An understanding of the *imbalance hypothesis* will help us think about that question effectively.
- How do emotions shape our students' thinking and learning? Check out work by Mary Helen Immordino-Yang and Louis Cozolino (Cozolino, 2013; Immordino-Yang, 2016).
- How should we help students manage stress? The more we know about *sympathetic and parasympathetic nervous systems*, the better we can interpret advice about our students' emotional lives.

The Goldilocks Rule, Part II: **when sources offer us broad conceptual frameworks, neurobiological background information might indeed help us do our own work better**. (And: if they change gears from "think this way" to "do this thing," we revert to Goldilocks Rule, Part I.)

With these rules in mind, you might now jump back to Chapter 2.

From Intermission I – A Practice Quest: Final Exams

As you consider your school's policy on final exams (see p. 87), you start at the Chasm of Self-Doubt. Do you dare to ask the source – in this case, the report's author – for his best evidence?

Yes: you *do* dare.

In fact, this adventure takes no time at all. The report's author *names his best evidence before you ask*. With his footnote, he lets you know that Cepeda's study provides the strongest research support for his claim.

His eagerness to highlight this research enhances his credibility and boosts your confidence. So far, so good. Time to start digging for Buried Treasure.

When you surf over to Google Scholar and put in the relevant information, you quickly get lots of good news. Basic sleuthing reveals that the journal is peer-reviewed. And, Google Scholar provides you with a PDF. After less than a minute, you've got more reasons to trust the source. He gives you his best evidence *and* relies on peer-reviewed research. It's looking good for this report.

Now it's time to cast your Breaking the Disguise spell. You've got your three questions handy. Did the source summarize the research accurately? Is his claim *exactly* what the research said? When you find Cepeda's abstract on Google Scholar, it certainly poses a few challenges:

"More than a century of research shows that increasing the gap between study episodes using the same material can enhance retention, yet little is known about how this so-called distributed practice effect unfolds over nontrivial periods. In two three-session laboratory studies, we examined the effects of gap on retention of foreign vocabulary, facts, and names of visual objects, with test delays up to 6 months. An optimal gap improved final recall by up to 150%. Both studies demonstrated nonmonotonic gap effects: Increases in gap caused test accuracy to initially sharply increase and then gradually decline. These results provide new constraints on theories of spacing and confirm the importance of cumulative reviews to promote retention over meaningful time periods." (Cepeda et al., 2009, p. 236)

The first sentence alone, clocking in at 36 words, feels intimidating. The abstract's stilted vocabulary – "nontrivial," "nonmonotonic" – creates extra puzzles. Despite those challenges, you focus on your three questions:

1. *What do the researchers want to know?* What happens if we increase the gap between restudy episodes over long ("nontrivial") periods of time?
2. *What did they do to find the answer?* They tested students on vocabulary, factual knowledge, and visual cues over various amounts of time – as much as six months later!
3. *What did they conclude?* The best ("optimal") restudy schedule increased students' learning by 150%. For that reason, "cumulative reviews" are important.

It's time to cast your spell: *is that exactly what the source said?* When you ask that question, you quickly notice alarming gaps.

First, Cepeda's team *didn't study exams.*

It might take a moment for that shocker to sink in. In his report, the source makes a Really Big Ask: *schools should stop giving final exams.* He insists that exams don't help students learn. He cites exactly one peer-reviewed study to support that claim. And that study never even uses the word "exam." Simply put, this source fails to cite research directly relevant to his claims.

Second, the research he does cite seems to *contradict* his claims. Cepeda's abstract concludes with these words: "These results … confirm the importance of cumulative reviews to promote retention over meaningful periods of time." Your school has long been in the habit of offering cumulative reviews – called "final exams." By any fair reading, Cepeda's study suggests that a well-structured review period followed by an exam could enhance learning. After all, a cumulative exam would require students to review information they have learned since September.

When they return to that material in June, they are – as Cepeda's research encourages – "restudying over nontrivial periods of time."

Cepeda's study wouldn't necessarily persuade us to *start* offering final exams. After all:

- Teachers can ensure year-end cumulative review in many ways: capstone projects or internships.
- Well-structured exams might accomplish Cepeda's goal. But badly structured exams wouldn't. (Of course, badly structured capstone projects wouldn't either.)
- Cepeda's research doesn't address the stress that exams create.

But this source doesn't cite Cepeda's study to encourage exams; he cites it to *forbid* them. And this study simply doesn't arrive at that conclusion. It doesn't even ask that question.

Has someone else done research showing that exams are ultimately counterproductive? Perhaps. If yes, *the source should have cited those studies* when he gave you his best evidence. (Perhaps Chapter 8 will inspire you to quest after them on your own.)

If you favor final exams, you might not be surprised to reach this conclusion. If you oppose exams, you might be disappointed. As Goldilocks, however, you set those feelings aside. Your just-right balanced process led you to an informed decision.

And so you report back to your principal with a clear conclusion: this source claimed that research discourages exams. The one study he cited doesn't even ask that question; by implication, it even contradicts his conclusion. Whatever our ultimate decision about exams, our school should look elsewhere for research-based guidance.

With this successful quest under your belt, you can return to Part III.

From Chapter 7: Laptop Notes and Neural Networks

As seen in Chapter 7 (see p. 149), Mueller and Oppenheimer's study on lecture notes (2014) might make sense from a *psychology* research perspective. Alas, it doesn't make sense from a *classroom teacher's* perspective. It relies, remarkably, on the assumption that students can't learn to do new things. If that's true, you and I are out of a job. If it isn't true, then their own data suggest that laptop note-takers – who can *both* write more words *and* reword the lecturer's ideas – should get double the benefits and therefore learn more.

This analysis – although perfectly straightforward – often prompts firm resistance. Rather than refute the argument, most objections sound like this:

Yes, but surely the physical act of writing adds an additional level of neural encoding that matters for memory. We've got lots of research showing that. So that's why handwriting helps more than laptop note-taking.

For three reasons, that response doesn't make a persuasive argument.

First, this argument *changes the subject*. If Mueller and Oppenheimer believe that handwritten notes boost learning because they create additional neural pathways, they should say so. (They don't.) If a source believes that the neural argument is the "best evidence," he should give us that research right away. (He didn't.)

In fact, this observation leads to a general rule. If we point out an obvious weakness in a source's "best evidence," he should imitate Goldilocks and say: "That's fascinating. Maybe it's time for me to change my mind. Let's see what else Google Scholar has to tell us."

If, instead, he changes the subject – "I meant to say that this *other field of brain research* has the best evidence" – we start to suspect his methodology. We might worry that he began with a *conclusion* – "good old handwriting is best" – and then tried to find evidence for it.

To be clear: people who follow such an approach needn't be wicked or deliberately deceptive. As human beings, teachers form opinions based on our experiences. *Of course we do.* When we find scientific evidence that matches our beliefs, we find it deeply persuasive. *Of course we do.* When people ask us for our opinions, we share our convictions and the research that confirms them. *Of course we do.* That process seems natural, perhaps inevitable.

I, as the author of this book, and you, as its reader, think we should escape that tempting pathway. We prefer a source who adopts this approach: "I believe that psychology research can give teachers helpful guidance. I'll review that research, see what conclusions arise from my analysis, and encourage teachers do those things." He starts with a *method*, and lets that method shape his conclusions and advice. If research contradicts his prior beliefs, well, he's glad to have learned something new.

A second reason the "additional neural pathways" argument shouldn't persuade us: it's *neuroscience* (à la 20th century), not *psychology*. We know that neuro-terminology has great power to persuade. This hypothesis certainly makes sense: maybe handwriting associates new neural pathways with specific memories, and thereby makes later recall easier. Until we test that hypothesis directly, we simply can't know.

The third reason: what the heck, let's give it the old college try. Again. It didn't work in Chapter 3, but maybe it will this time. What's the best evidence that handwriting creates new neural pathways that enhance memory?

Happily, recent research addresses this very question. An online article offers us this encouraging headline: "Why writing by hand makes kids smarter." It begins with a two-sentence summary: "Children learn more and remember better when writing by hand, a new study reports. The brains of children are more active when handwriting than typing on a computer keyboard" (NeuroscienceNews, 2020). The article then summarizes an fMRI study from Norway (Ose Askvik et al., 2020).

Given these findings, handwritten notes suddenly sound essential. If children get smarter – "learn more," "remember better" – when they write by hand, we should forbid laptops right away. Little wonder that reputable people retweeted these claims with enthusiasm.

Yet our Goldilocks training might already have raised some concerns. At a minimum, we've got some codes to crack. How does this source define "smarter," "learn more," "remember better"? What did the researchers measure to claim such impressive success?

With a greater degree of concern, we keep coming back to these words: "The brains of children are more active when..." We've known since Chapter 2 that, when it comes to neural activity, "more" isn't necessarily "better"; why is the source implying the contrary?

When we start cracking this code, our discoveries prompt genuine dismay. How did the researchers measure "learning" and "remembering"? *They didn't.* No, really. They did not ask participants to learn anything or remember anything. This study did not include any memory tasks.

Instead, they asked participants to write by hand, and then to use a keyboard. They measured "oscillatory neuronal activity" in "brain areas … important for memory and for the encoding of new information" (Ose Askvik et al., 2020, p. 1). Based on observed theta patterns, they drew inferences about learning and memory. But they did not – I repeat – actually test those predictions.

What happens if, instead of guessing based on theta patterns, we in fact measure students' learning? As detailed in Chapter 8, we get contradictory results. The Mueller and Oppenheimer study (2014) reached one set of conclusions. When other scholars tried to replicate those findings, however, they didn't find significant results in either direction (Morehead et al., 2019). We can, with a little skilled sleuthing, find lots of contradictory studies (Jarry, 2019). Research into "oscillatory neuronal activity" sounds impressive. But we teachers don't need to know what happens to our students' *theta patterns*; we need to know what happens to their *learning*. Ose Askvik's research doesn't, and can't, answer that question.

Someday, a wise combination of psychology and neuroscience research might give us and our students clear note-taking guidance. So far, we just don't have enough evidence to make any Big Ask persuasive. I suspect that, ultimately, our best advice will be carefully tailored to the students' age and preferences, the topic they're studying, their background knowledge – and, who knows, maybe their theta patterns.

Once again, giving this side quest the old college try takes up time without yielding much benefit. We can – of course – undertake such quests to be thorough. However, this map tries to balance thoroughness with efficiency. If we discover that our source's "best evidence" simply does not make classroom sense (Really? Students can't learn new things?), we can with full Goldilocks honor return to our hamlet and celebrate a quest well done.

From Intermission II – A Practice Quest: Learning with Music

This quest (see p. 151) starts off smoothly. Drawing on information from the podcast, you plug the words "Scullin," "Beethoven," and "Chopin" into Google Scholar. You discover that this research has been peer-reviewed (Gao et al., 2020). Chasm crossed, treasure found.

The abstract contains lots of technical information, much of it beyond our experience: theta activity, some obscure stats, a new abbreviation. At the same time, it offers plenty of useful information. It describes the participants (!), calculates Cohen's d (d = 0.63!!), and combines psychology and neuroscience (!!!). It's not nearly as turgid as other abstracts you've read. You've got lots to work with here.

In fact, the abstract's richness reveals several practical concerns: problems not articulated by the podcast. Scullin's team had college students listen to, say, a Chopin nocturne while watching an economics lecture. They then replayed that same nocturne for students *while they slept*. That replay did help students on a test the next day, but did not lead to improvement nine months later.

This research lends itself to dramatic claims: "listening to music helps students learn!" However, *Scullin does not make those claims*. And, when considered from a classroom teacher's perspective, this paradigm raises several practical questions:

- Should there really be music playing *while the teacher explains a new concept to students*? Teacherly instincts suggest that such music might distract students more than it helps them. Heck, it would certainly distract me.
- Do students need different music for each topic covered: Chopin for comets, Beethoven for Bismarck's biography, Vivaldi for the science of seasons? If yes, students will need a huge musical library devoted to the topics they learn over the years.
- Practically speaking, how do students replay the right music for themselves at night. Won't the sound wake them up?
- If the learning gains don't last, why bother?

The podcaster summarized Scullin accurately – as far as he went. A more complete understanding of this research makes that source's enthusiasm seem deeply implausible. This quest, by incorporating the *practical* questions that teachers know to ask, leads to a firm conclusion: we shouldn't try this strategy until we get some answers to those questions.

Happily, Scullin himself enthusiastically wants teachers to know about his research, and so cheerfully answers questions about it. (If you went so far as to email him on your quest, you get the Goldilocks Prize for Exemplary Bravery and Tenacity!) In our email conversation, he said:

- Music probably shouldn't play *while* the teacher speaks; perhaps students could listen to the music at low volume while doing homework?
- Yes, each topic would need its own music for night-time reactivation to help. For that reason, the technique should be used sparingly – perhaps only for those subjects that are hardest to learn and understand.
- To ensure that music plays at the right time – and very quietly – as students sleep, we will need a technology solution. Watch This Space. (M. Scullin, personal communication, May 2020.)

Clearly, Scullin agrees that such teacherly questions require practical solutions before we put this research to work in schools. (He also thinks we need LOTS more research to ensure we've explored boundary conditions.)

This quest, I suspect, ends with a split verdict. You're probably unlikely to trust this podcast's teaching recommendations going forward. But you certainly plan to follow Scullin's work to see when this music strategy is ready for primetime classroom use.

From Appendix I (p. 194)

If you'd like a handy, humorous shorthand guide to accepting or rejecting research advice, Christian Bokhove, associate professor in mathematics education at the University of Southampton in the UK, has got you covered (see Figure 29. I've tweaked this diagram from his original for clarity).

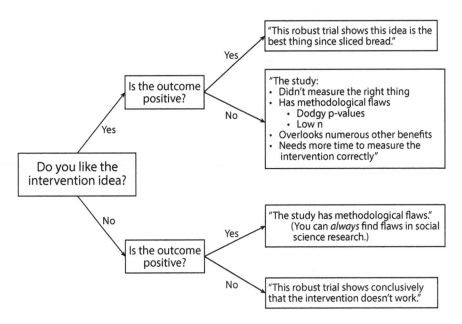

Figure 29. (Source: Christian Bokhove)

References

Adesope, O. O., Trevisan, D. A., & Sundararajan, N. (2017). Rethinking the use of tests: A meta-analysis of practice testing. *Review of Educational Research, 87*(3), 659–701. https://doi.org/10.3102/0034654316689306

Agarwal, P. K., & Bain, P. M. (2019). *Powerful teaching: Unleash the science of learning.* Jossey-Bass.

Agarwal, P. K., Bain, P. M., & Chamberlain, R. W. (2012). The value of applied research: Retrieval practice improves classroom learning and recommendations from a teacher, a principal, and a scientist. *Educational Psychology Review, 24*(3), 437–448. https://doi.org/10.1007/s10648-012-9210-2

Aschwanden, C. (2015, November 24). *Not even scientists can easily explain p-values.* FiveThirtyEight. https://fivethirtyeight.com/features/not-even-scientists-can-easily-explain-p-values

Ashman, G. (2018, January 16). Is "metacognition and self regulation" an actual thing? *Filling the Pail.* https://gregashman.wordpress.com/2018/01/16/is-metacognition-and-self-regulation-an-actual-thing

Author Guidelines. (n.d.). Wiley Online Library. Retrieved October 14, 2020, from https://onlinelibrary.wiley.com/page/journal/10990720/homepage/forauthors.html

Autin, F., & Croizet, J.-C. (2012). Improving working memory efficiency by reframing metacognitive interpretation of task difficulty. *Journal of Experimental Psychology: General, 141*(4), 610–618. https://doi.org/10.1037/a0027478

Bando, R., Näslund-Hadley, E., & Gertler, P. (2019). *Effect of inquiry and problem based pedagogy on learning: Evidence from 10 field experiments in four countries.* National Bureau of Economic Research. https://doi.org/10.3386/w26280

Bauer, C. C. C., Caballero, C., Scherer, E., West, M. R., Mrazek, M. D., Phillips, D. T., Whitfield-Gabrieli, S., & Gabrieli, J. D. E. (2019). Mindfulness training reduces stress and amygdala reactivity to fearful faces in middle-school children. *Behavioral Neuroscience, 133*(6), 569–585. https://doi.org/10.1037/bne0000337

Blakemore, S.-J. (2018). *Inventing ourselves: The secret life of the teenage brain.* Penguin Books.

Brod, G. (2020). Generative learning: Which strategies for what age? *Educational Psychology Review.* https://doi.org/10.1007/s10648-020-09571-9

Brown, P. C., Roediger, H. L., & McDaniel, M. A. (2014). *Make it stick: The science of successful learning.* Belknap Press/Harvard University Press.

Brumfiel, G. (2011, September 23). *Particles break light-speed limit.* Nature. www.nature.com/news/2011/110922/full/news.2011.554.html

Butler, A. C. (2010). Repeated testing produces superior transfer of learning relative to repeated studying. *Journal of Experimental Psychology: Learning, Memory, and Cognition, 36*(5), 1118–1133. https://doi.org/10.1037/a0019902

Cartwright, K. B., Bock, A. M., Clause, J. H., Coppage August, E. A., Saunders, H. G., & Schmidt, K. J. (2020). Near- and far-transfer effects of an executive function intervention for 2nd to 5th-grade struggling readers. *Cognitive Development, 56.* https://doi.org/10.1016/j.cogdev.2020.100932

Casey, B. J., Jones, R. M., & Somerville, L. H. (2011). Braking and accelerating of the adolescent brain. *Journal of Research on Adolescence, 21*(1), 21–33. https://doi.org/10.1111/j.1532-7795.2010.00712.x

Cepeda, N. J., Coburn, N., Rohrer, D., Wixted, J. T., Mozer, M. C., & Pashler, H. (2009). Optimizing distributed practice: theoretical analysis and practical implications. *Experimental Psychology, 56*(4), 236–246. https://doi.org/10.1027/1618-3169.56.4.236

Chan, J. C. K. (2009). When does retrieval induce forgetting and when does it induce facilitation? Implications for retrieval inhibition, testing effect, and text processing. *Journal of Memory and Language, 61*(2), 153–170. https://doi.org/10.1016/j.jml.2009.04.004

Cho, A. (2012, June 8). *Once again, physicists debunk faster-than-light neutrinos.* Science. www.sciencemag.org/news/2012/06/once-again-physicists-debunk-faster-light-neutrinos

Cimpian, A., Arce, H.-M. C., Markman, E. M., & Dweck, C. S. (2007). Subtle linguistic cues affect children's motivation. *Psychological Science, 18*(4), 314–316. https://doi.org/10.1111/j.1467-9280.2007.01896.x

Cohen, G. L., Steele, C. M., & Ross, L. D. (1999). The mentor's dilemma: Providing critical feedback across the racial divide. *Personality and Social Psychology Bulletin, 25*(10), 1302–1318. https://doi.org/10.1177/0146167299258011

Cohen, J. (1988). *Statistical power analysis for the behavioral sciences* (2nd ed.). Lawrence Erlbaum Associates.

Colé, P., Duncan, L. G., & Blaye, A. (2014). Cognitive flexibility predicts early reading skills. *Frontiers in Psychology, 5.* https://doi.org/10.3389/fpsyg.2014.00565

Cook, C. R., Fiat, A., Larson, M., Daikos, C., Slemrod, T., Holland, E. A., Thayer, A. J., & Renshaw, T. (2018). Positive greetings at the door: Evaluation of a low-cost, high-yield proactive classroom management strategy. *Journal of Positive Behavior Interventions, 20*(3), 149–159. https://doi.org/10.1177/1098300717753831

Cowan, N. (2017). The many faces of working memory and short-term storage. *Psychonomic Bulletin & Review, 24*(4), 1158–1170. https://doi.org/10.3758/s13423-016-1191-6

Cozolino, L. (2013). *The social neuroscience of education: Optimizing attachment and learning in the classroom.* W. W. Norton & Company.

Davidson, R. J., & Lutz, A. (2008). Buddha's brain: neuroplasticity and meditation. *IEEE Signal Processing Magazine, 25*(1), 176–179. https://doi.org/10.1109/MSP.2008.4431873

De Abreu, P. M. J. E., Abreu, N., Nikaedo, C. C., Puglisi, M. L., Tourinho, C. J., Miranda, M. C., Befi-Lopes, D. M., Bueno, O. F. A., & Martin, R. (2014). Executive functioning and reading achievement in school: A study of Brazilian children assessed by their teachers as "poor readers." *Frontiers in Psychology, 5.* https://doi.org/10.3389/fpsyg.2014.00550

De Waal, F. (2019). *Mama's last hug: Animal emotions and what they tell us about ourselves.* Granta Books.

Diamond, A., & Lee, K. (2011). Interventions shown to aid executive function development in children 4 to 12 years old. *Science, 333*(6045), 959–964. https://doi.org/10.1126/science.1204529

Doidge, N. (2007). *The brain that changes itself: Stories of personal triumph from the frontiers of brain science.* Viking.

Dornhecker, M., Blake, J. J., Benden, M., Zhao, H., & Wendel, M. (2015). The effect of stand-biased desks on academic engagement: An exploratory study. *International Journal of Health Promotion and Education, 53*(5), 271–280. https://doi.org/10.1080/14635240.2015.1029641

Doss, K. K., & Bloom, L. (2018). Mindfulness in the middle school classroom: Strategies to target social and emotional well-being of gifted students. *Gifted Education International, 34*(2), 181–192. https://doi.org/10.1177/0261429417716352

Eliot, L. (2009). *Pink brain, blue brain: How small differences grow into troublesome gaps – and what we can do about it.* Houghton Mifflin Harcourt.

Ericsson, A., & Pool, R. (2017). *Peak: Secrets from the new science of expertise.* Eamon Dolan/Mariner Books.

Fenesi, B., Lucibello, K., Kim, J. A., & Heisz, J. J. (2018). Sweat so you don't forget: Exercise breaks during a university lecture increase on-task attention and learning. *Journal of Applied Research in Memory and Cognition, 7*(2), 261–269. https://doi.org/10.1016/j.jarmac.2018.01.012

Fisher, A. V., Godwin, K. E., & Seltman, H. (2014). Visual environment, attention allocation, and learning in young children: When too much of a good thing may be bad. *Psychological Science, 25*(7), 1362–1370. https://doi.org/10.1177/0956797614533801

Franke, A. G., Gränsmark, P., Agricola, A., Schühle, K., Rommel, T., Sebastian, A., Balló, H. E., Gorbulev, S., Gerdes, C., Frank, B., Ruckes, C., Tüscher, O., & Lieb, K. (2017). Methylphenidate, modafinil, and caffeine for cognitive enhancement in chess: A double-blind, randomised controlled trial. *European Neuropsychopharmacology, 27*(3), 248–260. https://doi.org/10.1016/j.euroneuro.2017.01.006

Gabrieli, J. D. E. (2009). Dyslexia: A new synergy between education and cognitive neuroscience. *Science, 325*(5938), 280–283. https://doi.org/10.1126/science.1171999

Ganimian, A. J. (2020). Growth-mindset interventions at scale: Experimental evidence from Argentina. *Educational Evaluation and Policy Analysis, 42*(3), 417–438. https://doi.org/10.3102/0162373720938041

Gao, C., Fillmore, P., & Scullin, M. K. (2020). Classical music, educational learning, and slow wave sleep: A targeted memory reactivation experiment. *Neurobiology of Learning and Memory, 171.* https://doi.org/10.1016/j.nlm.2020.107206

Gladwell, M. (2008). *Outliers: The story of success.* Little, Brown.

Gligorić, V., & Vilotijević, A. (2020). "Who said it?" How contextual information influences perceived profundity of meaningful quotes and pseudo-profound bullshit. *Applied Cognitive Psychology, 34*(2), 535–542. https://doi.org/10.1002/acp.3626

Gogtay, N., Giedd, J. N., Lusk, L., Hayashi, K. M., Greenstein, D., Vaituzis, A. C., Nugent, T. F., Herman, D. H., Clasen, L. S., Toga, A. W., Rapoport, J. L., & Thompson, P. M. (2004). Dynamic mapping of human cortical development during childhood through early adulthood. *Proceedings of the National Academy of Sciences, 101*(21), 8174–8179. https://doi.org/10.1073/pnas.0402680101

Goodman, S. (2008). A dirty dozen: Twelve p-value misconceptions. *Seminars in Hematology, 45*(3), 135–140. https://doi.org/10.1053/j.seminhematol.2008.04.003

Grebe, N. M., Kristoffersen, A. A., Grøntvedt, T. V., Emery Thompson, M., Kennair, L. E. O., & Gangestad, S. W. (2017). Oxytocin and vulnerable romantic relationships. *Hormones and Behavior, 90,* 64–74. https://doi.org/10.1016/j.yhbeh.2017.02.009

Greenberg, D. M., Warrier, V., Allison, C., & Baron-Cohen, S. (2018). Testing the Empathizing-Systemizing theory of sex differences and the Extreme Male Brain theory of autism in half a million people. *Proceedings of the National Academy of Sciences, 115*(48),12152–12157. https://doi.org/10.1073/pnas.1811032115

Greene, J. P., Erickson, H. H., Watson, A. R., & Beck, M. I. (2018). The play's the thing: Experimentally examining the social and cognitive effects of school field trips to live theater performances. *Educational Researcher, 47*(4), 246–254. https://doi.org/10.3102/0013189X18761034

Guskey, T. R. (2019). Interpreting average effect sizes: Never a center without a spread. *NASSP Bulletin, 103*(4), 273–280. https://doi.org/10.1177/0192636519889151

Harvard, B. (2017, November 29). The pyramid of myth. *The Effortful Educator.* https://theeffortfuleducator.com/2017/11/29/the-pyramid-of-myth

Harvard, B. (2019, January 3). The most dangerous phrases in education. *The Effortful Educator.* https://theeffortfuleducator.com/2019/01/03/dangerous-phrases-in-education

Hattie, J. (2009). *Visible learning: A synthesis of over 800 meta-analyses relating to achievement.* Routledge.

Hattie, J. (2012). *Visible learning for teachers: Maximizing impact on learning.* Routledge.

Hölscher, C. (1999). Stress impairs performance in spatial water maze learning tasks. *Behavioural Brain Research, 100*(1–2), 225–235. https://doi.org/10.1016/S0166-4328(98)00134-X

Hong, Y., Chiu, C., Dweck, C. S., Lin, D. M.-S., & Wan, W. (1999). Implicit theories, attributions, and coping: a meaning system approach. *Journal of Personality and Social Psychology, 77*(3), 588–599. https://doi.org/10.1037/0022-3514.77.3.588

Howard-Jones, P. (2018). *Evolution of the learning brain: Or how you got to be so smart.* Routledge.

Huijbers, W., Pennartz, C. M. A., Cabeza, R., & Daselaar, S. M. (2011). The hippocampus is coupled with the default network during memory retrieval but not during memory encoding. *PLoS ONE, 6*(4). https://doi.org/10.1371/journal.pone.0017463

Hyatt, K. J. (2007). Brain Gym®: building stronger brains or wishful thinking? *Remedial and Special Education, 28*(2), 117–124. https://doi.org/10.1177/07419325070280020201

Hyde, J. S. (2005). The gender similarities hypothesis. *American Psychologist, 60*(6), 581–592. https://doi.org/10.1037/0003-066X.60.6.581

Immordino-Yang, M. H. (2016). *Emotions, learning, and the brain: Exploring the educational implications of affective neuroscience.* W. W. Norton & Company.

Izquierdo, J., Benítez, J., Berenguer, A., & Lago-Alonso, C. (2016). I decide, therefore I am (relevant!): A project-based learning experience in linear algebra. *Computer Applications in Engineering Education, 24*(3), 481–492. https://doi.org/10.1002/cae.21725

Janes, J. L., Dunlosky, J., Rawson, K. A., & Jasnow, A. (2020). Successive relearning improves performance on a high-stakes exam in a difficult biopsychology course. *Applied Cognitive Psychology, 34*(5), 1118–1132. https://doi.org/10.1002/acp.3699

Jarry, J. (2019, September 20). Pen and paper versus laptop: Is there a clear winner in the note-taking olympics? *McGill Office for Science and Society.* www.mcgill.ca/oss/article/technology-general-science/pen-and-paper-versus-laptop-there-clear-winner-note-taking-olympics

Jerrim, J., Macmillan, L., Micklewright, J., Sawtell, M., & Wiggins, M. (2016). *Chess in schools: Evaluation report and executive summary.* Education Endowment Foundation. https://files.eric.ed.gov/fulltext/ED581100.pdf

Johann, V., Könen, T., & Karbach, J. (2020). The unique contribution of working memory, inhibition, cognitive flexibility, and intelligence to reading comprehension and reading speed. *Child Neuropsychology, 26*(3), 324–344. https://doi.org/10.1080/09297049.2019.1649381

Johnson, Z. D., & LaBelle, S. (2017). An examination of teacher authenticity in the college classroom. *Communication Education, 66*(4), 423–439. https://doi.org/10.1080/03634523.2017.1324167

Kandel, E. R. (2006). *In search of memory: The emergence of a new science of mind.* W. W. Norton & Company.

Karakowsky, L., & Mann, S. L. (2008). Setting goals and taking ownership: understanding the implications of participatively set goals from a causal attribution perspective. *Journal of Leadership & Organizational Studies, 14*(3), 260–270. https://doi.org/10.1177/1071791907308047

Kornell, N. (2009). Optimising learning using flashcards: Spacing is more effective than cramming. *Applied Cognitive Psychology, 23*(9), 1297–1317. https://doi.org/10.1002/acp.1537

Kruger, J., & Dunning, D. (1999). Unskilled and unaware of it: How difficulties in recognizing one's own incompetence lead to inflated self-assessments. *Journal of Personality and Social Psychology, 77*(6), 1121–1134. https://doi.org/10.1037/0022-3514.77.6.1121

Kvarven, A., Strømland, E., & Johannesson, M. (2020). Comparing meta-analyses and preregistered multiple-laboratory replication projects. *Nature Human Behaviour, 4*(4), 423–434. https://doi.org/10.1038/s41562-019-0787-z

Lemov, D. (2015). *Teach like a champion 2.0: 62 techniques that put students on the path to college* (2nd ed.). Jossey-Bass.

Lewis, N., & Watson, A. (2020, September 29). How psychologists and teachers can talk about research most wisely. *Learning and the Brain.* www.learningandthebrain.com/blog/how-psychologists-and-teachers-can-talk-about-research-most-wisely

Lowel, S., & Singer, W. (1992). Selection of intrinsic horizontal connections in the visual cortex by correlated neuronal activity. *Science, 255*(5041), 209–212. https://doi.org/10.1126/science.1372754

Luthar, S. S., & Becker, B. E. (2002). Privileged but pressured? A study of affluent youth. *Child Development, 73*(5), 1593–1610. https://doi.org/10.1111/1467-8624.00492

Macnamara, B. N., Hambrick, D. Z., & Oswald, F. L. (2014). Deliberate practice and performance in music, games, sports, education, and professions: A meta-analysis. *Psychological Science, 25*(8), 1608–1618. https://doi.org/10.1177/0956797614535810

McEwen, B. S. (1998). Protective and damaging effects of stress mediators. *New England Journal of Medicine, 338*(3), 171–179. https://doi.org/10.1056/NEJM199801153380307

McGreal, S. A. (2013). The illusory theory of multiple intelligences. *Psychology Today.* www.psychologytoday.com/us/blog/unique-everybody-else/201311/the-illusory-theory-multiple-intelligences

Medina, J. (2018). *Attack of the teenage brain! Understanding and supporting the weird and wonderful adolescent learner.* ASCD.

Melby-Lervåg, M., Redick, T. S., & Hulme, C. (2016). Working memory training does not improve performance on measures of intelligence or other measures of "far transfer": Evidence from a meta-analytic review. *Perspectives on Psychological Science, 11*(4), 512–534. https://doi.org/10.1177/1745691616635612

Michigan State University. (2018, February 5). *Does dim light make us dumber?* [Press Release]. ScienceDaily. www.sciencedaily.com/releases/2018/02/180205134251.htm

Minear, M., Coane, J. H., Boland, S. C., Cooney, L. H., & Albat, M. (2018). The benefits of retrieval practice depend on item difficulty and intelligence. *Journal of Experimental Psychology: Learning, Memory, and Cognition, 44*(9), 1474–1486. https://doi.org/10.1037/xlm0000486

Monty Python. (2012, February 16). John Cleese considers your futile comments [Video]. YouTube. https://youtu.be/x8Afv3U_ysc

Morehead, K., Dunlosky, J., & Rawson, K. A. (2019). How much mightier is the pen than the keyboard for note-taking? A replication and extension of Mueller and Oppenheimer (2014). *Educational Psychology Review, 31*(3), 753–780. https://doi.org/10.1007/s10648-019-09468-2

Mueller, P. A., & Oppenheimer, D. M. (2014). The pen is mightier than the keyboard: Advantages of longhand over laptop note taking. *Psychological Science, 25*(6), 1159–1168. https://doi.org/10.1177/0956797614524581

Mullender-Wijnsma, M. J., Hartman, E., Greeff, J. W. de, Doolaard, S., Bosker, R. J., & Visscher, C. (2016). Physically active math and language lessons improve academic achievement: A cluster randomized controlled trial. *Pediatrics, 137*(3). https://doi.org/10.1542/peds.2015-2743

Mullender-Wijnsma, M. J., Hartman, E., Greeff, J. W. de, Doolaard, S., Bosker, R. J., & Visscher, C. (2019). Follow-up study investigating the effects of a physically active academic intervention. *Early Childhood Education Journal, 47*, 699–707. https://doi.org/10.1007/S10643-019-00968-Y

Neuroscience News. (2020, October 1). *Why writing by hand makes kids smarter.* https://neurosciencenews.com/hand-writing-smart-kids-17113

Nijboer, M., Borst, J., van Rijn, H., & Taatgen, N. (2014). Single-task fMRI overlap predicts concurrent multitasking interference. *NeuroImage, 100*, 60–74. https://doi.org/10.1016/j.neuroimage.2014.05.082

Ose Askvik, E., van der Weel, F. R. (Ruud), & van der Meer, A. L. H. (2020). The importance of cursive handwriting over typewriting for learning in the classroom: A high-density EEG study of 12-year-old children and young adults. *Frontiers in Psychology, 11*(1810). https://doi.org/10.3389/fpsyg.2020.01810

Pashler, H., McDaniel, M., Rohrer, D., & Bjork, R. (2008). Learning styles: Concepts and evidence. *Psychological Science in the Public Interest, 9*(3), 105–119. https://doi.org/10.1111/j.1539-6053.2009.01038.x

Pittenger, D. J. (1993). The utility of the Myers-Briggs Type Indicator. *Review of Educational Research, 63*(4), 467–488. https://doi.org/10.3102/00346543063004467

Pittenger, D. J. (2005). Cautionary comments regarding the Myers-Briggs Type Indicator. *Consulting Psychology Journal: Practice and Research, 57*(3), 210–221. https://doi.org/10.1037/1065-9293.57.3.210

P-value. (2020, September 22). In *Wikipedia.* https://en.wikipedia.org/wiki/P-value

Quigley, A. (2018). *Closing the vocabulary gap.* Routledge.

Ratey, J. J., & Hagerman, E. (2008). *Spark! The revolutionary new science of exercise and the brain.* Little, Brown.

Rattan, A., Good, C., & Dweck, C. S. (2012). "It's ok – not everyone can be good at math": Instructors with an entity theory comfort (and demotivate) students. *Journal of Experimental Social Psychology, 48*(3), 731–737. https://doi.org/10.1016/j.jesp.2011.12.012

Richland, L. E., Kornell, N., & Kao, L. S. (2009). The pretesting effect: Do unsuccessful retrieval attempts enhance learning? *Journal of Experimental Psychology: Applied, 15*(3), 243–257. https://doi.org/10.1037/a0016496

Rippon, G. (2019). *Gender and our brains: How new neuroscience explodes the myths of the male and female minds.* Pantheon Books.

RMIT University. (2018, October 3). *Sans Forgetica: RMIT creates typeface designed to help students study* [Press Release]. www.rmit.edu.au/news/newsroom/media-releases-and-expert-comments/2018/oct/sans-forgetica-media-release

Rodrigues, P. F. S., & Pandeirada, J. N. S. (2018). When visual stimulation of the surrounding environment affects children's cognitive performance. *Journal of Experimental Child Psychology, 176,* 140–149. https://doi.org/10.1016/j.jecp.2018.07.014

Rodrigues, P. F. S., & Pandeirada, J. N. S. (2019). The influence of a visually-rich surrounding environment in visuospatial cognitive performance: A study with adolescents. *Journal of Cognition and Development, 20*(3), 399–410. https://doi.or g/10.1080/15248372.2019.1605996

Rodrigues, P. F. S., & Pandeirada, J. N. S. (2020). The influence of the visual surrounding environment in older adults and young adults' cognitive performance: An alternative paradigm. *Journal of Cognitive Psychology, 32*(3), 332–343. https://doi.org/10.1080/20445911.2020.1749642

Roediger, H. L. (2013). Applying cognitive psychology to education: Translational educational science. *Psychological Science in the Public Interest, 14*(1). https://doi.org/10.1177/1529100612454415

Roediger, H. L., & Karpicke, J. D. (2006). Test-enhanced learning: Taking memory tests improves long-term retention. *Psychological Science, 17*(3), 249–255. https://doi.org/10.1111/j.1467-9280.2006.01693.x

Rohrer, D., & Taylor, K. (2006). The effects of overlearning and distributed practise on the retention of mathematics knowledge. *Applied Cognitive Psychology, 20*(9), 1209–1224. https://doi.org/10.1002/acp.1266

Rose, T. (2015). *The end of average: How we succeed in a world that values sameness.* HarperOne.

Sala, G., & Gobet, F. (2017). Does far transfer exist? Negative evidence from chess, music, and working memory training. *Current Directions in Psychological Science, 26*(6), 515–520. https://doi.org/10.1177/0963721417712760

Sala, G., & Gobet, F. (2020). Cognitive and academic benefits of music training with children: A multilevel meta-analysis. *Memory & Cognition, 48,* 1429–1441. https://doi.org/10.3758/s13421-020-01060-2

Sapolsky, R. M. (2018). *Behave: The biology of humans at our best and worst.* Penguin Books.

Schlosser, M., Sparby, T., Vörös, S., Jones, R., & Marchant, N. L. (2019). Unpleasant meditation-related experiences in regular meditators: Prevalence, predictors, and conceptual considerations. *PLoS ONE, 14*(5). https://doi.org/10.1371/journal. pone.0216643

Seabrooke, T., Hollins, T. J., Kent, C., Wills, A. J., & Mitchell, C. J. (2019). Learning from failure: Errorful generation improves memory for items, not associations. *Journal of Memory and Language, 104,* 70–82. https://doi.org/10.1016/j. jml.2018.10.001

Sibinga, E. M. S., Webb, L., Ghazarian, S. R., & Ellen, J. M. (2016). School-based mindfulness instruction: An RCT. *Pediatrics, 137*(1). https://doi.org/10.1542/ peds.2015-2532

Sisk, V. F., Burgoyne, A. P., Sun, J., Butler, J. L., & Macnamara, B. N. (2018). To what extent and under which circumstances are growth mind-sets important to academic achievement? Two meta-analyses. *Psychological Science, 29*(4), 549–571. https://doi.org/10.1177/0956797617739704

Slavin, R. (2018, June 21). John Hattie is wrong. *Robert Slavin's Blog.* https:// robertslavinsblog.wordpress.com/2018/06/21/john-hattie-is-wrong

Smeets, T., Wolf, O. T., Giesbrecht, T., Sijstermans, K., Telgen, S., & Joëls, M. (2009). Stress selectively and lastingly promotes learning of context-related high arousing information. *Psychoneuroendocrinology, 34*(8), 1152–1161. https://doi.org/10.1016/j. psyneuen.2009.03.001

Soderstrom, N. C., & Bjork, R. A. (2015). Learning versus performance: An integrative review. *Perspectives on Psychological Science, 10*(2), 176–199. https://doi. org/10.1177/1745691615569000

Søndergaard Knudsen, H. B., Jensen de López, K., & Archibald, L. M. D. (2018). The contribution of cognitive flexibility to children's reading comprehension – the case for Danish. *Journal of Research in Reading, 41*(S1), S130–S148. https://doi. org/10.1111/1467-9817.12251

Spear, L. P. (2010). *The behavioral neuroscience of adolescence.* W. W. Norton & Company.

Squire, L. R. (2004). Memory systems of the brain: A brief history and current perspective. *Neurobiology of Learning and Memory, 82*(3), 171–177. https://doi.org/10.1016/j.nlm.2004.06.005

Steinberg, L. D. (2014). *Age of opportunity: Lessons from the new science of adolescence.* Eamon Dolan/Houghton Mifflin Harcourt.

Sundararajan, N., & Adesope, O. (2020). Keep it coherent: A meta-analysis of the seductive details effect. *Educational Psychology Review, 32*(3), 707–734. https://doi.org/10.1007/s10648-020-09522-4

Talbert, R. (2020, January 6). Negative results about flipped learning from a randomized trial: A critique (part 1). *Robert Talbert, Ph.D.* https://rtalbert.org/negative-results-about-flipped-learning-1

Taylor, A., Sanson, M., Burnell, R., Wade, K. A., & Garry, M. (2020). Disfluent difficulties are not desirable difficulties: The (lack of) effect of Sans Forgetica on memory. *Memory, 28*(7), 850–857. https://doi.org/10.1080/09658211.2020.1758726

Thomas, A. K., Smith, A. M., Kamal, K., & Gordon, L. T. (2020). Should you use frequent quizzing in your college course? Giving up 20 minutes of lecture time may pay off. *Journal of Applied Research in Memory and Cognition, 9*(1), 83–95. https://doi.org/10.1016/j.jarmac.2019.12.005

Tufte, E. R. (2001). *The visual display of quantitative information* (2nd ed.). Graphics Press.

Tyner, A., & Kabourek, S. (2020). *Social studies instruction and reading comprehension: Evidence from the Early Childhood Longitudinal Study.* Thomas B. Fordham Institute. https://fordhaminstitute.org/national/resources/social-studies-instruction-and-reading-comprehension

Underwood, E. (2016, January 5). *Brain game-maker fined $2 million for Lumosity false advertising.* Science. www.sciencemag.org/news/2016/01/brain-game-maker-fined-2-million-lumosity-false-advertising

Van den Broek, G., Takashima, A., Wiklund-Hörnqvist, C., Karlsson Wirebring, L., Segers, E., Verhoeven, L., & Nyberg, L. (2016). Neurocognitive mechanisms of the "testing effect": A review. *Trends in Neuroscience and Education, 5*(2), 52–66. https://doi.org/10.1016/j.tine.2016.05.001

Van Heukelum, S., Mogavero, F., van de Wal, M. A. E., Geers, F. E., França, A. S. C., Buitelaar, J. K., Beckmann, C. F., Glennon, J. C., & Havenith, M. N. (2019). Gradient of parvalbumin- and somatostatin-expressing interneurons across cingulate cortex is differentially linked to aggression and sociability in BALB/cJ mice. *Frontiers in Psychiatry, 10*(809). https://doi.org/10.3389/fpsyt.2019.00809

Watson, A. C. (2017). *Learning begins: The science of working memory and attention for the classroom teacher.* Rowman & Littlefield.

Watson, A. C. (2019). *Learning grows: The science of motivation for the classroom teacher.* Rowman & Littlefield.

Willingham, D. T. (2009). *Why don't students like school? A cognitive scientist answers questions about how the mind works and what it means for the classroom.* Jossey-Bass.

Willingham, D. T. (2012). *When can you trust the experts? How to tell good science from bad in education,* Jossey-Bass.

Willingham, D. T. (2018, Summer). Ask the cognitive scientist: Does tailoring instruction to "learning styles" help students learn? *American Educator.* www.aft. org/ae/summer2018/willingham

Willingham, D. T. (2019). *How to teach critical thinking.* NSW Department of Education. https://education.nsw.gov.au/content/dam/main-education/teaching-and-learning/education-for-a-changing-world/media/documents/How-to-teach-critical-thinking-Willingham.pdf

Wolchover, N. (2012, February 22). *Loose cable explains faulty "faster-than-light" neutrino result.* LiveScience. www.livescience.com/18603-error-faster-light-neutrinos.html

Wong, Y. J., Cheng, H., McDermott, R. C., Deng, K., & McCullough, K. M. (2019). *I believe in you!* Measuring the experience of encouragement using the academic encouragement scale. *The Journal of Positive Psychology, 14*(6), 820–828. https://doi.org/10.1080/17439760.2019.1579357

Wong, Y. J., Zounlome, N. O. O., Goodrich Mitts, N., & Murphy, E. (2020). *You can do it!* An experimental evaluation of an encouragement intervention for female students. *The Journal of Positive Psychology, 15*(4), 427–437. https://doi.org/10.1080/17439760.2019.1651887

Wooldridge, C. L., Bugg, J. M., McDaniel, M. A., & Liu, Y. (2014). The testing effect with authentic educational materials: A cautionary note. *Journal of Applied Research in Memory and Cognition, 3*(3), 214–221. https://doi.org/10.1016/j.jarmac.2014.07.001

Yeh, R. W., Valsdottir, L. R., Yeh, M. W., Shen, C., Kramer, D. B., Strom, J. B., Secemsky, E. A., Healy, J. L., Domeier, R. M., Kazi, D. S., & Nallamothu, B. K. (2018). Parachute use to prevent death and major trauma when jumping from aircraft: Randomized controlled trial. *BMJ, 363*(k5094). https://doi.org/10.1136/bmj.k5094

Zoogman, S., Goldberg, S. B., Hoyt, W. T., & Miller, L. (2015). Mindfulness interventions with youth: A meta-analysis. *Mindfulness, 6*(2), 290–302. https://doi.org/10.1007/s12671-013-0260-4

CPSIA information can be obtained
at www.ICGtesting.com
Printed in the USA
JSHW020751060521
14286JS00002B/4

9 781913 622558